THE APPALACHIAN TRAIL
DAY HIKERS' GUIDE:

Downhill to Fine Wine and Accommodations
GEORGIA, NORTH CAROLINA, AND TENNESSEE

Carol and Jim Steiner

The Appalachian Trail Day Hikers' Guide: Downhill to Fine Wine and Accommodations
Georgia, North Carolina, and Tennessee

Published by Downhill Adventures Press, LLC, Atlanta, Georgia
Cover designed by Chris Bogan
Interior designed by Jera Publishing

Unless otherwise acknowledged, interior photographs taken by Carol B. Steiner or James B Steiner.
Maps and elevation profiles created by Stewart Holt, using data from CalTopo website (www.CalTopo.com)

Disclaimer:
THIS BOOK IS A GUIDE. Although the authors and publisher have taken reasonable care to verify the accuracy of the information contained in this book, the authors and publisher do not assume, and hereby disclaim, any liability to any party for any loss, damage, or disruption caused by the use of information contained in this book, or by any errors or omissions herein. HIKE AT YOUR OWN RISK.
The pictures and stories depicted in this book are the personal experiences and opinions of the authors, Carol B. Steiner and James B. Steiner. In order to maintain anonymity in some instances the authors have changed the names and some identifying characteristics of certain individuals.

Distances, downhill miles, and elevations for each hike are based on data from www. CalTopo.com (September 2017). Note, trail data change as trails are upgraded or relocated. Trail data taken from different sources may vary based on the manner of collection and computation. For example, the mileage between points and the profiles may differ slightly from guidebook to guidebook. Information relating to fine wine and accommodations is current as of April 2017.

Prior to hiking, the authors recommend that readers independently verify the information contained herein and obtain up-to-date information about trail maps/conditions, profiles, destinations, businesses and weather reports.

If you find that the information reflected herein is no longer accurate or up-to-date, please email the authors at TheATDayHiker@gmail.com.

ISBN 978-0-9996641-0-0
Libary of Congress Control Number: 2018937182

Contents

Hikes

The Appalachian Trail through the
Great Smoky Mountains National Park

Pondering

By John Newlon, 2013

If one did not stop to see the
Newly formed leaves unfolding
And listen to the little brown
Wren warbling over one's head
And smell the fresh damp of
The woods after a shower
And feel the cool breeze
Blowing in one's face from
Across the lake
Plus taste a pinch of snow
Hiding in the shade of granite
Rock
Then one would miss a lot
Of what Nature is offering

John was a friend and hiker who loved nature. He died October 19, 2013.
His poem is reprinted with permission from Jane Newlon, his wife.

Foreword

I wish that I had had this book when I hiked the Appalachian Trail.

For four months, I hiked up and down mountains, across streams and through valleys enjoying the beauty and camaraderie that the trail had to offer. However, the things that I remember the most are the special little surprises that I found in the communities that the trail traveled through. Local micro-breweries, retreat centers nestled in the woods and tiny pop-up bluegrass festivals were just waiting to be stumbled upon as I trekked North. These little gems were always the result of luck and serendipity. How many other wonderful things did I miss?

So, when Carol told me that she and Jim were writing this book, I immediately knew that it was far overdue. In a sea of publications about thru-hiking, blisters and struggle, what has long been missing is a book that focuses on the Appalachian Trail as a part of the fabric of the larger community that it travels through. One that shines a light on all the amazing hidden jewels that exist along the trail corridor. Whether it be a glass of local muscadine wine, a small-town creamery, or a monument to a WW II soldier, these treasures can take a regular hike and make it sublime. Carol and Jim Steiner have opened a new world to future hikers, trekkers and weekend explorers. A world where hiking is easily combined with a larger sense of exploration, community and comforts.

Thank you, Carol and Jim for celebrating the Appalachian Trail and its community in all its fullness.

Anna Huthmaker
Founder, Trail Dames

Why This Guide

Jim and I want to share with you the things we have learned over the last ten years while day hiking eight hundred miles of the Appalachian Trail---what we see and how we feel as we hike in the depths of the forest, how we handle the challenges the trail presents, how we get to and from the trailheads, and where we find comfortable places to stay at night as well as fine dining and hidden gems in the small towns along the A.T.

There is never a day hike during which we do not discover one or more of the veiled treasures of the A.T.: the rare red salamander sunning on the stepping stone, tiny bluets just beginning to bloom, the box turtle moving slowly down the middle of the trail, the gravestones of the Shelton brothers from the Civil War, or the smiles and stories of hikers we meet. Our lives have been enriched by hiking the Appalachian Trail one day at a time and pausing to enjoy the sights and sounds.

We want to inspire you to day hike the Appalachian Trail. It requires lots of planning, but the rewards are great. Plus, day hiking demands no tenting out in the woods overnight. You have the opportunity to touch and feel the solitude of nature in its finest array of beauty as you walk the Appalachian Trail and the opportunity to explore the Appalachian Communities and meet their people.

With the help of family and friends, this book blossomed from my hiking-journal entries and Jim's pictures of our hiking trips into *The Appalachian Trail Day Hikers' Guide: Downhill to Fine Wine and Accommodations.* It has been a labor of love, memories, and details to help you experience a safe, enjoyable day-hiking trip.

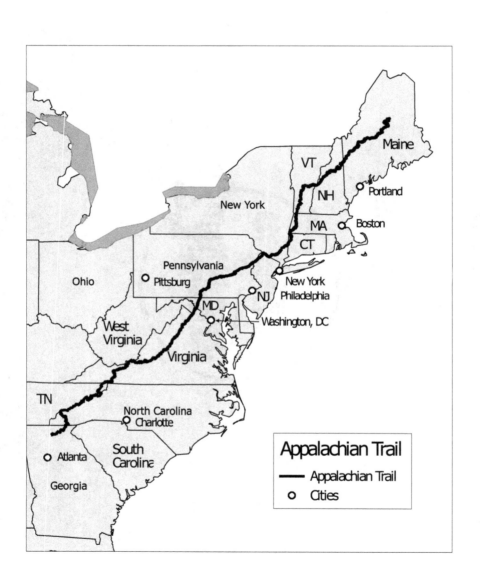

The Appalachian Trail from Georgia to Maine

Introduction

The Appalachian Trail is a cathedral in the wilderness waiting for you to partake of its stillness and beauty and to feel the harmony evoked by the cascading streams, the birds singing, and the trees, plants, and flowers whispering their secrets. The day hikes in this guidebook are a good place to begin to fulfill your dream of exploring the Appalachian Trail one day at a time.

The A.T., as it is commonly known, is a continuous footpath winding through the remote Appalachian Mountains for more than twenty-one hundred miles, crossing through fourteen states from Georgia to Maine. The plan for the Appalachian Trail was conceived by Benton MacKaye in 1921. As a forester, environmental steward, and visionary, MacKaye saw the A.T. as a way to give workers from the industrialized cities in the East a retreat from the daily grind in the factories. The Appalachian Mountains were within a day's ride from these major population centers.

In 1925 the Appalachian Trail Conference was created to organize volunteers to blaze the Appalachian Trail and to support outdoor recreation. Under the leadership of Arthur Perkins and later Myron Avery, members of the ATC, along with members of regional trail clubs, cleared the path, painted white blazes to mark the A.T., built shelters, and organized a system for ongoing trail maintenance. The Appalachian Trail was completed in 1937.

In 1968, Lyndon B. Johnson signed the National Trails System Act, and the Appalachian Trail became a public-private partnership between the Appalachian Trail Conference (now the Appalachian Trail Conservancy), the National Park Service (NPS), and the United States Forest Service (USFS).

Today the National Scenic Appalachian Trail includes over 250,000 acres of protected public land for all to explore and use as a retreat from the hectic pace of the electronic world. Over 99 percent of the Appalachian Trail is on public land.

The Appalachian Trail Day Hikers' Guide: Downhill to Fine Wine and Accommodations is written for both experienced hikers and those who are new to day hiking. It includes information about how to prepare for day hiking as well as essential information about each day hike, nearby accommodations, fun places to visit, and our story of hiking that section of the A.T. You will laugh at the times our hikes did not go exactly as planned. And you will find yourself laughing when your hike doesn't go quite as you had planned.

This guide covers the first 238 miles of the Appalachian Trail, from Springer Mountain, Georgia, to Davenport Gap, Tennessee. Other guidebooks are planned to cover additional sections of the A. T. that we have hiked.

We hope you enjoy *The Appalachian Trail Day Hikers' Guide: Downhill to Fine Wine and Accommodations* as much as we have enjoyed planning these trips, hiking the A.T., and finding comfortable lodging, choice restaurants, fine wines, and fun places to visit. When asked, "How long do you think it will take you to finish the Appalachian Trail?" Jim laughs and says, "Our son hiked the A.T. in a hundred and twelve days; we hope to finish it in a hundred and twelve years." Our goal is to enjoy each hike one day at a time and to explore the small towns along the way but not necessarily to complete the entire Appalachian Trail from end to end.

Our Story Begins in 2005

As I approached retirement, I planned a backpacking trip on the Appalachian Trail for my husband, Jim; our son, Harmon; and myself. The idea was to hike from Hot Springs, North Carolina, to Erwin, Tennessee: sixty-nine miles in five days. We planned to leave our car in Erwin for the end of the hike and we asked a friend to take us to Hot Springs to begin the hike. I selected this section of the A.T. because we were scheduled to attend the Appalachian Trail Conference in nearby Johnson City, Tennessee, after the hike.

I am the outdoor enthusiast, hiker, trip planner, and writer; Jim is the computer nerd and self-proclaimed non-hiker who takes the pictures,

Harmon, Jim, and I begin our hike in Hot Springs, North Carolina, in June of 2005

tracks the journey on his GPS, and analyzes the trip data; our son is the 1997 Appalachian Trail thru-hiker who joined us for my retirement celebration. Section hiking the A.T. was one of the things I wanted to do when I retired.

But this backpacking trip was an eye-opener for me. The three of us had never backpacked together for five days. I was surprised at what Jim didn't like about backpacking. After all, we had been married almost all our lives; I thought that surely I would have known these things.

My Hiking Journal

JUNE 2005: On a warm summer day, Bert, a friend of ours, shuttles us to the trailhead. With a little uncertainty showing on our faces, we smile when Bert takes our inaugural picture. About nine o'clock, as we climb down the banks of the French Broad River, the reality of the pack weight and what I have planned begins to sink in.

Our son sets a steady, quick pace. In the first mile, we climb five hundred feet to the rocky ledge at Lover's Leap, overlooking Hot Springs. We stop for a breather.

"This isn't too bad. Hot Springs looks romantic as the French Broad River winds around it," I say.

After five miles of up, up, up, my hair is wringing wet and my face is beet red. Jim opens his shirt for air.

Harmon and I stop to look at the map.

"How many more miles to Rich Mountain?" I ask.

"Three," Harmon says. "We can stop for lunch at the fire lookout tower."

About twelve thirty, we reach Rich Mountain, which has a tall fire lookout tower on top. Stairs lead to a platform overlooking the mountains.

Hot and with my thighs aching, I plop onto the ground and whine, "I've got to rest."

Jim hurries up the stairs to see what he can see. Not wanting to be left behind, Harmon and I follow after resting a few minutes.

"This seems surreal. It is so peaceful up here, looking out over the mountains," I say.

The views are magnificent. The ridgeline

The Smoky Mountains, July 2005

of the Smoky Mountains to the south is covered with floating, billowing clouds. The sky is clear blue.

We relax and eat our lunch of sardines, crackers, apple slices, and cookies. Then we stretch out on the platform and close our eyes for a little rest.

About one o'clock, with a big smile on his face and looking refreshed, Harmon says, "Let's get started."

Hot and with our eyes drooping, Jim and I put on our packs.

Looking at the map, I say, "Well, at least it is mostly downhill."

As we descend through the trees and rhododendrons, we pass two gopher tortoises and see a black centipede with yellow legs crawling slowly downhill.

Gopher Tortoise, July 2005

I ask, "Can you believe these little creatures out here in the hot sun, making their way down the trail?"

When we get to Allen Gap, I say, "The guidebook says the store is just down here on the right. Maybe we can get some ice cream."

We walk that way and to our chagrin, we see an old store with boards over the windows.

Jim says, "I don't think this store has been open for a long time."

I say, "I am so disappointed. I really wanted that ice cream."

We look at the map and I say, "It is another five miles uphill to Little Laurel Shelter, where I plan for us to stay tonight."

Harmon says, "We better get going."

As we are walking up the trail, Jim sees handwritten signs nailed to a tree that read, *Hemlock Hollow, Cabins/Campground,* and *Showers/ Supplies*. He turns to us and says, "Let's try them."

I reply, "Oh, I don't know. This place wasn't in the guidebook."

Harmon and me, July 2005

When we get to the road, Jim turns left toward the cabins. Without any discussion, Harmon and I follow.

I smile broadly when I see Hemlock Hollow, with cabins and a shower house. Jim finds the owners and checks us in. With every muscle in our body aching, we crash on the beds. After a long rest, we head for the hot showers. Feeling refreshed, I heat our supper of almond chicken and rice. We enjoy cookies for dessert.

The next day is a little cooler as we trudge up, up, up under the trees and through the rhododendron tunnels. We stop at Little Laurel Shelter for an early lunch of peanut butter sandwiches, dried apples, and cookies.

"Well, this isn't too bad today," I say.

Harmon says, "We haven't gone very far yet, only five miles."

Jim groans and asks, "How far are we going today?"

"Oh, another ten miles," Harmon replies.

As we head up the trail, we see a sign that reads, *10 MPH*. I smile and say, "What a joke. We're doing good to go two miles per hour."

Harmon and I walk down the road. July 2005

I walk through the rhododendrons. July 2005

We hike up the mountain over rocks and cliffs covered with small trees and bushes. We stop for a break. Jim takes pictures, enjoying the views. Harmon takes off his shoes and socks to give his feet a breather. I put on my hat and sunscreen.

"This is so pretty, strolling along the ridgeline, one rock at a time under the clear, blue sky with clouds drifting high in the sky," I say.

About four o'clock, we stop at Jerry's Cabin Shelter.

Harmon says, "Let's cook supper here."

I feel hot, tired, and grimy. "I need to rest first," I reply. I lie down on the picnic bench and take a little nap.

Harmon goes to the spring to filter water so we can refill our water bladders.

After a short rest, I set up our Jetboil stove, boil water, and cook yellow rice and chicken. We dive in.

Jim says, "Yellow rice and chicken is my favorite. It tastes just like my mother used to cook."

After supper, with our legs aching, Jim and I slowly get up and put on our packs while Harmon waits, ready to go.

Harmon says, "We still have a ways to go before the next shelter."

I look at the map and say, "We have six miles to go and it is already five o'clock. At this rate, we won't be there before it gets dark about eight o'clock."

With the wind blowing gently across the meadow, we walk lightly through the tall grasses and look out over the mountains. At the end

Jim and I walk through the meadow. July 2005

of the ridge crest, we scamper down the steep, rocky trail to the cool, thick hardwood forest canopy.

Jim stops and says, "Look at these graves of the Shelton brothers and a teenage boy. They are from the 1860s."

When I look the Shelton brothers up later, I find that the graves are from the Laurel Shelton Massacre, which occurred near this spot on

Gravestones, July 2005

the A.T. during the Civil War. The Shelton brothers (Unionists) and a thirteen-year-old scout were ambushed and killed by the Confederates.

Harmon leads the way through a maze of hunting trails and old logging roads, making sure we follow the white A.T. blazes. As the sun is waning, we are deep in the heart of the forest.

I look at my watch and say, "It's seven o'clock. I know the next shelter must be nearby, but I don't know how far it is. I am exhausted. I cannot go one more step. Let's camp here for the night."

Jim and Harmon nod in agreement.

The A.T. does not have mileposts to tell us where we are, only signs at trailheads and shelters noting how far the next shelter or trail crossing is. We have not seen a sign since we ate supper at Jerry's Cabin Shelter.

Harmon looks around and finds a flat place for us to camp in the unnamed gap where we have ended up. Jim and I pitch our tent, and Harmon puts up his hammock.

I sit in the tent. July 2005

Jim says, "We need to throw a rope over a limb and hang our food bag to keep it away from the bears." Jim and Harmon find a tree and hoist our food bag.

I look at the map and say, "We hiked at least fifteen miles today. No wonder I am so tired." I crawl into my sleeping bag and fall asleep quickly.

The next morning, Jim says, "I stayed awake all night listening for bears. I'm ready to go."

We quickly take the tent and hammock down, eat our

Jim at Devil Fork Gap, July 2005

cereal, and cram our gear into our packs. We hike uphill less than a mile and see the Flint Mountain Shelter.

"I can't believe the shelter was so close!" I exclaim.

Jim looks at his map and says, "Show me where we are!"

I point to the shelter symbol on the map and say, "Here is where we are, and this is the way we will be hiking today."

He turns and takes off up the trail like a jackrabbit. Harmon and I can't keep up with him.

"I think he has had more fun hiking than he can stand," I say.

In about an hour, we reach Devil Fork Gap and a road crossing.

Jim says, "I have had enough. I'm hitching a ride to Erwin." Jim crosses the road and sticks out his thumb.

Harmon says, "Oh, come on, Dad, you can make it to the next gap."

Jim turns his head the other way.

I feel sorry that he finds backpacking to be too much for him. Finally, I say, "I guess we should just leave him here. He'll get a ride."

As Harmon and I walk across the pasture and up the hill into the quiet, cool forest, I worry about whether Jim will, in fact, be able to get a ride. We are out in the middle of nowhere. Erwin must be at least fifteen miles away.

We walk along, talking, and before we know it, we have climbed fifteen hundred feet, hiked eight miles, and are now descending to a roadway.

I point and say, "There's the interstate. We must be at Sam's Gap." On second look, I see a white Suburban. I smile and say, "I think that is our car. Your dad must have come to give us a ride to Erwin."

When we get closer to the car, Jim smiles broadly and asks, "Want a ride?"

"Yes. I am pooped. I'm ready to try the fine wine and accommodations in Erwin, Tennessee," I say.

Harmon and I walk to the car. July 2005

Erwin is a small town where the Holiday Inn Express, the local diner, and the Mexican restaurant are considered to be the answer to "fine wine and accommodations." Erwin and Unicoi County are dry, but we have beer and wine in the cooler in our car.

As we are riding into Erwin, Jim recounts the story of his afternoon. "I wait at Devil Fork Gap for an hour while cars and trucks pass me. I was beginning to think I was going to have to walk to town when a little pickup truck pulls to the side of the road and the man hollers, 'Jump in the back.' Then he asks, 'Have you seen any strangers on the trail?'

"I answer, 'No.'

"The driver says, 'They are looking for an escaped prisoner who used to live around here.'

"Now I know why no one has given me a ride. I look scruffy. They are afraid I am the escaped prisoner."

When we get to the Holiday Inn Express, Jim says, "The manager gives every hiker a pint of ice cream."

I reply, "Finally, I am getting the ice cream I wanted the first day when that little store was boarded up."

Jim and I split the pint. Harmon, who is a vegan, foregoes the ice cream, waiting for our next stop, the Mexican restaurant.

At the restaurant, we fill up on chips, salsa, and burritos. It is just the spicy taste we need. We go back and fall into bed. I am exhausted, and my legs feel like they cannot carry me one more step.

After this hiking trip, I wonder if I'll ever be able to talk Jim into another one. Two years later, I suggest day hiking and staying in a nearby hostel each night.

Jim says, "Okay, as long as we don't have to sleep in the woods." Follow our adventures in **My Hiking Journal** included with each hike.

How to Use This Guide

Look over the **Table of Contents** and select the state you'd like to explore and the hikes that you feel you could comfortably complete. The descriptions of the hikes are followed by listings of lodgings, restaurants, and fun places to visit in the town(s) nearest the hikes. For example, **Georgia Hikes 2 and 3** are described, and then **Fine Wine and Accommodations: Dahlonega and Suches.**

Hikes are listed consecutively from south to north, from Springer Mountain, Georgia, to Davenport Gap, Tennessee. In the **Table of Contents**, each hike is listed with its number, the names of the beginning and ending trailheads, miles and the level of difficulty. For example: **Georgia Hike 2: Springer Mountain to Hightower Gap, 9.5 miles, Moderate.**

Each Hike Page includes basic information:

- **DISTANCE** is based on data from www.CalTopo.com. Because trail data change when the trail is relocated, check the latest version of the *Appalachian Trail Data Book.*

- **HIKE TIME** is the estimated number of hours it will take to complete the hike at an average rate of two miles per hour (mph). If the hike is challenging, thirty minutes have been added for each thousand feet of elevation gain or mile of difficult terrain. This estimate includes short breaks for snacks and pictures.

  Remember that this is only an estimate. If you are new to hiking, you should keep a record of your hike times for four or five hikes and create your own Hike Time based on your personal average.

- **LEVEL OF EFFORT** is rated as Easy, Moderate, and Challenging.
  - ○ **EASY:** A hike over gently rolling hills with elevation changes of two hundred feet or less on a path with small rocks and tree roots.
  - ○ **MODERATE:** A hike with elevation changes between two hundred and five hundred feet on a path with rocks, logs, or streams.
  - ○ **CHALLENGING:** A hike with elevation gains of more than five hundred feet or steep ups and downs on a path with large rocks, a river, or tree obstacles; or a hike of fifteen miles or longer.

  Most hikes will have stretches of varying degrees of difficulty, but the rating listed will indicate the most difficult portion of the hike. Ratings are subjective, but ours will give you an indication of how hard or easy Jim and I found that particular hike to be. Sometimes Jim and I disagreed about the level of effort that a hike required. In those cases, I noted both ratings.

- **RECOMMENDED DIRECTION** is the direction that has the most miles going downhill. When the trail has more miles going uphill than downhill regardless of which direction you hike, we suggest that, when possible, you tackle first the steepest part or the part with more miles going uphill. That way, you will hike the most difficult parts when you are the freshest.

- **DOWNHILL** includes the estimated number of miles you will hike downhill with the estimated elevation loss. This section also notes the estimated number of miles you will hike uphill with the estimated elevation gain. This information is extrapolated from the CalTopo hike profiles.

  "Downhill" means an overall decline in elevation from the beginning trailhead to the ending trailhead. It does not mean you will always be walking downhill; you may find yourself hiking over rolling hills or along a ridgeline, but the overall elevation will still decrease. The same can be said for "uphill." You may be hiking over rolling hills with an overall elevation gain, or you may be hiking up steep inclines.

- **FOLLOW THE BLAZES** includes mileage estimates for key features along the trail in relationship to the trailhead where we recommend you start. These estimates are based primarily on data from www.CalTopo. com/m/17QA and supplemented by data from the *Appalachian Trail Data Book 2017* and *Exploring the Appalachian Trail Georgia North Carolina Tennessee.*

- **PEAKS AND VALLEYS** is the trail profile noting significant mountains and gaps. The ups and downs on the trail profile will give you a good indication of the difficulty of the hike.

  Please note that the size of the profile graph for each hike is the same, but the scales for the elevation and the mileage change based on the total elevation change and total miles. For example, **Georgia Hike 1a** is only five miles and each square represents one half of a mile; **Georgia Hike 7** is over sixteen miles and each square represents two miles. The profiles were created using CalTopo data and may look slightly different from profiles in other guides using other data sets.

- **ALTERNATE HIKES** are shorter hikes that can be taken on the same section of the A.T. when there is access by car.

- **MY HIKING JOURNAL** is the story of our adventure on this particular section of the Appalachian Trail.

- **CAROL'S REMINDERS** are important safety tips that Jim and I are reminded of on each hike.

- **NEAREST TOWNS** are towns that are close to each segment of the trail.

- **DIRECTIONS TO TRAILHEADS** are driving directions and estimated miles and times to the trailheads from the nearest town. These mileage estimates are based on our personal experiences and supplemented with information from US Forest Service (USFS) maps and Google Maps. Driving times are calculated for travelers going fifty mph on federal and state highways, thirty mph on paved county roads, and fifteen mph on USFS roads. USFS roads are rough dirt and gravel roads and may not be passable during rainy periods or when it snows.

  If You Plan to Shuttle Using Two Cars is a section providing directions and the estimated miles and driving times from the nearest town to the trailheads. This is useful if you wish to leave one car at the trailhead where you plan to end your hike, then drive a second car to the trailhead where you will begin. After the hike, you will have to go back for the second car.

  ALTERNATIVE TRANSPORTATION tells how to use shuttle services and where to find contact information for providers for each hike.

Fine Wine and Accommodations

After every one or two hikes, **Fine Wine and Accommodations** are listed for the towns nearest that segment of the Appalachian Trail. Listings include: **Lodging and Restaurants; Hiker Essentials, Splurges, and Emergency Stops; and Fun Places to Visit**.

Lodging and Restaurants

Lodging includes hostels, local hotels, bed-and-breakfast accommodations (B&Bs), cabins, and national hotel chains near the Appalachian Trail with good reviews on TripAdvisor or with hiker-friendly services. Symbols for the price per room per night are as follows: ½$ (less than $50), $ (less than $100), $$ ($100–$199), and $$$ ($200 or more).

   Restaurants is comprised of full-service eateries located near the A.T. that have good reviews and are open in the evening when day hikers are looking for that wonderful meal after a long day of hiking. Restaurants open only for lunch or breakfast and fast-food places are not included. Symbols for the average price per *entrée* are: ½$ ($10 or less), $ ($11–$20), $$ ($21–$30), and $$$ ($31 or more). We have also noted whether or not beer and wine are served and if you are allowed to bring your own bottle (BYOB). A few counties along the A.T. are dry (do not allow alcohol to be sold) and these are noted.

Hiker Essentials, Splurges, and Emergency Stops includes shuttle-service providers, car rental agencies, outfitters, grocery shops, wine and beer stores, ATMs, urgent-care facilities, and emergency services.

Shuttle-Service Providers are those nearest each segment of the A.T. Prices for shuttle services vary. A shuttle-service provider may charge a flat price or a rate per mile plus a fee for more than one person, or an operator may just ask for a donation. Ask what they charge when you call to arrange shuttle services. We have paid as little as five dollars and as much as a hundred.

Fun Places to Visit includes fine-arts shops, events, historic buildings, museums, gardens, vineyards, outdoor-adventure businesses, and natural wonders.

If you have bad experiences at any of the places listed in this guide, please let us know. You can email us at TheATDayHiker@gmail.com.

Common Terms and Abbreviations and What They Mean for Hikers

APPALACHIAN TRAIL COMMUNITY: A community recognized by the Appalachian Trail Conservancy for promoting and protecting the Appalachian Trail by rolling out the welcome mat for hikers, hosting annual A.T. events, and preserving the environment around the Appalachian Trail.

A.T.: Appalachian Trail.

ATC: Appalachian Trail Conservancy (previously known as the Appalachian Trail Conference): the umbrella organization for the local hiking clubs that maintain the Appalachian Trail, educate the public about the A.T., and lead hikes. The ATC works with its federal partners, the National Park Service and the United States Forest Service, to promote and protect the Appalachian Trail.

A.T. COMMUNITY SUPPORTER: Businesses in a designated Appalachian Trail Community that are hiker friendly and support the A.T., local A.T. hiking clubs, and the ATC.

Balds in the Roan Highlands, June 2016 Courtesy of Fran Laprade

BALDS: Areas on mountaintops without trees, often with 360-degree views. Some balds are covered with low bushes, such as mountain laurel, rhododendron, blueberry, and huckleberry; others are covered with grasses. Balds are found along the A.T. from Georgia to southwest Virginia at elevations of four to five thousand feet.

The origin of balds is a mystery. Some scientists say that hot, dry conditions thousands of years ago killed the spruces and firs. Later, according to this scenario, cooler weather killed the hardwoods that were beginning to be established in these places, permitting the grasses and low bushes to take over. Others say that Indians cleared and periodically burned these areas for sacred sites or that settlers cleared the areas for pasture land.

BEAR PULLS: High wire lines with pulleys, placed near shelters or campsites for raising your pack or food bag out of the reach of bears.

White blazes on a tree, May 2009

BLAZES: Trail markers placed on a tree, post, or rock. Blazes on the Appalachian Trail are white rectangular markers. Hikers will also find the following: blue rectangular markers for side trails that angle oom the A.T.; white diamond-shaped markers for the Benton MacKaye Trail; yellow rectangular markers for the Bartram Trail in North Carolina and yellow diamond markers in Georgia; lime-green rectangular markers for the Len Foote Hike Inn Trail; different colors and shapes of other trails. In the picture above is a tree with two white rectangular blazes; this indicates a turn in the A.T. is coming up.

CAIRN: Conical-shaped pile of rocks used as a trail marker in an area above the tree line.

CAT HOLE: A hole six to eight inches deep used to bury human waste.

ELEVATION PROFILE: Graphical depiction of the Appalachian Trail, marking mountains, knobs, and gaps.

Friend John standing by a cairn, September 2015

FIRE RING: Circle of rocks designated for use in building a fire. These are usually found near shelters or tent-camping sites.

FIRE LOOKOUT TOWER: A small one-room building or platform, known as a cab, located on the summit of a mountain and once used to house fire lookout personnel. The fire lookout kept watch for wildfires in the wilderness, reported weather changes, and plotted lightning strikes during storms. Some lookout cabs sit on wooden or steel structures, some in trees, and others, when the summit is unobstructed, on the ground. Because of declining budgets, most fire lookout towers are now either unmanned or manned by volunteers.

FLIP-FLOP: In thru-hiking, this is a term for starting at one end of the Appalachian Trail and hiking to the middle or to a designated place, then going to the other end of the A.T. and hiking back to the previous destination. In day hiking, it means to hike south to north one day and north to south another day.

GAITERS: Water-resistant synthetic coverings extending from the foot up to the lower legs or knees to keep water out of shoes and protect the lower legs.

HEADLIGHT: A flashlight that you wear on a headband so that your hands are free for other activities, such as using hiking poles, drinking water, or eating snacks.

HIKER REGISTERS: Log books placed in shelters and at some trailheads for hikers to note that they stopped by this place or began their hike here. Hikers often blog about their hike here.

When you stop by a shelter or a trailhead with a hiker register, it is important for you to make an entry and record you name and the date. Rescue teams read these registers when they are looking for lost hikers.

HOSTEL: Lodging that provides basic overnight accommodations for hikers with bunk rooms, toilets, and showers. Some hostels also provide laundry facilities, Wi-Fi, shuttle service, food, and hiking supplies.

HOT SPOTS: Small, painful red spots on your feet. Left unprotected or untreated, they can become blisters.

HYDRATION SYSTEM: Water bladder and small hose leading from the bladder to your mouth. This system allows you to drink water hands free.

KNOBS: Small mountaintops.

NPS: National Park Service.

OUTFITTERS: Stores that sell hiking equipment and supplies.

PORTABLE TOILET: A temporary waterless toilet housed in a container with a door. These portable toilets are placed along the A.T. at high-use areas such as a road crossings and emptied and cleaned periodically by service companies.

Privy near Wayah Bald Shelter, April 2008

PRIVY: Outhouse with a toilet seat. These may be pit, composting, or moldering privies. Moldering is a slow, cool composting process. Privies are built, maintained, and cleaned periodically by A.T. hiking clubs.

PURIFY WATER: To remove contaminants with chemicals, water filters, water pumps, or ultraviolet light; or by boiling. Contaminants, such as Giardia, bacteria, and other microorganisms may cause stomach cramps, diarrhea, fever, and/or bloating.

SECTION HIKER: A backpacker who hikes one or more parts of the Appalachian Trail over several years.

SHELTER: A three-sided structure to protect hikers from the elements, featuring one or more sleeping shelves. Common shelter designs include a simple lean-to with one sleeping shelf, built with logs or logs and stone; a multistory lean-to with several sleeping shelves; and a Nantahala design with an extended roof covering a table, benches, a fireplace, and one or two sleeping shelves. The simple and multistory lean-tos often have uncovered tables, benches, and fire rings. Most shelters have a nearby water source, and many have nearby privies. In extremely bear-prone areas, most shelters have either bear pulls or bear boxes. The style, construction, and age of shelters vary.

Nantahala design

Log lean-to

Shelters are usually positioned every six to eight miles along the A.T. in the Southeast and are for use by all hikers. Shelters are a good place for day hikers to rest, have lunch, and get out of inclement weather.

SIDE TRAIL: Path that angles off from the A.T. and goes to a point of interest, such as a shelter, water source, or waterfall. The side trail is usually marked with a blue blaze.

SHUTTLE-SERVICE PROVIDERS: Individuals or company providing transportation to hikers for a fee or donation or for free. It is best to arrange this transportation before your trip.

SLACKPACKER: Hiker without a backpack and with no intention of sleeping out in the woods overnight. This hiker carries the essentials for a day hike in a small pack.

You will not find the word *slackpacker* in *Webster's Dictionary*. The term is often used to describe thru-hikers who have the opportunity to leave their backpacks at a hostel, have someone shuttle them up the A.T. ten or fifteen miles, and then walk back to the hostel carrying only the essentials for that day in a small pack. As the term *slack* means "without," thru-hikers began to refer to hiking without a backpack as slackpacking. Day hikers are by definition slackpackers.

STAMPS: Large grassy areas along the trail without trees or scrubs, where cattle once gathered after a summer in the forest. As you hike north from Springer Mountain, Georgia, Whiteoak Stamp in North Carolina is the last stamp along the A.T.

SWITCHBACKS: Paths that zigzag up or down the mountains instead of going straight up or down. Switchbacks are constructed to protect the trail from erosion and to ease the hiker's ascent and descent up and down the mountains.

THRU-HIKER: Backpacker who plans to hike the entire Appalachian Trail in one twelve-month period.

TRAIL ANGELS: Volunteers who support thru-hikers by providing free food, drink, lodging, or transportation.

We found Trail Angels at road crossings cooking hamburgers and hot dogs for hikers during the peak thru-hiker season. We met a Trail Angel on the A.T. in May in Virginia at a fence crossing a mile from the nearest road. Every morning during thru-hiker season, he brought peanut butter crackers and sodas and left them for hikers.

TRAILHEAD: Juncture where the Appalachian Trail crosses a road, allowing access to the A.T. to begin or end your hike. Typically, there's designated parking nearby.

TRAIL MAGIC: Free food, drink, lodging, or transportation provided unexpectedly by Trail Angels to thru-hikers. Sometimes Trail Magic is designated for thru-hikers. Other times it's not; it's for any hiker.

We've found fruit, peanut butter crackers, and beverages left under a tent for hikers by a local church youth group.

TRAIL NAME: Quirky name taken by or given to a hiker on the Appalachian Trail. This name is often inspired by a trait, a mishap, or a feeling the person has about himself on this hiking adventure. The name releases the person from his life outside the Appalachian Trail.

"Inspector Gadget," July 2010

My trail name is "Ink Pen."
I chose it because I am writing about our Appalachian Trail day hiking adventures. Jim's trail name is "Inspector Gadget." It was given to him by a friend who saw all the electronic gadgets that Jim carries when he hikes. At one time, he had a GPS antenna attached to his hat as well as cords attaching his camera and GPS to his belt.

TROWEL: Small spade used to dig a hole and bury human waste.

USFS: United States Forest Service.

WATER DIPS OR WATER BARS: Shallow troughs cut diagonally across the trail or to the side to drain water away from the trail and slow erosion.

WATER SOURCES: Springs or creeks along the Appalachian Trail. Water from these sources should be considered contaminated and in need of purification before drinking. Be aware that in the summer, some water sources may be dry.

Get Ready

Prepare Your Body and Mind

How healthy are you? Get a checkup. If the doctor finds you have health problems, such as, hypertension, diabetes, heart disease, arthritis, or have had a joint replacement, ask the doctor if day hiking is right for you and if there are any precautions you should take.

If you are healthy but aging, be aware of your visual and hearing limitations. If you don't see as well in low light, be prepared to let your eyes adjust as you enter the forest, and if needed, use a flashlight or headlight. If you do not hear well, take extra care to be visually alert to changes along the trail, such as the presence of any streams or road crossings that you may be approaching.

Start your hiker fitness program.

Your goal is to have the strength and endurance to comfortably hike in the mountains with your daypack with a moderate level of effort.

If you already have a regular exercise program and consider yourself fit but are new to hiking, allow four to six weeks to get your body ready for day hiking. Your goal is to increase your cardiovascular endurance, muscle strength, and stability. You can do this at home or at the gym with a trainer. Design your own plan or follow the weekly plan described below. Train intensely five days a week, then let your body recover one day with leisurely walking, swimming, or biking; and give yourself a day off each week.

Two days a week, perform physical activity to increase your cardiovascular endurance, expanding the sessions from forty-five minutes to ninety minutes per day. These activities can include walking briskly, running, swimming, or bicycling.

Two days a week, perform muscle-strengthening exercises and interval training. Muscle-strengthening exercises can be done with free weights or weight machines. Interval training refers to physical activity performed at a fast pace for a minute or two and then at a slow pace for the same period of time. Do this for twenty minutes a day.

Increase flexibility with slow stretches of your arms and legs daily.

One day each week, hike with your daypack. Start by hiking a mile or two with a lightly filled daypack, and gradually work up to hiking with a full daypack, matching the distance and elevation changes that you will experience on your planned hike. If you live in an area with no hills or significant elevation changes, use stairs in a tall building or the StairMaster at the gym, and climb with your daypack once a week.

If you do not have a regular exercise routine and do not consider yourself fit, allow three to six months to prepare your body for day hiking. Design your own weekly routine or ask a trainer to help you set up a plan. Here is one example.

- Start out slowly by walking thirty minutes a day.
- Stretch your muscles slowly each day.

- Add muscle-strengthening exercises, first with one-pound or two-pound weights, and gradually building up to heavier ones.
- Add interval training.

Do not overdo. You should feel comfortable while exercising and not exhausted when you finish. Make physical fitness a part of your daily routine. Take walks weekly in local parks or on local trails.

With exercise, you will find that you feel better and think more clearly. When you feel moderately fit, complete the **Hiker Fitness Program** described above.

Improving your fitness should be the first step in preparing for your hike. Don't wait until the last few weeks before your hike to ensure your physical fitness. If you do, you will *not* be prepared for the hike, you will *not* enjoy the trip, and you will give up the joy of day hiking before you begin.

We learned the importance of hiker fitness the hard way when we first started day hiking. We were both healthy and fit. We had normal checkups each year. I ran or walked three to five miles five days a week. Jim is a high-energy guy and was always walking around and getting up and down. Neither one of us was overweight. So I thought, "Oh, we can easily hike five to ten miles." After our first day hike, we came back to the hotel room with our legs aching. When we got back home, our legs were stiff. We could hardly walk up a flight of stairs without hurting.

Now we consciously prepare for the hiking season with the **Hiker Fitness Program** described above. We practice with full packs before we go on day-hiking trips.

During the off-season and in between hikes, we exercise thirty to forty-five minutes five days a week.

This has made the difference. Now, when we come back from hiking trips, we are refreshed instead of sore. Our minds are buzzing with ideas and our bodies are relaxed.

Learn What to Expect on the Appalachian Trail in the Southern Appalachian Mountains

The A.T. is a narrow earthen or rocky footpath that goes deep into the forest, through wilderness areas, and across mountaintops. Shortly after you begin your hike at the trailhead, you enter the solitude of the forest and mountains and savor the mystique of the A.T., a sanctuary away from the commercial world, as Benton MacKaye envisioned it

The Appalachian Trail goes up and down the mountains, sometimes gently and sometimes sharply. Trail maintenance crews often design paths called *switchbacks* that zigzag up the mountain. Crews also construct log or stone steps to slow erosion and help hikers make the sharp climb. You will marvel when you have the opportunity to walk along an open, gentle ridgeline.

As you cross the mountaintops, some are covered with trees or scrubs and have no views, some have cliffs with views, and some are balds with

Appalachian Trail, May 2016
Courtesy of Fran Leprade

views. As you hike down into the valleys and gaps, you cross creeks and rivers on wooden bridges, logs, or rocks. Be careful crossing on logs and rocks; they can be slippery. Use your hiking poles to steady yourself.

Occasionally, you must ford small streams. Look for a place to cross where the stream has a low current and is not very deep. Do not cross in a narrow place where the current is strong. Be cautious of stream crossings after heavy rains.

Always follow the white blazes when the A.T. path differs from your map. The trail path and mileage changs as the A.T. is relocated or improved to protect it from development, prevent erosion, or make it more scenic. The Appalachian Trail has grown from 2025 miles in 1937 to 2190 miles in 2017.

How is the Appalachian Trail marked? The A.T. is marked by two-by-six-inch white rectangular blazes on trees, posts, or rocks and above the tree line by cairns (conical piles of rocks). The frequency of white blazes or cairns varies. In wilderness areas, there may be only four to five blazes per mile. If you hike fifteen minutes without seeing a blaze or cairn, turn around and retrace your steps to the last one that you passed.

One day when Jim and I were hiking down the mountain with snow on the ground, I thought we were on the A.T., but when I looked up, I didn't see any blazes. My heart was racing. My eyes were darting up and down the trail as I looked for blazes.

I asked Jim, "When did you last see a blaze?"

He replied, "Oh, I don't know, maybe ten minutes ago."

We turned around and retraced our tracks in the snow to the last white blaze. We saw that we had not made a turn when the A.T. zigzagged. As we were the first hikers on the trail that morning, there were no tracks to follow in the snow.

The Appalachian Trail often joins other trails or logging roads for a short period of time. These include the Benton MacKaye Trail in Georgia. Be sure to follow the white rectangular blazes of the Appalachian Trail and not the white diamond-shaped blazes of the Benton MacKaye Trail or rectangular blazes in other colors.

In addition to blazes, you will find small signs at trailheads, shelters, and trail crossings noting the names of the next trailheads or shelters along with directional arrows and mileage. But there are not many signs noting other trail features such as mountains, knobs, creeks, or views.

What kind of light, weather, flora, and fauna can I expect along the Appalachian Trail in Georgia, North Carolina, and Tennessee? In the summer, as you enter the cathedral of tall trees in the forest with the wildflowers blooming and the trees in full foliage, you'll feel the cool temperature, and your eyes will have to adapt to the reduced light on the trail. In the valleys and coves, it will be still and quiet. The light will be dim with shadows, except for when the sun peeks through holes in the umbrella of trees.

On the mountaintops covered with trees, you'll have reduced light as the sun seeps through the leaves and branches. On balds, you will walk through tall grasses or scrubs with full light overhead. In the winter when the trees and scrubs are bare, you will walk in full light and be able to see from mountaintop to mountaintop.

In these remote southern Appalachian Mountains, where the elevation ranges from twenty-five hundred to sixty-six hundred feet, you can expect weather variations including cooler temperatures and more winds in the mountains than in the valleys and coves. These mountains stall storms coming from the west, which drop more precipitation in the valleys and coves and increase the lightning and winds on the mountaintops. According to the National Weather Service, the temperature can decrease three to five degrees for every thousand feet of elevation gain.

The weather can surprise you. One spring break when we left Atlanta, it was sunny and a pleasant fifty degrees. When we arrived in the Smokies that afternoon to begin our hike, there was snow on the ground, a strong wind was blowing, and it was cold but sunny. This was an unexpected change!

The increased precipitation in these mountains enhances the variety and growth of woodlands and wildflowers. The southern hardwood forest in the mountains, with elevations between two thousand and four thousand feet, consists primarily of different species of oaks and hickories, but there are over forty other varieties of trees. In the small valleys between ridges, the cove hardwood forests contain the most diverse mid-latitude woodlands and wildflowers outside of China. On the mountaintops and ridges below forty-five hundred feet, hemlocks grow along the streams and slopes. Above forty-five hundred feet, there are spruce, fir, and northern hardwood forests. On the drier slopes, there are pine forests.

Over fifteen hundred varieties of flowering plants can be seen emerging from midwinter through late fall. In May and June, you may walk through rhododendron and mountain-laurel tunnels covered with beautiful white or pink blooms and see bright orange flame azaleas peeking through the scrubs.

Wild creatures are abundant in the southern Appalachian Mountains. There are over 150 species of mammals, amphibians, and reptiles and more than 200 species of birds. If you are hiking at dusk, you may see deer or bear, and during the day you may see chipmunks scampering along the ground or turkeys ambling through the underbrush. You will hear birds and often see them whisk through the tall trees or scrubs. If you are lucky, you may see rare salamanders hiding under rocks in the streams or sunning themselves on stepping stones.

Always look to see what you can see. Stop and watch the wildlife, but do not disturb. Respect them in their home in the wilderness. Read about our encounters with wildlife in **My Hiking Journal**.

Will others be hiking on the Appalachian Trail? During thru-hiker season, from February to May in the Southeast, you can expect to see other hikers. Stop and talk with them; hear their stories of where they are from, where they are going, and why they are hiking the A.T. You will meet people of all ages who share your dream of hiking the Appalachian Trail.

Other times of the year, you and your partner may be the only ones on the A.T. Enjoy the solitude of nature at its finest and renew your spirit.

Are dogs allowed on the A.T.? Dogs *on* leashes are allowed on most parts of the A.T., but dogs are *not* allowed in the Great Smoky Mountains National Park. The A.T. is challenging. Dogs should be in good physical condition and well mannered if hiking with you on the A.T.

Keep dogs away from springs, shelters, and food. Do *not* let your dog off the leash to run in the woods where your pet might disturb small animals and other hikers or get lost. Be aware that dogs may attract bears.

What facilities are along the A.T.? You won't find the things the civilized world calls the necessities of life: treated running water, flush toilets, comfy beds, fast-food restaurants, and urgent-care centers. But every six to eight miles in the Southeast, you will find rustic shelters (three-sided structures with sleeping shelves, not beds), fire rings, and picnic tables. Most will have nearby privies and untreated water sources. These are good places to relax, have lunch, escape the rain, and read the hiker register to see who was there last.

You must bring the physical necessities of life with you in your day-pack, be prepared for those unexpected mishaps, and when nature calls, use the outdoors discretely. Always practice the outdoor code known as "Leave No Trace."

Leave No Trace Principles:

1. **Plan Ahead and Prepare.** Know the type of terrain and possible weather conditions you might encounter. Minimize impacts by keeping groups small and avoiding high use times for the Trail. Walking single file and avoiding shortcuts will limit damage to the trail and surrounding ecosystems.
2. **Travel and Camp on Durable Surfaces.** Focus activity on resilient ground. Surfaces consisting of sand, gravel, rock, snow, or dry grass are durable and can withstand heavy use.

3. **Dispose of Waste Properly.** Pack it in, pack it out! This includes not only food wrappers, but also biodegradable waste such as banana peels, etc. Also practice "negative trace" by picking up trash left by others. Dispose of human waste in cat holes dug 6-8 inches deep in soil at least 200 feet from any water source. Pack out all toilet paper and hygiene products.

4. **Leave What You Find.** You can look, but please don't take. Leave everything that you find in the wilderness where it belongs. Avoid moving rocks, picking plants, and disturbing cultural or historic artifacts.

5. **Minimize campfire impacts.** Keep your campfire small—or go without. Use previously constructed fire rings or mounds. Only burn small diameter wood found on the ground. Do not damage live or fallen trees. Be aware of the level of fire danger of the area. Make sure your campfire is completely smothered before you leave camp. Small camping stoves are much more efficient for cooking, and leave no impact on site.

6. **Respect Wildlife.** Let the wild be wild. Keep your distance and do not attract or approach animals. Never feed them food intended for humans as this disrupts their natural foraging habits. Control pets in natural areas and always keep them restrained.

7. **Be Considerate of Other Visitors.** Show respect for other trail users. Keep voices/noises from getting intrusively loud. Obey any posted trail rules including rights of way. Orient rest spots and campsites away from the trail. Attempt to minimize visual impacts by wearing clothes that are earth tone colors (unless, of course, hiking in the vicinity of hunters): brown, green, tan or black.

This **LEAVE NO TRACE** fact sheet was created by and is used with the permission of the American Hiking Society.

Find a Hiking Partner, Join a Hiking Club, or Bring Friends with You on Your Hiking Trips

Hiking is more fun and safer with a partner or group to share your experiences. If there is a problem or an emergency, there is someone to help you. As the Appalachian Trail is remote, cell phone reception may be poor, and you might find yourself miles from urgent-care or emergency services, a partner might be a lifesaver if an unexpected mishap occurs.

Hiking Partner: If you are new to hiking, find a partner who is also new to hiking, who walks at a pace similar to yours, and who, like you, wants to hike the Appalachian Trail. As you and your partner become familiar with each other's hiking patterns, decide who will lead, who will set the pace, how far apart from each other you are comfortable hiking, and when you plan to stop to wait for each other. Don't let more than ten minutes go by without seeing or hearing your partner before you stop and wait for him or her.

Friends: Hiking with friends is not only fun but can be a source of support as well. Friends often encourage each other to take that next step on the A.T. In the **My Hiking Journal** entries, you will notice that friends join us on many of our hiking adventures.

Hiking Clubs: Join the local hiking club or Appalachian Trail Club to meet friends who love to hike. Each of the fourteen states that the A.T. goes through has one or more of these outdoor clubs. The clubs that cover the portion of the A.T. that are the subject of this book include the Georgia Appalachian Trail Club, the Nantahala Hiking Club, and the Smoky Mountains Hiking Club. Members of these clubs maintain the trail, lead hikes, educate the public, and sponsor events. Plan to go on an A.T. day hike with one of the clubs. The Georgia Appalachian Trail

Club leads day hikes each year covering various sections of the A.T. in Georgia. Check club websites for hike schedules:

www.georgia-atclub.org
www.nantahalahikingclub.org
www.smhclub.org

Day Hiker Essentials

Your Shoes and Socks are the most important items. For hiking, you must have happy feet. Shoes and socks should be comfortable, a good fit, lightweight, sturdy, ready for hiking, cool when it is hot, and warm when it is cold.

Check out the athletic shoes and socks that you wear often. How do your feet feel after you have worn them while doing physical activity all day? Do both shoes together weigh a pound or less? Do your shoes hold your heels securely so that your feet do not slip? Do you have plenty of toe room so that your toes don't bump the end of the shoe when going downhill? Are your shoes trail-ready with firm heels, flexible bodies, and treads on the soles?

Do your socks fit snuggly without squeezing your feet? Do your socks keep your feet dry? Cotton socks will retain water and cause your feet to be wet, but polyester, nylon, or wool socks will wick water away from your feet. Wet feet are susceptible to blisters.

If you need different socks, go to your local big-box store to check out their selection. If you find synthetic, nylon, or wool quick-drying socks that your feet like, buy them before you go shoe shopping. If you do not find them at the big-box store, the outdoor retailer will have a variety of hiking socks.

If you need to look for new shoes, go online to read reviews by Backbacker.com or the American Hiking Society. Each year, the

April issue of *Backpacker* rates the latest gear. Examine the ratings for hiking, cross-training, or trail-running shoes or for lightweight boots. Check out the websites of retailers such as REI, Eastern Mountain Sports, High Country, and Sierra Designs to see what brands of hiking or trail-running shoes or boots they carry. Look for details on the weight, fabric, sole composition, and treads of the footwear that interests you.

For day hiking, you need shoes or boots that are lightweight (both shoes together weighing one pound or less), have synthetic fabric uppers, rubber or Vibram soles, and treads with grooves. During the rainy season, wear the GORE-TEX version of the hiking shoes or boots you choose. Whether you buy a hiking shoe or hiking boot depends on individual preference, the type of terrain you will be walking on, and any need you might have for additional ankle support.

Now you are ready to go to your local outdoor retailer to see what they have and which shoes or boots feel comfortable on your feet. Go shopping at the end of the day when your feet are tired and may be a little swollen. Try the shoes on with the socks you will be wearing when you hike.

Ask the sales clerk to measure your feet. Try on lightweight hiking shoes or boots half a size larger than your feet measure. Since your feet will swell a little when you are hiking, it is better to buy shoes one half size larger than you normally wear so your feet will not feel squeezed after a day of hiking.

Remember that your feet will let you know what is comfortable and fits just right. Each person is different. You need to find the shoes or boots that your feet like.

What kinds of shoes and socks do Jim and I like? Jim's latest trail shoes are by Salomon. They are lightweight, comfortable with padded insoles, and have quick-release laces, which he really likes. He wears his regular polyester socks.

I have tried and liked many lightweight trail shoes made by Salomon, La Sportiva, New Balance, and Asolo. The only time I felt I needed lightweight boots was in the steep, rocky terrain of the White Mountains.

Some of these hiking shoes have good insoles; some do not. If they don't, I change them out and put in Superfeet padded insoles, which can be found at an outdoor retailer.

In the past, I have worn thin polyester or nylon quick-drying socks that I buy at big-box stores. Now I wear lightweight Wrightsocks, which have a patented double-layer design with a blister-free guarantee. These are comfortable and keep my feet blister free. I like Smartwool socks for winter hiking. I have tried polyester padded hiking socks, but I find that my feet perspire too much and I get blisters.

Your Daypack is the next most important item. It should fit right, be lightweight, and hold what you need for day hiking. You want a pack that will allow you to walk comfortably and easily up and down hills and mountains.

What pack capacity will you need for day hiking? 1500–2500 cc or 25–40 L. Some manufacturers list their capacity in cubic centimeters (cc) and some in liters (L).

What features should your pack have? Padded hip and shoulder belts, a hydration sleeve (if you plan to use a hydration system, consisting of a water bladder with a hose that goes from the bladder to your mouth) or mesh pockets that are easy to reach (if you plan to use water bottles), and a rain cover. Some packs have attached rain covers; others do not. If your pack does not, buy a rain cover specifically for your pack so that it fits snuggly.

Do you need a top-loading or panel-loading daypack? If you like to have everything together and do not mind hunting for items in your pack, the top-loader is for you. If you like to have everything segregated so that you can go directly to what you want, then the panel-loading daypack is what you need. The trade-off is the weight of the daypack; the panel-loading models are often heavier.

When is a pack considered to be lightweight? A lightweight pack weighs two and a half pounds or less. You want a pack made of lightweight nylon or polyester durable fabric such as ripstop. Cotton packs are too heavy.

What individual pack size do you need? Ask a friend to measure down your back along the spine from the bony prominence at the base of your neck to the top of your hip bones; this is your torso size. If you are less than sixteen inches, you need an extra small; if you are sixteen to eighteen inches, a small; if eighteen to twenty inches, a medium; if twenty to twenty-two inches, a large; if greater than twenty-two inches, an extra large. Try on the size pack that matches your torso length. Some packs come in only one size. If you like a one-size pack, try it on to see if it fits.

Should women buy a unisex pack or a women's pack? If you are a woman, try both on and see which fits better. Your pack should ride snuggly on your hips, not your shoulders. A women's pack is usually more narrow than a unisex pack.

Do you need a pack with a hip belt? Yes, the hip belt attaches to the bottom of the pack and allows the pack weight to rest on your hips and not your shoulders. You want to carry the weight on your hips.

What features should your hip belt have? The hip belt should be well padded all the way around the back and across your hips. The belt should be adjustable so that it fits snuggly across your hips.

How do you find the daypack you need?

Ask your hiking friends. They might have a daypack they will loan you to try out.

Check the April issues of *Backpacker* magazine from the last few years to read reviews and ratings for daypacks.

Go to the manufacturer and retail websites to check details about the fabric, weight, compartments, water bladder sleeves or pockets for water bottles, and sizes of daypacks that you like.

Call your local outfitter to see which brands they carry and if they carry the one you would like to try. If they carry the brand but do not have the specific model you would like to try, ask them if they can order it. Ask about end-of-season sales or periodic garage sales of returned or rental daypacks.

Now you are ready to go to the retailer and try on daypacks. Find one that fits your body, that is light, and that has the capacity you need for day hiking. Once you find a daypack you like in your size, ask the salesperson to put one ten-pound weight in it so you can try it out.

If you are not near an outfitter, select an online retailer with a good return policy and order one to try.

What kind of daypacks do Jim and I use? My body is narrow and I find that a women's pack fits me better. We love our Osprey packs with their ventilated mesh back panels that allow air to flow across our backs. I have several with different pack capacities, including an Osprey Sirrus 24 for short hikes and an Osprey Aura 35 for longer hikes when I need to carry extra things. Jim has an Osprey Stratos 24.

We both have larger-capacity packs for times when we are hiking hut-to-hut and need to carry a sleeping bag, toiletries, and a change of clothes. (In the White Mountains, there are huts with sleeping and dining facilities that you can reserve for an overnight stay, allowing you to hike hut-to-hut.)

Your Navigation Equipment and Supplies are a must for any day hike. Carry a compass and the latest official map of the section of the Appalachian Trail you plan to hike. Although this guidebook includes overview maps, directions to the trailheads, and trail profiles, it does not include the detailed topographical maps that you will need to hike the A.T. If you wander off the A.T., you will need to know how to use a compass and map to navigate back to the trail or trailhead.

Official maps for the hikes in this guide include *The Appalachian Trail Guide, North Carolina–Georgia, Set #10 and The Appalachian Trail Guide, Tennessee–North Carolina,* Set #11, both published by the Appalachian Trail Conservancy (ATC); and *The Appalachian Trail, Springer Mountain to Davenport Gap, Topographic Map Guide,* published by the National Geographic Society. You will need one of these map sets or guide. Either can be purchased from the Appalachian Trail Conservancy website at www.appalachiantrail.org or from www.amazon.com as well as at local outfitter stores.

Optional: A recreational GPS with the Appalachian Trail map card or your charged iPhone with an Appalachian Trail app can be useful, *but do not leave the paper map at home.* If your GPS or iPhone batteries are down, you will need the paper map and compass. Note: The recreational GPS is different from the version in automobiles; it does not tell you when you will be arriving at the trailhead or how much farther you have to go. You have to estimate distances and timing based on how far you have gone and how fast you are hiking. If you are bringing a GPS, be sure to practice how to use it before you hike the Appalachian Trail. You have to dial in the hiking settings and turn on the Appalachian Trail map.

What we do: We each take a copy of the Appalachian Trail map for the section of the A.T. we plan to hike and a compass. I place the map in a waterproof sleeve that I wear around my neck.

Jim and I each have a Garmin recreational GPS with an Appalachian Trail map card. We use these to see where we are and how far we have hiked. There are usually signs at the trailheads with the mileage to the next shelter or trailhead, but there are few signs in between to let you know how close you are to your destination. With the GPS telling us how far we have hiked and the map telling us how long the hike is, we can calculate how much farther we have to go. This is what we like.

What Other Clothes, Supplies and Equipment Do You Need?

My philosophy is to prepare for the worst while traveling as lightly as you can.

What to Wear

Pants and Shirts: Check the weather forecast and layer accordingly. In the summer, wear light-colored, lightweight, polyester/nylon, breathable, fast-drying shirts and hiking pants, shorts, or skorts. Do *not* wear cotton. When cotton gets wet, it stays wet and you get chilled.

In the spring and fall, add an extra layer, such as polyester long underwear. If it is expected to be frigid all day, add a lightweight wool or fleece shirt and heavier polyester pants, then add a down or fleece jacket. During hunting season wear a bright orange hat and vest or jacket.

When you start your hike in cool weather, you may need all the layers, but as you warm up, take off a layer before you begin to sweat. Shirts wet with sweat may cause you to get chilled. When you stop, you will cool down. Put on that jacket you brought along so that you will not get chilled.

What we like: Long-sleeved polyester shirts and long pants to protect our arms and legs from sun, ticks, stinging insects, and tall or wet grasses and bushes. If we get hot, we roll up the sleeves and put on sunscreen. When it is cool in the spring and fall, we add a layer of lightweight long underwear and take lightweight fleece shirts or jackets. In the winter we add wool long underwear and take heavier down or fleece jackets.

We like shirts with two pockets and pants with cargo pockets so we have places to put our personal belongings, including our keys, insurance cards, money, and wipes for when nature calls. As styles change, it is often difficult to find shirts and pants for women that have pockets.

Hat: Wear a polyester, broad-brimmed hat to protect your face and neck from the elements. If it is hot, wear a ventilated version. If you anticipate rain, wear a hat that is waterproof. If it is frigid and windy, wear a wool skull cap under your broad-brimmed hat.

What we like: For ten years we have worn the same hats by Columbia with long front brims and drop-downs in the back to protect our faces and necks from the sun. We added nylon cords to secure our hats when it is windy. We wear ventilated versions in the summer. If it is frigid, we wear neck scarves and wool skull caps under our broad brimmed hats.

Underwear: Quick-drying polyester underwear.

What we like: Boxers, undershirts, pants, and camisoles by ExOfficio. I find comfortable polyester sports bras at big-box stores.

What to Take in Your Pack

Food: Carry enough protein, fruit, and carbohydrate snacks to eat at least twice a day or nibble on throughout the day. If it is hot and humid, take salty snacks because you will be losing body fluids and electrolytes as you hike.

Take a nutritious lunch that is easy to eat, such as a sandwich and fruit. If it is going to be a long hike, take a high-energy bar or drink to give you that extra boost to propel you over that last mountain.

Prepare for the worst and take extra nutrition bars in case you find yourself unexpectedly out in the woods overnight because you've wandered off the trail, gotten hurt, or had to stop in a shelter because weather or trail conditions prevented you from completing your day hike.

Water: Bring one to three liters of water, depending on the length and difficulty of the hike, elevation changes, temperature, and your personal hydration needs. Calculate your water usage on practice hikes.

In the morning before you begin your hike, drink plenty of water. Plus, bring at least six to eight ounces per mile for the hike you've planned. If it is a hot, humid day, add electrolytes (in a powder form from a hiking outfitter) to your water, eat salty snacks, or drink sports drinks. It is easy to become dehydrated.

Be safe. Take extra water. If you are new to hiking and plan to hike eight to ten miles, take at least two liters of water. After you have day-hiking experience and know what your hydration needs are, take what you know you need plus extra.

Should you use a water hydration system or water bottles? This is a personal preference. Are you a sipper or a gulper? With a water hydration system, consisting of a water bladder with tubing that leads to your mouth, you can sip water hands-free all day long. With water bottles, you can drink water at a fast rate when you stop. Which would you rather do?

What we do: We use a CamelBak hydration system. We find that the water bladder is easy to fill and easy to use all day long. We carry three liters of water because we want to have plenty of water available and do not want to stop to purify additional water. We check our water usage at the end of each day.

If we don't need the water, someone else may need it, or water might be needed for a medical emergency. Several times we have come upon backpackers who needed water and have given them our extra by taking off the mouthpiece of our hose and draining water into their containers from our water bladder.

When we first started day hiking, we carried water bottles. We found that we did not drink often enough and were always exhausted at the end of the hike because we were dehydrated.

Do you need to take a water-purification device or water-purifying tablets or liquid on a day hike? For safety, always take water-purifying tablets or liquid or a water-purification device to use for those unexpected emergencies or overnight stays.

Water-purifying tablets or liquids are light, but take thirty minutes to four hours to work, depending on the type of purifying chemicals and the cleanliness and temperature of the water. Dirty, cold water takes longer to purify.

Water-purification devices weigh four ounces or more. You must stop at streams along the way to purify water and fill up your water bottles or bladder. You can purify one liter of water with some water purification devices in two minutes or more. These devices are useful if you are hiking more than ten miles on a challenging hike in hot weather or on shorter hikes when you want to reduce the weight you carry. Water weighs 2.2 pounds per liter.

What do we do? If we plan a hike of ten miles or less and are carrying three liters of water, we take Katadyn Micropur purifying tablets to use in an emergency. If we plan a longer hike or plan to hike in hot weather, we add a SteriPEN ultraviolet light or Sawyer mini-filter water purification device to use if our water runs low.

Extra Clothing: Always carry a rain jacket, an extra pair of socks, and a bandana. In the spring, fall, or winter, add a warm synthetic fleece or down lightweight jacket, a warm wool or synthetic skull cap, synthetic or wool gloves, and a neck wrap. If the weather forecast calls for rain with declining temperatures, add waterproof pants, gloves, and short gaiters (synthetic coverings to keep rain out of your shoes), and line your pack with a plastic garbage bag to keep everything dry. Always be prepared for the worst. Pack additional clothing in small waterproof bags.

Rain gear: Your rain jacket and pants should be lightweight, waterproof (not just water resistant), and breathable. The rain jacket and pants can be used against both rain and wind.

Umbrella (optional): When you expect light showers, an umbrella is nice to have because it will keep you dry and cool and you will not need your rain jacket.

What we like: Rain jacket and rain pants by LightHeart Gear and the Euroschirm telescope hands-free umbrella.

Extra socks: Bring an extra pair of the same kind that you plan to wear hiking. You do not want your feet to be wet with perspiration or water. I often change my socks at midday if it is a hot, humid, or rainy day. These extra socks can also substitute for gloves if the weather unexpectedly turns cold.

Bandana or handkerchief: *A* lightweight bandana can be used for many things, including wiping perspiration, washing your face in a cool stream, wiping rain from your glasses, and compressing a wound to stop bleeding.

Personal Necessities: Pack hand cleaner, sunscreen, lip balm, insect repellant, toilet paper or Kleenex, and a trowel. Bring the toilet paper in a plastic bag with an extra plastic bag to pack out the dirty wipes. You will use the trowel (small spade) to dig a cat hole in which to dispose of human waste. Bring a plastic bag to put the trowel in after you use it.

Camera or iPhone with camera: You will want a lightweight megapixel camera with at least a 10X zoom or an iPhone camera to capture your adventure, the views from the mountaintops, and the beautiful flora. Each Appalachian Trail day hike is an amazing journey that you will want to remember with your pictures.

The advantage of the megapixel camera is the quality of the pictures. The advantage of your iPhone camera is that you can immediately send pictures to your family and friends.

What we do: Jim has an Olympus camera that he likes because it is protected against damage from drops up to seven feet and from water up to seventeen feet. Although he never wants to drop it or submerge it, Jim wants this kind of protection for his camera.

I have a Sony that I like because of the high quality of color pictures it produces.

A.T. Passport (Optional): This is a small folded document with squares on which hiker-friendly lodging, outfitters, restaurants, and national parks can place their stamp to verify you have visited their location. This is only a memento of your trip, not a required document. Go to www. atpassport.com or www.appalachiantrail.org to purchase an A.T. Passport.

The ATC is sponsoring the 14-State Challenge. When you have hiked on the A.T. in each state, purchase a 14-State Challenge badge. Have your A.T. Passport stamped by a hiker-friendly business in each state. Be proud of your accomplishment and show your friends that you have hiked in each of the fourteen states that the A.T. traverses. Put your new badge on your daypack.

Essential Safety Equipment and Supplies

1. **Headlight** *with extra batteries* to use when the light is dim or it is dark.
2. **Cell phone** to call or text in an emergency. (Keep the cell phone off unless you need to use it in an emergency. If you leave your cell phone on in remote areas where you do not have service, it will continue to search for service towers and drain your battery more quickly.)
3. **Whistle** to alert your partner where you are if you get separated or to alert other hikers that you need help. Sound three whistle blasts every fifteen minutes to alert others you need assistance.
4. **Emergency blanket** to use to keep you warm if you are injured or have an unplanned overnight stay. A blanket specifically designed for this purpose is lightweight, low bulk, and made of heat-reflective thin, plastic sheeting. (This sheeting was developed by NASA to be used on the exterior surface of spacecraft for heat control.)
5. **Waterproof matches or a lighter** to ignite a fire to keep you warm in an emergency, such as an injury or unplanned overnight stay. Take these matches or lighter in all seasons. At higher elevations, the weather can change quickly and be much cooler than expected.

6. **Small pocketknife** to cut supplies or repair equipment.
7. **Reflective mirror** to signal your location to rescuers if you are lost or have an accident.
8. **Pencil and paper** to leave notes for friends or rescuers. For example, if you get off the trail because nature calls while your partner is hiking behind you, you might want to leave him a note to let him know where you are.
9. **One foot of duct tape** to use to repair your pack or other equipment.
10. **Fifty feet of small nylon parachute rope** for rescue purposes if someone falls.

Optional: *Satellite tracking device.* If you are hiking in a remote part of the Appalachian Trail at a time when there are few hikers, you might consider taking a satellite tracking device to send your GPS location to family and friends; this signal can give them peace of mind by letting them know where you are. You can also use it to send an emergency signal if you have an accident or get lost.

What we do: We take a SPOT satellite tracking device when we day hike the Appalachian Trail in remote places, such as the White Mountains in New Hampshire. My sister, who is my emergency contact, says, "I feel better knowing you have a SPOT. I worry when you are hiking."

Optional: *Bear spray.* Check the ATC, National Park Service, and US Forest Service websites for any warnings about high bear activity in the area where you plan to hike. If there is high bear activity, buy bear spray and learn how to use it.

Essential First-Aid Supplies

1. **Synthetic gloves** to protect you and any sick or injured person from bacteria and viruses.
2. **Six to ten bandages** for small cuts or abrasions.

3. **Four to six sterile pads** *(two inches by three inches or four inches by four inches)* to use to compress a wound if a hiker ends up with a cut that is bleeding profusely.

4. **Clear one-inch-wide medical tape** *(by 3M)* to secure sterile pads, compress a wound, use with padding to stabilize a broken bone, or apply to hot spots or areas susceptible to hot spots.

5. **Scissors** to cut bandages.

6. **Tweezers** to remove splinters or ticks.

7. **A small water bottle** to use when washing wounds. Experts recommend that you use water to flush out wounds to clean them rather than using alcohol wipes.

8. **Products to prevent or treat blisters.** There are several options: Moleskin, Second Skin, and New-Skin. Moleskin is cotton padding with adhesive to put around the blister to protect it from further abrasion. Second Skin is a moist pad that helps cool a hot spot. (A hot spot is a red spot that hurts and is caused by friction.) New-Skin is a liquid bandage to paint the hot spot with in order to ease pain and promote healing. Potential problem areas can also be painted in order to prevent hot spots from developing. These products can be found in the foot-care section of most pharmacies.

9. **Elastic wrap or bandana** to wrap a sprained ankle or knee in case of injury.

10. **Over-the-counter medications and protective creams:** sunscreen with an SPF of at least 30; insect repellant; Polysporin antibiotic ointment to protect any cut or burn you might sustain and to prevent infection; pain relief medication, such as aspirin, Advil, or Tylenol; Claritin or Benadryl for allergic reactions; and insect-bite ointment to reduce any itching or swelling.

Know how to use these essential first-aid supplies, and take a first-aid course, such as the ones offered by the Wilderness Medicine Institute or the American Red Cross.

Place all supplies in a small waterproof bag and have it readily available near the top of your pack. If you use some of the supplies during your hike, restock the same day after completing that day's hike. If you do not want to make your own first-aid kit, outfitters sell small sets for day hiking.

What we do: Jim takes an REI Day Hiker First-Aid Kit. I take a homemade kit with all the items described above. I take a small Victorinox tool that has a pocketknife, scissors, and tweezers. When we are hiking multiple days, I take extra supplies plus ice packs that activate when squeezed. I leave these behind in the hotel room in case we need to replace items we have used or need the ice packs for injuries.

Hiking Poles

Some people use hiking poles and some do not. Hiking poles increase your stability and take the weight and stress off your knees as you hike downhill. At streams, they help you stay upright as you cross on rocks or slippery logs.

Use lightweight, adjustable, anti-shock aluminum or carbon poles with cushioned hand grips. Poles should be adjusted to the height that you need. When you are standing and the hiking pole is parallel to your body, the grip should meet your hands when your elbows bend at a ninety-degree angle.

What we take: For years, I used Leki adjustable, anti-shock hiking poles. On his thru-hike, our son used Leki hiking poles, and Leki sent him a replacement when a pole bent and became unusable.

In 2013 I discovered the Black Diamond carbon hiking poles at just the right length for me. They fold into short fourteen-inch lengths, have rubber and steel tips, and are very easy to use. They are not for everyone because they only come in three lengths and do not have the anti-shock feature.

Jim, on the other hand, is very agile and carries only one pole, which has a camera mount on top that holds the camera still for good shots. He sees no need for two hiking poles except at stream crossings. He picks up a heavy stick or borrows one of my poles to make a safe stream crossing.

Plan Your Hiking Trip

Choose your hike(s). With your hiking partner, select a hike or hikes that you both feel comfortable with, considering the distance, level of effort, and trail profile. If the main hike that we list for an area seems too challenging or too long, select one of the alternate shorter hikes.

Select the time of year you would like to go. Each season is beautiful in its own way, but each has challenges as well. In the early spring and late fall, the weather can be iffy; storms, snow, rain, and muddy trails are all possibilities. In the summer, be prepared for heat, insects, and dry springs. In the winter, you might deal with extreme chill and winds.

Set potential dates and check the weather history for those dates.

Learn more about your hike(s)

Explore official A.T. maps and guidebooks. Examine the map for the section of the A.T. you plan to hike as you would a road map. It will show you where the roads to the trailheads are; which roads, streams, mountains, and gaps the trail crosses; and how the elevation profile looks.

The profile will tell you whether there are steep changes in elevation, such as five hundred feet in half a mile, or if you'll experience a more gradual change, such as five hundred feet over a distance of two or three miles.

Explore US Forest Service and National Park maps. If the A.T. is in one of the national forests or national parks as it is in the Southeast, these maps will show the A.T., other trails, and most roads, including Forest Service roads; county, state, and federal roads. These are particularly useful for driving to the trailheads. For Georgia, examine the map for the Chattahoochee-Oconee National Forest; for Southwest North Carolina, examine the map for the Nantahala National Forest; and for the Smokies, examine the map for the Great Smoky Mountains National Park.

Explore the *Delorme Atlas & Gazetteer.* This book is also useful for driving to the trailheads. There is one book for each state. These books have topographic maps showing back roads, recreational sites, and GPS grids.

Explore electronic maps and profiles. For hikes in this guide go to www.CalTopo/m/17QA. Select the hike you plan to take and then select "profile." This will bring up the map and the profile. On the profile, you can move the line back and forth and see the dot on the map move. If you want to know the name of one of the peaks, you can zoom in on the dot until you can read the name of the peak. You can also see the terrain, roads, and streams.

Find pictures and hiking stories for this portion of the A.T. Go to our website, www.atdayhiker.com, to see pictures we have posted. Google the hike and go to www.trailjournals.com and www.thetrek.co to see what other hikers have posted.

Plan the logistics

Length of each hike: If this is a multi-day trip, vary the number of miles you hike each day.

What we do: If we are taking a multi-day hiking trip, I plan an easy hike the first day. In the middle of the trip, we take a day off for relaxation or we do another easy hike.

Lodging: If you need lodging, select a place to stay as close to the A.T. as possible.

Restaurants: Once you have picked a restaurant, be sure to check the hours and days that it is open. In small towns, restaurants tend to close early and are not open every day. Choose a backup restaurant in case your restaurant of choice unexpectedly closes early.

What we do: We try local restaurants. We choose a restaurant and then have a backup plan. Occasionally, we bring precooked food with us in a cooler for the first night. When we plan a long hiking day and think we might be too tired to go out, we buy prepared food at a nearby grocery the day before to eat in our room after the hike.

Transportation to and from the trailheads where you plan to start and end your hike: You will need to use a shuttle-service provider or plan to shuttle yourselves using two cars so you will have a car at the ending trailhead when you finish your hike. Don't try to schedule a shuttle service to pick you up when you expect to arrive at the end because your hiking time may vary, and shuttle-service providers don't like to wait for you. Don't count on being able to call a shuttle-service provider when you arrive at the end because cell phone service is not reliable in remote areas.

What we do: When we are hiking near our home, we take two cars. When we are hiking farther away, we either hire a shuttle service or rent a car, whichever is easier and more cost effective.

Be Safe

Leave a copy of your itinerary with at least two friends or family members. Leave it with someone who will check on you if you do not return when expected. Don't forget to let them know when you do return.

Sign the hiker registers in the shelters along the A.T. When rescuers are looking for people who are lost, they check hiker registers.

Follow the white A.T. blazes closely. Occasionally, when you are talking with your partner or enjoying the solitude of the forest, you might miss a turn along the trail and wander down an animal trail that looks like the A.T., or you might end up on another trail or logging road that crosses the Appalachian Trail.

If you have not seen a white blaze for fifteen minutes, stop, think, and retrace your steps until you find a white blaze.

Check the weather conditions before you leave home for a hiking trip, and then check for updates daily.

Be prepared for the worst weather. If it is raining but not lightning and you plan to hike, take full rain gear plus extra clothes to change into if your clothes get wet. Take a warm jacket as well. Protect the contents of your pack by lining it with a plastic bag and putting your clothes in waterproof ditty bags.

As you hike, follow the weather patterns in the sky. If the weather becomes stormy with lightning, avoid hills, balds, mountaintops, cliffs, and tall trees. Take cover in an area of the forest with smaller trees and bushes or in a shelter.

Change your plans for the day when forecasters predict unsafe conditions, such as extreme cold, ice, strong winds, lightning, tornadoes, and floods. This may be the day you check out nearby museums and shops in one of the towns described in **Fun Places to Visit** in this guidebook.

Check the trail conditions a few days before you leave on your trip. Ask the US Forest Service or the National Park Service in the area where you will be hiking what the trail conditions are. Check the ATC or local A.T. hiking club websites for notices about trail conditions.

Ask if there has been severe weather in the area that has taken down trees or caused floods or fires. If so, find out if parts of the trail have been closed or rerouted because of these events.

Ask if there have been recent rains or storms that have made the paths muddy or caused stream crossings to become more challenging.

Ask if there has been a drought that has left the streams and creeks dry.

Ask if there has been increased bear activity in the area and if any shelters or parts of the trail have been closed because of this.

Change your hiking plans if you or your partner (s) aren't feeling well. The Appalachian Trail is located in remote areas. You need to be healthy to enjoy your day hike. (In the section below, "you" refers to both you and your hiking partner (s).)

If you are sick, feel a little under the weather, or have had a recent injury or surgery before you leave, delay your trip.

If you become exhausted, injured, or sick while hiking, you are more likely to fall, slip, or go the wrong way. Stop and rest. If you become injured, administer first aid. If you feel exhausted and dehydrated, eat an energy bar, nuts, or something salty. Drink more water.

After you have rested, decide what you should do. Can you make it to the point where you had planned to end your hike? If so, go at a slower pace and stop to rest frequently. If you can't, devise an early exit strategy.

Know where you can make an early exit on your planned hike in case of an emergency. Have your A.T. map with you so that you know where the nearest roads are. As you hike along, be aware of landmarks you have passed, such as shelters, streams, trail crossings, and roads.

Know when the sun rises and sets. Plan your hike so that you are back at your car before the sun sets.

Be prepared for an unexpectedly long hiking day that leaves you on the trail as the light is waning. Occasionally you may find yourself in this situation because it has taken longer than expected to shuttle your cars, because the hike was more difficult than expected, or because you had an accident.

Have your headlight and extra batteries near the top of your pack. Put the headlight on as the light begins to wane so that you won't miss white blazes or stumble over rocks and roots.

Be prepared for the possibility that you may have to go back for your second car on a Forest Service road after dark; it can be tricky.

Check your car's GPS and your hiking GPS to see if they show any secondary and Forest Service roads. Have your hiking map and Forest Service map out to use for navigation; both will show you any Forest Service roads.

Driving on secondary or Forest Service roads after dark can be a little tricky because they have limited road signs. It is easy to take the wrong turn.

One night near Davenport Gap, Tennessee when we were hiking with friends, we experienced one of those situations. The hike had taken longer than expected. It was already getting dark when we finished the hike at six thirty p.m. We were ten miles from the nearest restaurant, located at a gas station, which was closing in thirty minutes. Fifteen miles away—in the other direction—was the second car we needed to retrieve.

We decided to eat first. About eight o'clock, we headed back to get the second car on a winding and remote Forest Service road. Jim was driving and I was navigating with the hiking map because the AAA map did not show Forest Service roads. We did not have our car GPS.

We were taking our friends to get their car at the place where we had left it when we began our hike. The car was near Max Patch, a beautiful mountain bald on the A.T. in the middle of nowhere near the North Carolina/Tennessee border. In the daylight, we'd had no problem finding Max Patch.

But the night was pitch black, and there were no lights from cars or houses. When we came to a crossroads, my heart was pounding as I wondered, "Which way should we turn? I'm not sure this is the same Forest Service road as the one the map shows. There is no sign." In rural areas, not all roads are on the hiking map and not all roads have signs.

Hoping this was the correct one, I said, "Turn left. I think this road goes to Max Patch." In ten more minutes, there was another crossroads with no road sign. I looked at the map again and said, "Go straight." Finally, after what seemed like an hour, our lights shone on our friends' car in the parking area. Every muscle of my body relaxed and I said, "We're here."

Use your hiking poles when the trail has rocks, roots, and slippery surfaces that could cause you to fall.

Cross streams carefully. Fortunately, in the southeast section of the A.T., the streams are usually shallow, but after heavy rains, they may be flowing fast and deep. Be careful. Use your hiking poles to steady yourself when crossing on stones or slippery logs.

If you must ford a stream, look for a place to cross where the stream has a low current and is not very deep. Do not cross in a narrow place where the current is the strongest. If the stream is above your knees, look for another place to cross.

Protect those feet that must take every step along the trail. Wear trail shoes or boots and socks that make your feet happy. Powder your feet to prevent dampness. Prevent hot spots by air-drying your feet and changing your socks at lunch or when your feet become damp. If you know your feet are susceptible to blisters, paint the potential hot-spot areas with New-Skin or wrap them with medical tape. I know I am repeating myself here, but taking care of your feet is a priority.

Be prepared for everyday hiker health challenges. Have your first-aid kit readily available and know how to use it.

Treat hot spots and blisters: If you feel a hot spot (a little red place hurting on your foot), stop, inspect, and protect the spot from further abrasion with moleskin, medical tape, New-Skin or Second Skin. If you already have a blister, cut a hole in the moleskin a little larger than the blister, apply the moleskin so that the blister peeks through it, put antibiotic ointment on the blister, and cover it with a bandage.

Prevent sunburn: When hiking on sections of the trail exposed to direct sunlight, such as balds and gaps, and in the forest when the trees are bare, wear long-sleeved shirts and pants and a broad-brimmed hat. Apply sunscreen to exposed areas such as your face.

Prevent insect bites: Put insect repellant on your exposed skin, particularly in the summer. If you are in a "tick-infested area," you might want to spay your clothes with clothing insect repellant. Avoid ticks in heavily wooded and grassy areas by walking in the middle of the trail away from tall grasses and bushes and by tucking your shirt into your pants and your pants into your socks. At the end of the day, inspect your body for ticks. Take a hot shower and wash with a cloth to remove any unattached ticks.

If you find ticks attached to your body, use tweezers to grasp and pull the ticks straight out. Save any tick you find. If you suspect that you have been bitten by a deer tick (a tiny black tick the size of a pinhead), seek medical treatment and show the doctor the tick. Do not wait until symptoms appear. Deer ticks can cause Lyme Disease, which can make you very ill.

Prior to your trip, Google "tick-infested areas" to see what kind of ticks you might expect when hiking. In the Southeast, it is dog ticks and not deer ticks that are most likely to be a problem, but be on the lookout for deer ticks.

Prevent mild dehydration: Symptoms include fatigue, thirst, confusion, and dark yellow urine. Drink plenty of water and in hot weather, eat salty snacks. If you do become dehydrated, drink water, sports drinks, or fruit drinks, and eat fruits, such as bananas, that are loaded with potassium, which your body needs.

Prevent overheating: Symptoms include extreme fatigue, headaches, and nausea. In hot weather, wear light-colored and lightweight clothes and a hat with mesh vents, hike early in the morning, rest in the shade in the middle of the day, hike slowly, drink plenty of water, eat salty snacks, add electrolytes to your water, and wet your body with cool water.

Prevent and treat mild to moderate hypothermia (subnormal body temperature): Symptoms include shivering, confusion, stumbling, fumbling, and slurred speech. Prevent this by wearing warm clothes, including a hat, gloves, and neck scarf in cold and windy weather; replacing wet clothes with dry clothes; putting on a jacket once you have stopped hiking in cool weather; drinking plenty of water; and eating high-energy food.

To treat mild or moderate hypothermia, move the ailing hiker from the trail to a sheltered environment out of the wind. Remove his or her wet clothes and replace them with dry, warm clothing. Have the ailing hiker snuggle with warm people, and give him or her tepid or warm fluids and snacks.

Be cautious of strangers. Don't tell them your plans. Don't hitch a ride. Follow your gut instincts. Leave any situation which makes you feel uncomfortable. Go to the nearest trailhead and alert the US Forest

Service or National Park officials if you have noticed something that you feel might pose a danger to others on the trail.

Unfortunately, the Appalachian Trail is not immune to criminal behavior, especially in spots where unsavory people have access to the A.T. near major roads. Locals may have beer or drug parties in shelters near paved roads on weekends. Although violence is rare, it has occurred.

One day when we were hiking along the A.T. in the Cherokee National Forest, we came upon a situation which made me feel uncomfortable. There was an old camper parked right next to the trail. We did not see anyone, but I wondered if the owner might be luring hikers to his trailer for unsavory reasons. Before we left the area, we went to the US Forest Service office and reported our findings. The ranger told Jim that anyone is permitted to camp in the national forest. Rangers check on people if a problem is reported and would check this trailer out.

Reduce opportunities for theft. Leave your jewelry at home, keep your money and credit cards hidden on your person, and don't leave your pack unguarded.

At trailheads, do not leave valuables in your car.

Be prepared for an unexpected meeting with a black bear or poisonous snake. The forest is their home; respect and do not disturb them. Do not leave food and wrappers out and give bears a reason to come near you. No hiker ever wants to get too close to a bear or snake, and guess what? Bears and snakes don't want to get too close to you either.

The ATC and NPS post signs on the A.T. or notices on the internet about areas with high bear activity. Before your hiking trip, check their websites. If you will be in an area with high bear activity, carry bear spray and know how to use it.

The ATC and NPS recommend the following actions when you unexpectedly meet a black bear or happen upon a poisonous snake.

Black bear sighting: Stop, keep your eye on the bear, and retreat slowly. **Do not run or climb a tree.** The bear can run faster and climb better than you can.

The few times that Jim and I have seen bears nearby, they have gone the other way when they heard us coming or when Jim yelled, "A bear!" and made noise.

In the rare situation when the bear comes toward you, stand your ground, wave your arms, create a commotion, and throw things at him. If he attacks, fight back by going for his face and eyes and using your bear spray.

Poisonous snakes: Snakes hide in tall grasses and piles of leaves or rocks, and can be found on top of boulders. Watch where you put your hands and feet.

If you encounter a rattlesnake, stop, stamp your feet, and move back slowly. The vibration of your moving feet will let the snake know you have moved away.

Evaluate the situation. Do you hear rattling noises? If so, the rattlesnake is alarmed and may strike. A rattler can spring one third to one half of its length or about one to three feet.

At a safe distance, wait to see if the rattlesnake slithers away after he stops rattling. If the rattlesnake stays and defends his position, wait until he stops rattling. Then give him a wide berth and walk around him, keeping his head and tail in view. Do not provoke him.

If you encounter a copperhead, wait and keep an eye on his head. Move back slowly. Do not provoke. Wait to see if he slithers away. A copperhead may freeze and stay where he is. If he does not move, give him a wide berth and walk around him.

Be prepared for the rare and unexpected medical emergency. Take a first-aid course and be prepared to assist in these situations. Experts in wilderness and backcountry first aid make the following recommendations. (In the situations below the terms, "he," "him," and "his," refer to the person in distress whether the person is male or female.)

In the medical emergencies described below, access the situation, keep the person in distress warm, and put him in a protected environment. If possible, move the person to the side of the trail, put an emergency blanket or pad underneath him, and cover the person with a jacket or emergency blanket.

Call and text 911, even if you have no signal, and prepare evacuation plans. Be ready to tell the emergency crew where you are, including what roads, shelters, or landmarks you have recently passed.

A cell phone carrier is required to deliver emergency calls and texts even if the caller is not using the carrier's service. In remote areas where there is limited reception, text messages may still go through. If you have a SPOT or other tracking device, send out an emergency signal.

If you are unable to contact emergency personnel from where you are and you have done as much for the person in distress as you can, try other ways to contact emergency services, such as climbing to the top of a mountain where cell phone reception is better or going to the nearest road and flagging down a passerby.

If the hiker has a broken bone, large cut, or head injury, stop and evaluate the situation. Is he bleeding? Is he breathing? Does he have a pulse? Is he conscious?

If the person is bleeding profusely, put pressure on the wound. When the bleeding stops, apply a tight bandage but make sure that it's not constricting.

If the person isn't breathing or has no pulse, check for airway obstruction, clear the airway if necessary, and initiate CPR.

If the injured person is unconscious, monitor his vital signs: pulse, breathing, and consciousness.

If the person has an injured limb and possibly a broken bone, immobilize the limb with splints.

If the hiker has severe chest pains, do not allow him to continue hiking. Keep him physically and emotionally calm. If he stops breathing and has no pulse, start CPR.

If the hiker has signs of a stroke, such as slurred speech, numbness, or paralysis in the arms, legs, or face, or if the person in distress has trouble seeing, do not let him continue hiking. Ask him to sit or lie down and monitor his vital signs.

In the rare situation where a hiker is bitten by a poisonous snake, move the person away from the snake. Stay calm. Take off any rings, bands, or clothing from the limb where the bite occurred. (The limb will swell and the ring or clothing will restrict circulation.) Wash the wound. Keep the hand, arm, or leg where the bite occurred below the victim's heart.

Do not give the person anything to eat or drink. Keep the injured hiker quiet and still. Do not continue to hike. Be prepared to tell emergency personnel what the snake looked like and whether or not it had rattles.

Carol's Tips for a Fun and Safe Hiking Trip

- Be physically and mentally prepared for the trip.
- Hike with a partner, and bring friends to enjoy the trip with you.
- Wear appropriate hiking clothes and shoes.
- Take a comfortable, lightweight pack with essentials for the day hike, including rain gear, first-aid supplies, safety gear, and a warm sweater or jacket if you are hiking in the fall, spring, or winter.
- Bring enough water for adequate hydration and snacks to provide you with that extra energy for hiking.
- Bring maps and a compass, GPS, and camera so you can navigate the trail easily and record and share special moments and sights.
- Know what to expect along the Appalachian Trail.
- Check the weather forecast each day before you start your hike.
- Hike at a comfortable pace. Do not hurry.
- Plan your hike so you have the whole day to savor the beauty of the Appalachian Trail and the scenery, wildflowers, trees, and creatures you will discover.
- Plan your hike so that you are not on the trail after dark when you will be more vulnerable to accidents.

- Learn about local towns near the Appalachian Trail. Select comfortable lodging and restaurants nearby. Leave time for **Fun Places to Visit.**

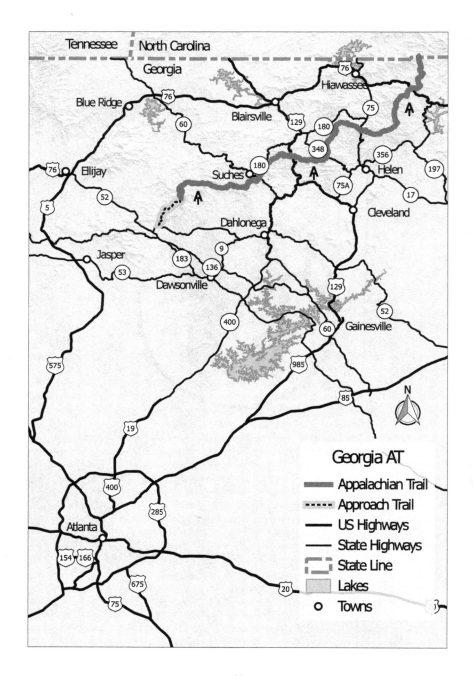

The Appalachian Trail in Georgia

Although the Appalachian Trail in Georgia is not for the timid, it *is* for those who enjoy the sights and sounds of the forest and the mountains. It winds up and down four four-thousand--foot mountains and twelve peaks that are over thirty-five hundred feet. It crosses streams, gaps, and roads but does not go through towns. The highest point is Blood Mountain, which stands at 4,460 feet.

The A.T. takes you through the depths of the Chattahoochee-Oconee National Forest and is covered with beautiful trees, plants, wildflowers, and rock outcroppings. In the late spring and summer, you will walk under the cover of trees

As I look out over the mountains, I ponder, "Will I be able hike all seventy-eight miles of the A.T. in Georgia?" May 2007

and through rhododendron and mountain-laurel tunnels. In the fall, you will delight in the reds, oranges, and yellows as the leaves change colors. In the winter, because the trees are bare, you will be able to see easily from one mountain to the next. Each season is special.

Springer Mountain, the southern terminus of the Appalachian Trail, is the place to be when thru-hikers are just beginning their trek. We like to stop and meet the hikers and hear their stories. They feel the call of the Appalachian Trail and are following their dream. Join them in April or May after the early spring crowd has started, and hike your own dream, one day at a time.

Peruse the eight hikes in Georgia and see which one you want to try.

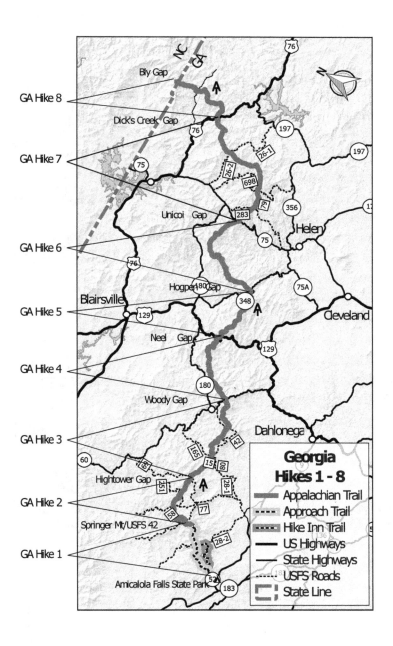

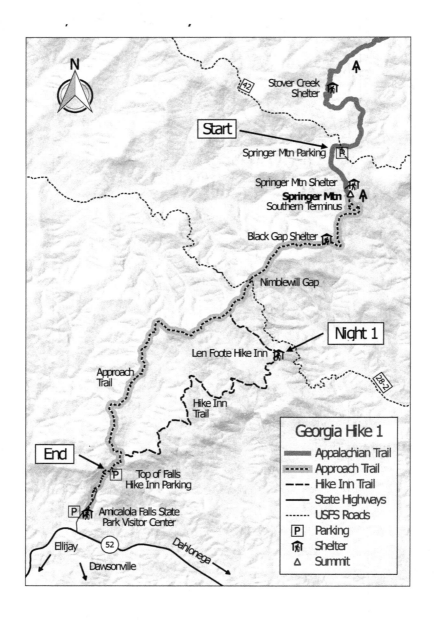

USFS 42 to Springer Mountain to Len Foote Hike Inn to the Top of Amicalola Falls

Day 1: 5.2 miles, Moderate;
Day 2: 4.8 miles, Easy

Georgia Hike 1 is a two-day hiking trip with an overnight at Len Foote Hike Inn. It is a one-mile taste of the Appalachian Trail.

I stand near the hiker plaque on Springer Mountain. April 2016.

Day 1: USFS 42 and Springer Mountain Parking to Springer Mountain, Then to Len Foote Hike Inn

HIGHLIGHTS: At Springer Mountain, look at thetwo bronze plaques and check the hiker register to see how many hikers have signed in for that year. The plaque with the embossed hiker in the picture above is near the first white blaze and was placed there by the Georgia Appalachian Trail Club when the southern terminus of the A.T. was moved from Mount Oglethorpe to Springer Mountain in 1958. The other plaque designates Springer Mountain as the southern terminus of the Appalachian National Scenic Trail and was placed there in 1993 by the US Forest Service.

At the end of day one, you will enjoy an overnight stay at Len Foote Hike Inn, Georgia's only backcountry inn. (A backcountry inn is one that is located in a remote, undeveloped rural area.) It is an environmentally friendly inn with basic accommodations, good meals, and a knowledgeable staff. For more information, go to **Fine Wine and Accommodations: Dawsonville, Lodging in Amicalola Falls State Park.**

DISTANCE: 5.2 miles.   **HIKE TIME:** 3 hours.

LEVEL OF EFFORT: Moderate to Easy.

RECOMMENDED DIRECTION: North to south, from USFS 42 and Springer Mountain parking to Springer Mountain to Len Foote Hike Inn.

DOWNHILL HIKE: 2.8 miles with an elevation loss of 1,350 feet. **UPHILL:** 2.4 miles with an elevation gain of 1,030 feet.

ALONG THE TRAIL: From USFS 42 to the summit of Springer Mountain, you will hike the A.T. under the shade of hardwood trees up and over rocks and more rocks. You will cross the Benton MacKaye Trail and the side trail to Springer Mountain Shelter. After exploring the summit and enjoying the views, you will hike south on the earthen A.T. Approach Trail and pass the side trail to Black Gap Shelter. At the next trail juncture, you will turn left and hike down the narrow Len Foote Hike Inn Trail through the rhododendron tunnels to the Len Foote Hike Inn.

Each trail is marked with a blaze that is a different color and sometimes a different shape. The Appalachian Trail is marked with white rectangular blazes, the Benton MacKaye Trail with white diamond-shaped blazes, the A.T. Approach Trail and the side trails to the shelters with blue rectangular blazes, and the Len Foote Hike Inn Trail with lime-green rectangular blazes.

SHELTERS: There are two shelters, one at Springer Mountain and one at Black Gap, just off the A.T. Approach Trail. Each has a picnic table, a nearby privy, and a nearby water source.

Follow the White Blazes

MILE 0.0: USFS 42 and Springer Mountain parking, 3,390 feet.
MILE 0.8: Southern terminus of Benton MacKaye Trail; Springer Mountain Shelter, 0.2 miles east.
MILE 1.0: Springer Mountain, 3,782 feet. On the rock to the right is the Georgia A.T. Club bronze plaque with the embossed hiker. On the rock to the left is the US Forest Service bronze plaque marking the southern terminus of the Appalachian National Scenic Trail and the black mailbox with the hiker register.

Follow the Blue Blazes of the A.T. Approach Trail

MILE 2.5: Black Gap Shelter.
MILE 3.6: Nimblewill Gap (USFS 28), 3,060 feet.

Follow the Lime-Green Blazes

MILE 4.2: Turn left down the Len Foote Hike Inn Trail.
MILE 5.2: Len Foote Hike Inn, 3,060 feet.

Peaks and Valleys

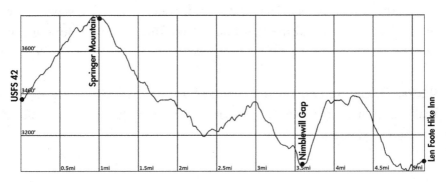

Day 2: Len Foote Hike Inn to the Top of Amicalola Falls

HIGHLIGHTS: Have a cup of coffee and watch the sun rise from the Sunrise Room porch or the granite Star Base of the Hike Inn. (See the picture below.) Along the trail, enjoy views of Atlanta and Stone Mountain rising from the haze. In the spring, look for wildflowers, mountain laurel, and rhododendrons blooming. In the fall, delight in the beautiful colors of the changing hickory, maple, and oak leaves and the smell of the pine trees. From the top of Amicalola Falls, the highest falls east of the Mississippi, you will be mesmerized by the sight of water cascading down the rocks.

DISTANCE: 4.8 miles.   **HIKE TIME:** 2.5 hours.   **LEVEL OF EFFORT:** Easy.

Len Foote Hike Inn, October 2011 Courtesy of Betty Brewer-Calvert

RECOMMENDED DIRECTION: North to south, from Len Foote Hike Inn south to the top of Amicalola Falls.

DOWNHILL HIKE: 3.0 miles with an elevation loss of 1,230 feet. **UPHILL:** 1.8 miles with an elevation gain of 700 feet.

ALONG THE TRAIL: The trail is an earthen path about three feet wide along the ridge with a drop-off on the eastern side. It winds over rolling hills, through trees and rhododendron tunnels, and crosses several small creeks over wooden bridges and on stepping stones.

SHELTERS: No shelters.

The granite Star Base is a celestial calendar and compass marking the extremes of the summer and winter solstices. Oct 2011, Courtesy of Betty Brewer-Calvert.

Follow the Lime-Green Blazes of the Len Foote Hike Inn Trail

MILE 0: Len Foote Hike Inn, 3,060 feet.

MILE 0.7: Views of Atlanta, Stone Mountain, Sawnee Mountain, and Kennesaw Mountain, 2,970 feet.

MILE 3.9: Vista with log bench, 2,780 feet.

MILE 4.6: Juncture of the Len Foote Hike Inn Trail and the A.T. Approach Trail.

MILE 4.8: Top of Amicalola Falls and parking, 2,570 feet.

Peaks and Valleys

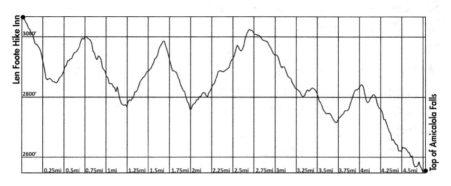

Alternative Hikes

If you want to drive one car and park nearby to make a loop hike to the Len Foote Hike Inn, use one of these hikes.

GEORGIA HIKE 1.1:
Northern Loop Hike, Day 1: 5.2 miles, Moderate;
Day 2: 5.2 miles, Moderate
DAY 1: USFS 42 and Springer Mountain parking to Springer Mountain, then to Len Foote Hike Inn.
DAY 2: Len Foote Hike Inn to Springer Mountain to USFS 42 and Springer Mountain parking.
DISTANCE: Day 1: 5.2 miles. Day 2: 5.2 miles.
HIKE TIME: Day 1: 3 hours. Day 2: 3 hours.
LEVEL OF EFFORT: Day 1: Moderate. Day 2: Moderate.

GEORGIA HIKE 1.2:

Southern Loop Hike, Day 1: 4.8 miles, Moderate; Day 2: 11.8 miles, Challenging

DAY 1: Top of Amicalola Falls to Len Foote Hike Inn.

DAY 2: Len Foote Hike Inn to Springer Mountain and then down the A.T. Approach Trail to the Top of Amicalola Falls.

DISTANCE: Day 1: 4.8 miles. Day 2: 11.8 miles.

HIKE TIME: Day 1: 2.5 hours. Day 2: 6 hours.

LEVEL OF EFFORT: Day 1: Moderate. Day 2: Challenging because of the total miles.

GEORGIA HIKE 1.3 :

Southern Loop Hike with a Second Night at Len Foote Hike Inn, Day 1: 4.8 miles, Moderate. Day 2: 8.4 miles, Moderate. Day 3: 4.8 miles, Easy

DAY 1: Top of Amicalola Falls to Len Foote Hike Inn.

DAY 2: Len Foote Hike Inn to Springer Mountain, then back to Len Foote Hike Inn.

DAY 3: Len Foote Hike Inn to the Top of Amicalola Falls.

DISTANCE: Day 1: 4.8 miles. Day 2: 8.4 miles. Day 3: 4.8 miles.

HIKE TIME: Day 1: 2.5 hours. Day 2: 4.5 hours. Day 3: 2.5 hours.

LEVEL OF EFFORT: Days 1 and 2: Moderate. Day 3: Easy.

My Hiking Journal

SOUTHERN LOOP HIKE, JANUARY 2010: We meet our friends John and Vicky in the parking area at the top of Amicalola Falls and begin our trek up the trail at about two o'clock. The skies are clear and the temperature is a little cool. Talking about hiking and future trips, we hike gingerly up and down over the rolling hills. We stop as Jim points out Stone Mountain and the tall buildings in Atlanta, about seventy miles southeast.

At four o'clock, we see the Hike Inn through the trees.

Vicky says, "I'm glad we are finally here."

We check in, get our linens, and go to the room.

John says, "Just bare bones, bunk beds with mattresses and blankets."

As we are making the beds, I say, "Woo. It is a little cold in here. We'd better turn on the heater. It's supposed to get colder tonight."

"How about a glass of wine?" Jim asks.

"Sure," we all say in unison. "Just what we need."

As we are finishing our wine, we hear a bell.

"Must be time for the tour of the Hike Inn," I say. "I think they are even going to show us the worms in the worm bed under the inn. The worms recycle leftover food and are their cash crop."

Vicky says, "Go ahead. I think I can miss that. We will see you for dinner."

At 6:30 p.m. the dinner bell rings. We join the others in the dining hall. There are families with small children, couples, and groups of adults, some young and some old. We find a place with Vicky and John and some new friends we have just met—Sam and Nancy and their young children, Matt and Grace.

I ask, "How did Matt and Grace do coming up the trail?"

Nancy replies, "They did just fine. We took our time and stopped when they wanted to rest."

As we settle in and pass the food around the table, Mike, the manager, says, "We are having ham, sweet potatoes, beans, salad, and apple cobbler tonight. Eat as much as you want. At the end of dinner, we will weigh the scraps from the plates at each table. I want to see who eats all of the food on their plates and has the least scraps by weight. Least is best. We don't want many leftovers. The worms cannot eat everything."

After dinner, we talk with Ann, a writer who is just beginning her annual week on the Appalachian Trail.

"I thru-hiked the Appalachian Trail in 1990," she tells us. "I come back every year to hike the A.T. and stay in the shelters for a week. It renews my spirit."

Robert, a 1970s thru-hiker, gives a slide presentation about another thru-hiking adventure, this one experienced with his son in 2000. When he hiked the A.T. the first time, he went north from Springer Mountain to Mount Katahdin, Maine. This time he and his son hiked from Mount Katahdin south to Springer Mountain. When they hiked the one-hundred-mile wilderness in Maine in June, the black flies were terrible. But other than that, the experience was great, he says. The equipment was better and lighter than on his previous trek, the trail food was good, and the friends they met were incredible.

I always enjoy hearing these thru-hikers' stories.

We awake the next morning to the beating of a drum, letting us know that the sun will soon be on the horizon. I open the door to check the weather.

"Brr. It is really cold out there," I say.

I bundle up and sit on the Sunrise Room porch with a cup of hot coffee to watch the red sun rise over the horizon in the clear, crisp air.

"The sunrise was beautiful," I say to Jim, John, and Vicky when I see them later in the dining hall.

At breakfast Mike announces, "The temperature is only twenty-eight this morning. We are expecting snow flurries."

As we get ready for our hike back to the car via the Approach Trail, we bundle up in warm caps, mittens, jackets, and long underwear.

When we get to the Approach Trail, Jim asks, "Do you want to go on up to Springer Mountain before we hike back down to the cars?"

John replies, "No, not today. It is too cold."

On the way down, we meet Tim, a thin young hiker moving quickly up the trail.

Jim asks, "Where are you from and where are you going?"

He says, "I'm a student at Ohio State and taking a long break. I'm going to Maine. I plan to be the first one to sign the hiker register at Springer Mountain this year."

Jim says, "Good luck."

A little further down the mountain, we meet Pam and Tom, an older couple bundled in their jackets, caps, and gloves, and carrying big packs.

Jim asks them, "Where are you from and where are you going?"

Pam says, "We're from Auburn. Tom's a retired professor, and I'm a retired medical technologist. We are beginning our thru-hike for the fourth time. The first time, I fell and got hurt. The next time, Tom got Lyme disease. The last time, we made it to Front Royal. This time, we hope to make it all the way."

Just as they head on up the trail, we look up and see snowflakes.

Jim calls to them, "Do you want a ride to the trailhead near Springer Mountain?"

After talking to each other, they turn and say, "Yes, we do."

They hike down to the car with us.

John and Vicky say, "We better head back to Atlanta."

The snow is falling lightly as Jim drives slowly out of Amicalola Falls State Park. We drive west on GA 52 and see more and more snow sticking on the road. The traffic is crawling. We see a car in a ditch.

Jim says, "I don't think we can make it to the trailhead near Springer Mountain. The forest service road will be too slippery. We'd better turn around and go back to Amicalola Falls."

I turn around and say to Pam and Tom, "I think we will go to the Amicalola Falls State Park Lodge for the night. Where would you like to go?"

Tom says, "Just let us out at the visitor's center. Our car is in the parking lot. We may just stay at the shelter behind the visitor's center tonight and start our thru-hike tomorrow."

With our car slipping a little on the hills, we slowly drive back to Amicalola Falls State Park and leave Pam and Tom at the parking lot near the visitor's center. We drive up the mountain toward the lodge, and the car begins to slide. We slow to a crawl. Finally, we make it to the snow-covered parking lot at the lodge.

After we check in at the lodge, we stop at the bar for wine. We sit down in the soft chairs in front of the big picture window in the lobby and watch the snow fall. As the light wanes, we go to the restaurant for dinner.

"I am so glad to be here and not on the road back to Atlanta," I say. "I am thankful we are warm and safe."

The next day as we are driving out of Amicalola Falls State Park, we look over in the parking lot at the visitor's center and Jim says, "I don't see Tom and Pam's car. I wonder where they stayed last night."

Carol's Reminders

- **Take time to stop on Springer Mountain, read the hiker register, and enjoy the view.** This is a historic place that you will want to explore.
- **Engage fellow hikers at Springer Mountain and at the Len Foote Hike Inn.** Hikers have interesting stories and they are fascinating people. Talking with them will enhance your hiking experience.
- **Check the weather forecast before you leave home and before you begin your hike each day.** Have alternative plans in case the weather turns bad. Never continue with your original plan if that puts you and your fellow hikers in danger.

Nearest Towns

Dawsonville is fifteen miles southeast of Amicalola Falls State Park. Ellijay is twenty miles west of the park, and Dahlonega is eighteen miles to the east.

Directions to the Trailheads

SOUTHERN TRAILHEAD, TOP OF AMICALOLA FALLS IN AMICALOLA STATE PARK: GPS coordinates 34.56693, -84.24358. From the visitor's center, follow the signs to the top of Amicalola Falls and Len Foote Hike Inn parking. This parking area is located one mile from the visitor's center.

NORTHERN TRAILHEAD, USFS 42 and Springer Mountain parking:: GPS coordinates 34.63777, -84.19499. From Amicalola Falls State Park, drive west or right on GA 52 and travel thirteen miles to Cartecay. Turn right on Roy Road between a gas station and Cartecay Methodist Church. Drive nine miles to the end of the road. Turn right and go two miles to Mt. Pleasant Baptist Church on the left. Turn right onto the dirt and gravel US Forest Service (USFS) Road 42. Go six miles to the point where the Appalachian Trail crosses USFS 42. Springer Mountain parking is on the left. The total trip is thirty miles; allow sixty minutes.

If you plan to shuttle using two cars, leave one car at the southern trailhead for the end of the hike, and then drive the other to the northern trailhead, where you will begin your hike. Allow seventy-five minutes to check in at the visitor's center and shuttle the cars. At the end of the hike, drive back to pick up the second car.

ALTERNATIVE TRANSPORTATION: Use a shuttle service to take you from the Hike Inn parking area at Amicalola Falls State Park, where you will leave your car for the end of the hike, to the A.T. as it crosses USFS 42 going up to Springer Mountain, where you will begin your hike. See the list of shuttle service providers in the **Hiker Essentials** section under Ellijay for Hike 1 or under Dahlonega for Hikes 2 and 3.

Driving Directions to Amicalola Falls State Park from Atlanta

OPTION 1: Drive north on GA 400. Exit left onto GA 53 West to Dawsonville. From Dawsonville, take GA 53 North, then GA 183 to GA 52. Turn right, and drive east to Amicalola Falls State Park on the left. The total trip will be seventy miles.

OPTION 2: Drive north on I-75, then turn right onto I-575, which becomes GA 515 and goes toward Jasper. Turn right onto GA 53 East (Waleska Highway), drive through Tate and Marble Hill, then turn left onto GA 356 East (Steve Tate Road), right onto GA 136 East, left onto GA 183, then right onto GA 52. Amicalola Falls State Park will be on the left in two miles. The total trip will be seventy miles.

Fine Wine and Accommodations
Dawsonville

DAWSONVILLE is a friendly small town tucked into the mountains at the southern terminus of the Appalachian Trail. It is home to Amicalola Falls, the highest cascading waterfall east of the Mississippi River.

Dawsonville is also known as the birthplace of NASCAR. (National Association for Stock Car Auto Racing, Inc).

Lodging

Lodging In Amicalola Falls State Park

LEN FOOTE HIKE INN: $$; includes dinner and breakfast; hiker bag lunches available for a fee; coffee, tea, and water are available in the early morning and evening; lemonade and cookies in the afternoon. This backcountry inn is accessible only by foot either from the top of Amicalola Falls north on the Len Foote Hike Inn Trail or from Springer Mountain south on the A.T. Approach Trail and then the Len Foote Hike Inn Trail. For reservations, call 1-800-581-8032 Monday through Friday, 10 a.m. to 5 p.m. or go to www.HIKE-INN.com.

SPECIAL LOGISTICS: You must check in at the Amicalola Falls State Park Visitor's Center by two p.m. The park ranger will give you a pass for overnight parking and a map to the parking area. Do *not* pay for a pass at the entrance to Amicalola Falls State Park because the parking pass is part of the lodging package.

The **Len Foote Hike Inn** is an environmentally friendly, rustic inn owned by the Georgia State Park Service and operated by the non-profit Appalachian Education & Recreation Service, an affiliate of the Georgia Appalachian Trail Club. The inn has twenty bunk rooms with extra-long bunk beds; a bathhouse with hot showers, soap, shampoo, and odorless composting toilets; a large family- style dining room for meals and programs; and the Sunrise Room for relaxing, playing games, and reading. On check-in, the manager will give you towels and sheets. (If you need en-suite facilities and room service, the Hike Inn is not for you.) There are no electrical outlets in the bunk rooms. No dogs are allowed, except for service dogs meeting Americans with Disability Act requirements.

The common areas are heated with wood heaters and cooled by open windows and ceiling fans. The bunk rooms are heated with electric ceiling heaters and cooled with ceiling fans.

SPECIAL FEATURES: The granite Star Base below the Sunrise Room is a celestial calendar and compass marking the extremes of the summer and winter solstices.

Cornbread, one of the local folk artists, has a painting hanging in the dining room. In his adult life, Cornbread began painting the memories of his youth, when he would often wander around the woods in North Georgia.

Dining: Family-style dinner and breakfast. For evening meals, there are vegetables, salad, hot homemade rolls, potatoes or rice, meat, and dessert. For breakfast, the inn serves grits, oatmeal, dry cereal, an egg dish, bacon, and biscuits. No beer or wine is served.

Activities: In the late afternoon, prior to dinner, there is an educational tour of the facility, and in the evening, there is a nature program. In the early morning, enjoy coffee and watch the sunrise in a rocker on the Sunrise Room porch or at the Star Base.

What to Bring: In addition to your day-hiking supplies and equipment, bring your personal toiletry items and a change of clothes. As the inn provides linens and blankets and the rooms are heated, no sleeping bags or towels are required.

If you enjoy a glass of wine at the end of the day, bring wine and plastic glasses. The Hike Inn does not serve wine or beer and does not permit drinking in the public areas, but you may drink discreetly in your room.

OUR EXPERIENCE: We have stayed at the Len Foote Hike Inn a number of times. The staff is friendly and helpful. The accommodations are simple but sparkling clean. In the summer, even though the rooms do not have air conditioning, the temperature feels comfortable as the inn is nestled under trees and small circular fans help keep things cool as well. In the winter, rooms are kept toasty warm with the ceiling heaters. The meals are tasty, nutritious, and homemade. We enjoy hearing the stories of guests and staff.

THE LODGE AT AMICALOLA FALLS STATE PARK: $-$$ for hotel rooms; $$ for 3 BR, 1 BA cabins or 1 BR, 1 BA cottages; ½ $ for campsites; dogs allowed in cabins and campground; restaurant on site; special events hosted throughout the year; 418 Amicalola Lodge Road; 1-800-573-9656; www.amicalolafallslodge.com

This two-story lodge has beautiful mountain views. Some cabins are on the mountaintop, and some cottages are at the base of the falls.

OUR EXPERIENCE: We have stayed at the lodge many times through the years. The rooms are clean and comfortable, and service is good. Recently they updated their rooms with upscale beds and linens as well as baths with contemporary fixtures.

Lodging Near Amicalola Falls State Park

FORREST HILLS MOUNTAIN RESORT & CONFERENCE CENTER: (Seven miles east of Amicalola Falls State Park) $ for room with breakfast, $$ for 2 BR cabin with breakfast, restaurant on site for guests, 135 Forrest Hills Rd, 706-864-6456, www.forresthillsresort.com.

National Chain Hotels *Near the Junction of GA 400 & GA 53*

(Twenty miles southeast of Amicalola Falls State Park)

QUALITY INN AND SUITES, : $ with free breakfast and pool, 706-216-1900, www.choicehotels.com.

DAWSON VILLAGE INN: $ with free breakfast and indoor pool, 706-216-4410, www.dawsonvilleinn.com.

SUPER 8: $ with free breakfast and indoor pool, 706-216-6801, www.wyndhamhotels.com.

Restaurants

Restaurant In Amicalola Falls State Park

THE MAPLE RESTAURANT AT THE LODGE is the only restaurant in the park. $ (discounts available for children and seniors), Southern, either buffet service or from the menu, beer and wine, 7 a.m. to 9 p.m. daily, 706-265-8888.

OUR EXPERIENCE: We have eaten here many times. When there is an event at the hotel or on weekends, the food is served buffet style, but at other times, guests order from the menu. The food is good, but not exceptional. The staff is very attentive, and the views are wonderful.

Restaurants In Marble Hill, GA

(Ten miles southwest of Amicalola Falls State Park.)

FORNO ITALIAN RESTAURANT AND PIZZERIA: $, Italian, beer and wine, 11 a.m. to 9 p.m. Mon through Sat, 12 to 9 p.m. Sun; 218 Foothills Parkway, 770-893-4222.

FUEGO MEXICAN GRILL: ½$, Mexican, beer and wine, 11 a.m. to 10 p.m. Mon through Thu, 11 a.m. to 11p.m. Fri and Sat, 11 a.m. to 9 a.m. Sun; 60 North Gate Station Drive, 770 893-3399.

HOME RESTAURANT: $–$$, American farm-to-table, beer and wine, 5 to 9 p.m. Tue through Fri, 5 to 9:30 p.m. Sat; 3909 Steve Tate Highway, 770-893-3389.

OUR EXPERIENCE, MARCH 2017: On our way to Amicalola Falls State Park for the A.T. Kickoff (Amicalola Falls State Park sponsors a weekend of workshops and vendors for thru-hikers who typically begin their thru-hike in the Spring.), we delight when we pull into the parking lot of the restaurant and see that the lot is filled with cars.

"This must be the place to eat. I'm glad I made reservations," I say.

"Yes. It is just past Big Canoe, and that must be why the restaurant is here," Jim says. Big Canoe is the site of many vacation mountain homes.

When we walk in, there is a line, but the hostess asks, "Do you have reservations?" We nod and she seats us immediately.

When the waiter asks what beverages we would like, I say, "A glass of wine sounds good after that traffic from Atlanta."

I order mountain trout and Jim orders a filet mignon. We look around. Every table is filled with couples, families, or friends; all are smiling and talking.

I say, "This is just the right place to be."

When the waiter serves our dinner, it is artistically arranged on the plate. The food is cooked just right and delicious. Passing up delectable-sounding pies and pastries, we share vanilla ice cream with amaretto for dessert.

SOURWOOD CAFÉ: $$, American, classy casual, full bar, 5:30 p.m. until closing (closing time varies) Mon through Sat, 60 Northgate Station Drive, 470-695-3600.

Selected Restaurants In Downtown Dawsonville

(Fifteen miles south of Amicalola Falls State Park.)

DAWSONVILLE TAVERN: $, American, full bar, 11 a.m. to 10 p.m. Sun through Thu, 11 a.m. to midnight Fri and Sat, 29 Main Street, 706-531-0050.

OLD TOWN PIZZA: ½ $, Italian, no wine or beer, 11 a.m. to 9 p.m. Mon through Thu, 11 a.m. to 10 p.m. Fri and Sat, noon to 9 p.m. Sun, 104 GA 9 North, 706-265-1520.

DAWSONVILLE POOL ROOM: a shrine to race car driver Bill Elliott and home of the "Bully Burger," ½ $, American, no beer or wine, 7 a.m. to 10 p.m. Mon through Thurs, 7 a.m. to 11 p.m. Fri and Sat, 8 a.m. to 10 p.m. Sun; 9 Bill Elliott Street South, 706-265-2782

OUR EXPERIENCE, MARCH 2016: On Sunday afternoon after the A.T. Kickoff, Jim and I stop to explore the Bill Elliott-themed restaurant and have a late lunch on our way back to Atlanta. A group of motorcycle riders are just coming out of the restaurant as we go in. The tables haven't been cleared after the Sunday lunch crowd.

We look around at the memorabilia on the wall and hanging from the ceiling. Jim takes pictures of the trophies.

I say, "I wonder how they got that piece of a race car to hang from the ceiling in here."

We find a clean table in the back and have a seat. I check out the menu and note that this is a typical short-order diner with burgers, hotdogs, sandwiches, salads, and plates with meat and two sides. The menus are stained with grease. I look over to see the cook pouring fries into hot grease and frying burgers on the grill.

I say, "I wonder what I should order that is the most nutritious and has the least grease."

I don't know if there is any such item on the menu.

Finally, the waitress has a chance to take our order. I order a broiled chicken fingers plate with fries and slaw. Jim orders a chicken sandwich with fries. The chicken fingers are good but a little dry. The slaw has too much mayonnaise, and the fries are good. Jim takes his sandwich apart and eats the chicken, lettuce, tomato, and fries, but leaves the bun.

Dawsonville Pool Hall is a real local place with a race-car flavor. You won't find this anywhere else.

Restaurants Near the Junction of GA 400 & GA 53

(Twenty miles southeast of Amicalola Falls State Park.)

Friends Sports Grill, Blue Bicycle, Chin Chin Chinese Restaurant, Fajita Grill, Osaka Steak & Sushi, Big D's BBQ, Applebee's, Ruby Tuesday, and LongHorn Steakhouse.

Hiker Essentials, Splurges, and Emergency Stops

Car Rental Agency

ENTERPRISE RENT-A-CAR: 8 a.m. to 5:30 p.m. Mon through Fri, 9 a.m. to noon Sat, 25 Beartooth Parkway, 706-429-0034.

Outfitters

OUTSIDE WORLD:10 a.m. to 7 p.m. Mon through Sat, 12 to 6 p.m. Sun, 471 Quill Drive, 706-265-4500.

Groceries

FOOD LION: groceries, beer and wine, 7 a.m. to 11 p.m. daily, 59 Main Street, Suite 100, 706-344-3979.

WALMART: 24/7, groceries, hiking supplies, beer and wine, 256 Power Center Drive, 706-265-8787.

FOOTHILLS IGA: groceries, beer and wine, 7 a.m. to 9 p.m. daily, 70 Foothills Parkway, Marble Hill, 770-893-3100.

Beer and Wine

DAWSON FINE WINE AND SPIRITS SUPERSTORE: 9 a.m. to 10 p.m. Mon through Thu, 9 a.m. to 11 p.m. Fri and Sat, 12:30 to 8 p.m. Sun, 46 Blue Ridge Parkway, 706-265-2065.

ATMs

BANK OF AMERICA ATM: 61 ATM Drive.

UNITED COMMUNITY BANK: 6372 GA 53 East.

Urgent Care and Emergency Services

NORTHSIDE FAMILY MEDICINE AND URGENT CARE: 8 a.m. to 8 p.m. Mon through Sat, 10 a.m. to 8 p.m. Sun, 81 Northside Dawson Drive, 706-344-6940.

NORTHEAST GEORGIA PHYSICIANS GROUP URGENT CARE: 8 a.m. to 8 p.m. daily, 108 Prominence Court, Suite 200, 706-216-3238.

NORTHSIDE HOSPITAL–FORSYTH, EMERGENCY SERVICES: 24/7, 1200 Northside-Forsyth Drive, Cumming, 770-844-3200.

Fun Places to Visit in or near Dawsonville

AMICALOLA FALLS VISITOR'S CENTER: 9 a.m. to 5 p.m. Mon through Wed, 9 a.m. to 7 p.m. Thu through Sun, 280 Amicalola Falls State Park Road, 706-265-4703.

Check in for the Len Foote Hike Inn here, buy snacks and some hiker supplies, and ask rangers your last minute questions before starting a hike on the Len Foote Hike Inn Trail, the A.T. Approach Trail, or the Appalachian Trail.

Look at the exhibit of Gene Espy's hiking equipment. Espy, a Georgia native, was the second person to thru-hike the Appalachian Trail in 1951. In 2017, at the age of ninety, he was still telling his story at Appalachian Trail events.

AMICALOLA FALLS: These 729-foot falls are the tallest cascading waterfalls east of the Mississippi. Best views are from the top of the falls or from the A.T. Approach Trail .

APPALACHIAN TRAIL APPROACH TRAIL AND ARCH: located behind the Amicalola Falls State Park Visitor's Center. The arch is the entryway to the eight-and-one-half-mile A.T. Approach Trail, the challenging trail to Springer Mountain. You might want to have your picture taken at the Arch.

DAWSON COUNTY EVENTS: listings available at www.Dawson.org, including a car show, Memorial Day weekend activities, Heritage Days, and Fourth of July weekend events.

AROUND BACK AT ROCKY'S PLACE: amazing folk art gallery, 11 a.m. to 5 p.m. Sat, 1 to 5 p.m. Sun, 3631 Highway 53 East, 706-265-6030, www.aroundbackatrockysplace.com.

BOWEN CENTER FOR THE ARTS: 10 a.m. to 4 p.m. Tue through Fri, 12 to 4 p.m. Sat, 334 Highway 9 North, 706-216-2787, www.dawsonarts.org.

HISTORIC DAWSON COUNTY COURTHOUSE & JAIL: free, 8:30 a.m. to 4 p.m. Mon through Fri, intersection of GA 53 & GA 9, 706-265-3980, www.dawsoncounty.org.

ATLANTA MOTORSPORTS PARK: 1 to 8 p.m. Tue through Sun, 20 Duck Thurmond Road, 678-381-8527.

DAWSONVILLE MOONSHINE DISTILLERY: 10 a.m. to 5 p.m. Mon through Sat, 12:30 p.m. to 5 p.m. Sun, 415 GA 53 East, 706-344-1210.

GEORGIA RACING HALL OF FAME: $6 for adults, $5 for seniors, $2 for children, free for children six and under; 10 a.m. to 5 p.m. Mon through Sat, 1 to 5 p.m. Sun, 415 GA 53 East, 706 216-7223.

CHESTATEE GOLF CLUB: 18-hole, par-71 course; prices vary but include cart and greens fee; 7 a.m. to 7 p.m. daily; Heron Grill 8 a.m. to 4 p.m.; 777 Dogwood Way, 1-800-520-8675.

GIBBS GARDENS: world-class gardens, walking trails, $20 for adults, $18 for seniors, $10 for children; 9 a.m. to 5 p.m. Tue through Sun, Mar 1 through June 11, 9 a.m. to 5 p.m. Wed through Sun, June 14 through

Dec 10; food available at Arbor Café, 11 a.m. to 2 p.m. 1987 Gibbs Drive, Ball Ground, GA, 770-893-1881 (20 miles south of Amicalola Falls State Park).

Fine Wine and Accommodations
Ellijay

ELLIJAY in Gilmer County is a recognized Appalachian Trail Community located at the foot of the Appalachian Mountains. It's twenty miles west of Amicalola Falls State Park. Known as a place to enjoy recreational activities in the mountains and on the lakes, Ellijay is the biking capital of Georgia, a wildlife sanctuary, and home of the Apple Festival. Ellijay hosts other festivals, art exhibits, and entertainment events throughout the year

Selected Lodging

BEST WESTERN MOUNTAIN VIEW: $, free continental breakfast and heated indoor pool, 73 Coosawattee Drive, East Ellijay, 706-515-1500, www.bwmountaininn.com.

STRATFORD MOTOR INN: $, free continental breakfast, outdoor pool, 79 Maddox Circle, East Ellijay, 706-276-1080, www.magnusonhotels.com.

Restaurants

Selected Restaurants in or near Ellijay

CHARLIE'S ITALIAN RESTAURANT: $, Italian, full bar, 11 a.m. to 10 p.m. Mon through Thu, 11:30 a.m. to 10 p.m. Sat, 706 West Cross Street, East Ellijay, 706-635-2205.

JOLLY ROGER SEAFOOD: $, American, no wine or beer but you may bring your own, 4 to 8 p.m. Thu through Sat, 716 Industrial Boulevard, 706-276-2090.

RIVER STREET TAVERN: $, American, full bar, 11 a.m. to 10 p.m. Tue through Thu and Sat, 11 a.m. to 11 p.m. Fri, 12:30 to 8 p.m. Sun, 40 River Street, Suite B, 706-635-6166.

Selected Restaurants in Blue Ridge *(Fifteen miles north of Ellijay.)*

CHESTER BRUNNENMEYER'S BAR & GRILL: $–$$, American, full bar, 4 to 11:30 p.m. Mon through Thu, 11:30 a.m. to 11:30 p.m. Fri and Sat, 12:30 to 11:30 p.m. Sun, 733 East Main Street, 706-258-2539.

HARVEST-ON-MAIN: $–$$, American, fine dining, full bar, 5 to 8 p.m. Sun through Thu, 5 to 9 p.m. Fri and Sat, 576 East Main Street, 706-946-6164.

MASSERIA KITCHEN & BAR: $-$$, Italian, full bar, 11 a.m. to 8 p.m. Sun through Thu, 11 a.m. to 9 p.m. Fri and Sat, 67 Roberts Way, 706-946-1511.

OTHER RESTAURANTS IN THE AREA: LongHorn Steakhouse, Ruby Tuesday, El Ray (Mexican), Bigun's (BBQ), Oki (Japanese), Ellijay Fish House.

Hiker Essentials, Splurges, and Emergency Stops in or near Ellijay

Shuttle-Service Providers

RON'S SHUTTLE SERVICE: 706-636-2825 or cell 706-669-0919, hikershuttles@outlook.com.

DICK ANDERSON: 706-276-2520.

DONALD (GRATEFUL) BALLARD: 706-400-9195, 772-321-0905.

KELLY FIELDS: 706-635-6730.

Outfitters

GEORGIA MOUNTAIN OUTFITTER: 10 a.m. to 6 p.m. Tue through Sat, 14244 Highway 515 North, Suite 1200, Ellijay, 706-698-4453.

BLUE RIDGE OUTDOOR EXCHANGE: 10 a.m. to 5:30 p.m. Mon and Thu through Sat, 10 a.m. to 4 p.m. Sun, 4118 East First Street, Blue Ridge (fifteen miles north of Ellijay), 706-632-0168.

Groceries

FOOD LION: groceries, beer and wine, 6 a.m. to 11 p.m. daily, 130 Fowler Street, 706-276-6300.

INGLES MARKETS INC.: groceries, beer and wine, 7 a.m. to 11 p.m. daily, 100 Old Orchard Square, 706-635-2585.

Wine and Beer

APPALACHIAN BEVERAGE: 9 a.m. to 9 p.m. Mon through Thu, 9 a.m. to 11 p.m. Fri and Sat., 399 Mountain View Drive, East Ellijay, 706-515-9463.

HILLTOP PACKAGE: 8:30 a.m. to 9 p.m. Tue through Thu, 8:30 a.m. to 11 p.m. Fri and Sat, 12 Hefner Street, East Ellijay, 706-636-5156.

HITCHING POST BEER & WINE: 9 a.m. to 9 p.m. Mon through Thu, 9 a.m. to10 p.m. Fri and Sat, 740 South Main Street.

ATMs

BBT ATM: 894 Maddox.

UNITED COMMUNITY BANK ATM: 558 Industrial Boulevard.

Urgent Care and Emergency Services

APPLE MEDICAL CENTER, affiliated with North Georgia Medical Center: 8 a.m. to 5 p.m. Mon through Fri, 9 a.m. to 2 p.m. Sat, 822 Industrial Boulevard, 706-635-5177.

Fun Places to Visit in or near Ellijay

TABOR HOUSE HISTORICAL MUSEUM & CIVIL WAR LIBRARY: 11 a.m. to 2 p.m. Thu through Sun, 138 Spring Street, 706-276-1861.

AARON FAMILY ORCHARDS: 9 a.m. to 6 p.m. daily Aug through Dec, 8350 GA 52 East, 706-273-3180.

APPLE PICKIN' FESTIVAL: market, apple and berry picking, animal rides, 9 a.m. to 6 p.m. daily Sep through Nov, 9696 GA 52 East, 706-273-3838.

B.J. REECE'S ORCHARD: "You Pick" starts in Aug, country store and bakery, 8 a.m. to 5 or 6 p.m. daily Jul through Dec, 9131 GA 52 East, 706-276-3048.

HUDSON'S APPLE HOUSE: 9 a.m. to 6 p.m. daily Sep through Nov, 8036 GA 52 East, 706-273-3160.

R&A ORCHARDS: bakery, market, and restaurant; 8:30 a.m. to 6:30 p.m. daily; 5505 GA 52 East, East Ellijay, 706-273-3821, www.randyorchards.com.

MERCIER'S ORCHARDS: apple orchard, bakery, deli, market store, and farm winery; 7 a.m. to 7 p.m. daily (hours may change in winter); 8660 Blue Ridge Drive, Blue Ridge, 706-632-3411.

CARTECAY VINEYARDS: cheese platters, tastings, 11 a.m. to 6 p.m. Mon through Sat., 12:30 to 5:30 p.m. Sun, music every Sat 1:30 to 5:30 p.m., 5704 Clear Creek Road, 706-698-9463.

WHITEPATH GOLF COURSE: public, 18 holes, $31–$36, 7 a.m. to 7 p.m. daily, 1156 Shenendoa Drive, 706-276-3080.

BLUE RIDGE SCENIC RAILWAY: twenty-six miles of history, scenery, and smiles with a stop in McCaysville to shop, tour, and dine; $42; Mar through Dec; 241 Depot Street; Blue Ridge; 706-632-8724

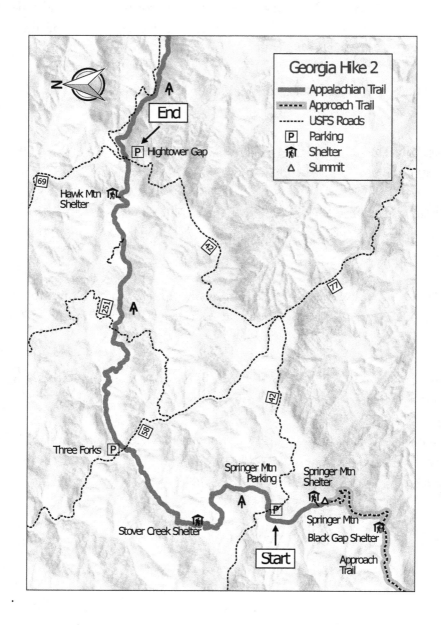

Georgia Hike 2

Appalachian Trail
Approach Trail
USFS Roads
P   Parking
Shelter
△   Summit

End

P Hightower Gap

69

Hawk Mtn
Shelter

42

77

251

58

Three Forks P

Springer Mtn
Parking

Springer Mtn
Shelter

Stover Creek Shelter

P

Springer Mtn

Black Gap Shelter

Start

Approach
Trail

Springer Mountain to Hightower Gap,
9.5 Miles, Moderate

GEORGIA HIKE

2

HIGHLIGHTS: In the spring, Springer Mountain is a special place to be. Thru-hikers hurry up the path, eager to see where the Appalachian Trail begins. They sign the hiker register to mark the fact that they are beginning their hike that day. They look at the commemorative A.T. plaques, take pictures, and say goodbye to loved ones.

At this southern terminus of the Appalachian Trail, you can feel the spirit of these thru-hikers who aspire to hike the entire 2,190 miles of the A.T., as well as the enthusiasm of those of us who aspire to hike a portion of it one day at a time.

The hiker plaque was placed at Springer Mountain by the Georgia Appalachian Trail Club in 1958.

Cross USFS 42 and enter the solitude and beauty of the Chattahoochee-Oconee National Forest, where you'll discover a stand of old-growth hemlocks. When you come to the blue-blazed trail to Long Creek Falls, take a one-tenth-mile side trip to see the beautiful falls cascading down the rocks and to swim in the pool at the bottom.

DISTANCE: 9.5 miles.　　**HIKE TIME:** 5–6 hours.

LEVEL OF EFFORT: Moderate to Easy.

RECOMMENDED DIRECTION: South to north, from Springer Mountain to Hightower Gap.

DOWNHILL HIKE: 6.0 miles with an elevation loss of 2,030 feet. **UPHILL:** 3.5 miles with an elevation gain of 1,490 feet.

This USFS plaque designates Springer Mountain as the southern terminus of the Appalachian National Scenic Trail.

ALONG THE TRAIL: The trail up and down Springer Mountain is about three-feet wide and rocky. The trail north of the Springer Mountain parking at USFS 42 is wide, covered with leaves, and speckled with tree roots. Under the cover of tall hardwood trees and hemlocks, the A.T. winds over rolling hills and crosses several creeks. Trail maintainers have built wooden bridges and placed stepping-stones for hikers to use at these creek crossings.

The A.T. joins old logging roads and merges with the Benton MacKaye Trail as it climbs gently along the side of the ridge of Hawk Mountain before it drops down into Hightower Gap. Be sure to follow the white rectangular A.T. blazes and not the white diamond Benton MacKaye blazes or the logging road.

SHELTERS: There are three shelters—Springer Mountain, Stover Creek, and Hawk Mountain—with privies and nearby water sources. Relax and stop for lunch at Stover Creek Shelter.

Follow the White Blazes

MILE 0.0: USFS 42, Springer Mountain parking, 3390 feet.

MILE 1.0: Springer Mountain, 3,782 feet.

MILE 1.2: The southern terminus of the Benton MacKaye Trail with white diamond blazes; Springer Mountain Shelter, 0.2 miles east on the blue-blazed trail.

MILE 2.0: USFS 42 and the Springer Mountain parking, 3,390 feet.

MILE 3.8: Stover Creek Shelter, 0.2 miles east.

MILE 4.3: Stand of old hemlocks. These trees are thought to be the only virgin stand of hemlocks between Georgia and the Great Smoky Mountains National Park.

MILE 4.8: Stover Creek.

MILE 5.3: Three Forks (USFS 58), 2,570 feet. Stover Creek, Chester Creek, and Long Creek merge here to form Noontootla Creek.

MILE 6.2: Long Creek Falls, 0.1 miles west; Benton MacKaye Trail; Duncan Ridge Trail.

MILE 7.2: USFS 251, 3,080 feet. To the west of this intersection is the Hickory Flats cemetery, the only remaining sign of the community of Hickory Flats and its people, who once farmed in this area in the early 1900s.

MILE 9.1: Hawk Mountain Shelter, 0.2 miles west.

MILE 9.5: Hightower Gap, 2,870 feet, USFS 42 and USFS 69.

Peaks and Valleys

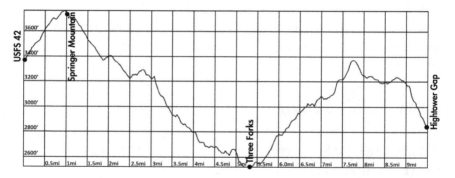

My Hiker Journal

MAY 2007: This is the first day of our five-day slackpacking trip. We drive from Atlanta to Springer Mountain in two cars with our friends Janice and John. John will be hiking with us for a few days. Janice will shuttle us. We leave one car at Hightower Gap, where we will end our hike, and then drive back to Springer Mountain parking, where our adventure begins.

With smiles on our faces, we excitedly hike up to Springer Mountain.

Jim says, "Stand over under the trees so I can get a good picture." He checks the hiker register and says, "Twelve people have signed in today. It was ten years ago when Harmon started his thru-hike about this same time of year at Springer Mountain." (Harmon is our son.)

The sky is blue and clear, and the temperature is about seventy degrees, making it a perfect day for hiking. As we walk under the cover of tall trees, we see that white mountain magnolias and flaming azaleas are blooming.

I stand with our friend John on top of Springer Mountain. May 2007

I say, "Let's stop at Stover Creek Shelter for lunch."

"Sure," Jim and John reply.

We check the hiker register. "It looks like six hikers stayed here last night," Jim says.

After lunch we stop to talk with four young guys sitting around a campsite. Jim asks them where they are going.

One of them says, "Oh, we are just out hiking for a few days. We started at Springer Mountain and are going to Neel Gap."

Jim asks, "Can you believe this big hole? A bear could hide in this tree." May 2007

We stop to check out Hawk Mountain Shelter. It looks weathered and worn. "I bet many thru-hikers stop here the first night," I say.

The miles and time fly by as we talk, meet other hikers, and stop to see what we can see. We hike these 9.5 miles in only four and a half hours.

Carol's Reminders

- **Invite friends to enjoy the A.T. with you.**
- **Bring a cooler with food and beverages.**
- **Make reservations in advance for lodging and shuttle services near the A.T.**
- **If you have kitchen facilities available at your lodging,** you may want to bring precooked food with you for the first night.

Nearest Towns

Dahlonega is thirty-eight miles and Ellijay thirty-one miles from the southern trailhead where the A.T. crosses USFS 42 north of Springer Mountain. Dahlonega is forty-five and Ellijay thirty-eight miles from the northern trailhead at Hightower Gap.

Directions to the Trailheads

SOUTHERN TRAILHEAD (USFS 42 AND SPRINGER MOUNTAIN PARKING): GPS coordinates 34.63777, -84.19499. From Dahlonega, drive west on GA 52 twenty-one miles to Cartecay. Turn right onto Roy Road between the gas station and Cartecay Methodist Church. Drive nine miles to the end of the road. Turn right and go two miles to Mt. Pleasant Baptist Church on the left. Turn right onto the unpaved dirt and gravel USFS 42. Go six miles to the point where the A.T. crosses USFS 42, and Springer

Mountain parking will be on the north side of the road. The total trip is thirty-eight miles. Allow seventy minutes.

NORTHERN TRAILHEAD (HIGHTOWER GAP): GPS coordinates 34.66358, -84.12978. Follow the directions above to Springer Mountain parking and USFS 42. From there, continue on USFS 42 seven miles to Hightower Gap, at USFS 42 and USFS 69. Park along the road. The total trip is forty-five miles; allow ninety-five minutes.

If you plan to shuttle using two cars, drive one car to Hightower Gap, the northern trailhead, for the end of the hike. Then drive the other car back on USFS 42 to Springer Mountain parking, where the A.T. crosses USFS 42. This is the southern trailhead, where you will begin your hike. The total trip from Dahlonega to Hightower Gap and back to Springer parking is fifty-two miles; allow two hours.

ALTERNATIVE TRANSPORTATION: Use a shuttle service to meet you at Hightower Gap where you will leave your car for the end of the hike and then drive you to Springer Mountain parking, where the A.T. crosses USFS 42, to begin your hike. See the list of shuttle-service providers for Dahlonega, Ellijay, and Suches in the **Hiker Essentials** section.

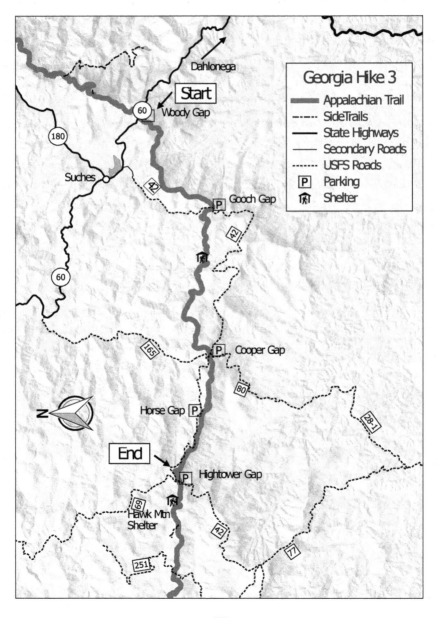

Mountain parking will be on the north side of the road. The total trip is thirty-eight miles. Allow seventy minutes.

NORTHERN TRAILHEAD (HIGHTOWER GAP): GPS coordinates 34.66358, -84.12978. Follow the directions above to Springer Mountain parking and USFS 42. From there, continue on USFS 42 seven miles to Hightower Gap, at USFS 42 and USFS 69. Park along the road. The total trip is forty-five miles; allow ninety-five minutes.

If you plan to shuttle using two cars, drive one car to Hightower Gap, the northern trailhead, for the end of the hike. Then drive the other car back on USFS 42 to Springer Mountain parking, where the A.T. crosses USFS 42. This is the southern trailhead, where you will begin your hike. The total trip from Dahlonega to Hightower Gap and back to Springer parking is fifty-two miles; allow two hours.

ALTERNATIVE TRANSPORTATION: Use a shuttle service to meet you at Hightower Gap where you will leave your car for the end of the hike and then drive you to Springer Mountain parking, where the A.T. crosses USFS 42, to begin your hike. See the list of shuttle-service providers for Dahlonega, Ellijay, and Suches in the **Hiker Essentials** section.

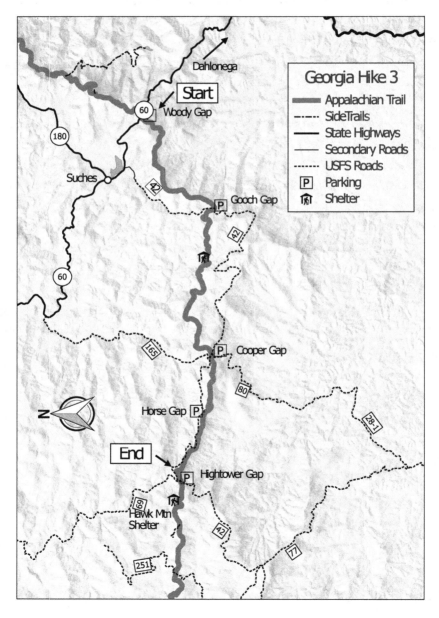

Georgia Hike 3

- Appalachian Trail
- Side Trails
- State Highways
- Secondary Roads
- USFS Roads
- P Parking
- Shelter

Dahlonega

Start

60 Woody Gap

180

Suches

42

P Gooch Gap

42

60

165

P Cooper Gap

80

28-1

Horse Gap P

N

End

P Hightower Gap

9

Hawk Mtn
Shelter

42

77

251

Woody Gap to Hightower Gap,
11.9 Miles, Challenging

GEORGIA HIKE
3

HIGHLIGHTS: If you are new to the Appalachian Trail in Georgia, this hike will give you a feel for what the A.T. is like. You will be challenged by treks up and down the steep, rocky trail to Ramrock, Justus, and Sassafras

Pointing at the map, I say, "John, we are on Ramrock Mountain. Those rolling hills to the south are in the Piedmont region." May 2007

Mountains, but the rewards are great. From outcroppings on Ramrock Mountain, you can see fifty miles to the south on a clear day, from the Blue Ridge Mountains to the Piedmont Region.

DISTANCE: 11.9 miles.   **HIKE TIME:** 7–8 hours.

LEVEL OF EFFORT: Moderate to Challenging because of the length of the hike.

RECOMMENDED DIRECTION: North to south, from Woody Gap to Hightower Gap.

DOWNHILL HIKE: 5.8 miles with an elevation loss of 2,880 feet. **UPHILL:** 6.1 miles with an elevation gain of 2,560 feet.

ALONG THE TRAIL: From Woody Gap, the trail is narrow, covered with leaves, and speckled with tree roots as it winds up and down the gentle hills. It

Large rock outcroppings along the A.T. May 2007

becomes rocky as it goes up and down the steep, lush green mountains with drop-offs on one side. On these steep slopes, there are log and stone steps and water dips to ease your climb and to slow erosion.

SHELTER: Gooch Mountain Shelter has two sleeping shelves and a picnic table under a sloping roof with a privy and water source nearby. You might want to eat lunch and relax at the shelter.

Follow the White Blazes

MILE 0: Woody Gap (GA 60), 3,170 feet. Parking, portable toilets, and water are available at the trailhead. Woody Gap is named for the Woody family who have lived in the area for generations. Arthur Woody, a family member and former chief ranger, who loved the land, flora, and fauna, reintroduced deer to this area after they had been hunted to extinction.

MILE 1.5: Ramrock Mountain, 3,260 feet.

MILE 3.6: Gooch Gap (USFS 42), 2,810 feet.

MILE 5.0: Gooch Mountain Shelter, 0.1 miles down a blue-blazed trail.

MILE 6.4: Justus Creek, 2,540 feet.

MILE 7.7: Justus Mountain, 2,970 feet.

MILE 8.5: Cooper Gap (USFS 42/USFS 80), 2,830 feet.

MILE 9.1: Sassafras Mountain, 3,350 feet.

MILE 10.0: Horse Gap (USFS 42 to the west), 2,680 feet.

MILE 11.9: Hightower Gap (USFS 42/USFS 69), 2,870 feet.

Peaks and Valleys

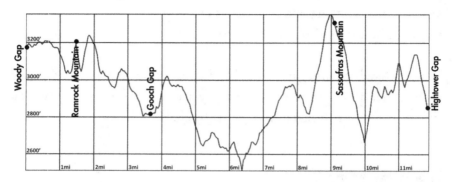

Alternative Hikes

As this was a long hike for us, we've divided it into two shorter hikes.

GEORGIA HIKE 3.1:

Hightower Gap to Gooch Gap, 8.3 miles, Moderate to Challenging

DISTANCE: 8.3 miles.

HIKE TIME: 5 hours.

LEVEL OF EFFORT: Moderate to Challenging.

RECOMMENDED DIRECTION: South to north, from Hightower Gap to Gooch Gap.

GEORGIA HIKE 3.2:

Woody Gap to Gooch Gap, 3.6 miles, Easy

DISTANCE: 3.6 miles.

HIKE TIME: 2 hours.

LEVEL OF EFFORT: Easy.

RECOMMENDED DIRECTION: North to south, from Woody Gap to Gooch Gap.

My Hiking Journal

MAY 2007: This is the second day of our five-day slackpacking adventure. Our friends Janice and John have joined us for a few days but will be leaving after lunch today. John will be hiking with us. Janice will meet us with lunch at Gooch Gap.

On this beautiful day, with the wind blowing through the trees and the blackberry bushes blooming with little white flowers, we hike up Ramrock Mountain. We stop and enjoy the views of the mountains and the valleys. Then we walk down into Gooch Gap.

Janice has lunch waiting for us. After a leisurely lunch, she and John leave to go see her brother in Tennessee.

I feel tired and sleepy; my eyes are drooping. I wonder what time we'll finish this hike. We have eight and a half more miles to hike, including two mountains to climb, and it is already one o'clock.

Our spirits lift as we pass some hikers that we saw yesterday.

One calls out to us, "I thought I passed you yesterday. Why are we seeing you again today?"

Jim replies, "We're day hikers. Yesterday we were hiking south to north as you were. Today we started at Woody Gap and are hiking south to Hightower Gap."

We stop for a break on the rock outcropping on Justus Mountain. The breeze blowing through my hair feels good.

We have just one more mountain to climb before we cross Horse Gap and walk along the ridgeline and down into Hightower Gap. Feeling tired, we finally trudge into Hightower Gap at six thirty p.m.

When I see the car, I say, "Finally, we're here."

We pull a cold beer from our cooler to share. We wet our bandanas and wipe the sweat off our faces and change shirts.

Jim says, "I'm driving back to Dahlonega slowly. It is dusk and I don't want to hit a deer or bear on the road. This is the time of day that they come out."

The clock on the courthouse square strikes eight as we pull into Dahlonega. We plan to try the Corkscrew Café, which was recommended at the Hiker Hostel this morning. After driving around a little, we find it just off the square. We grin when we see that it is still open.

As we enter the restaurant, we notice a plaque on the wall recognizing the Corkscrew Café as Restaurant of the Year, and we see white tablecloths and napkins.

I say, "We'll have fine dining tonight."

They seat us on the terrace. We enjoy glasses of pinot noir and listen to soft music being played by a band while we wait for dinner. The chef cooks us filet mignon, medium rare, just as we ordered. It is delicious and comes with baked potatoes and asparagus.

I say, "Oh, what a dinner. This is just the way to end our long day."

Carol's Reminders

- **Get an early start for a hike longer than five or six miles.** You want to be off the trail before dark.
- **Have a list of restaurants with you with hours of operation and phone numbers** for those hikes that end later than expected. In the next section of this guide, under **Fine Wine and Accommodations,** we give you a list of restaurants for the **Nearest Town** and hike number (for example, **Hike 2 and 3, Fine Wine and Accommodations: Dahlonega**).
- **When possible, notify your lodging hosts** if your day hiking trip takes longer than expected. They may be concerned about your

safety. (As cell service is often limited in the mountains, you may have to wait until you get back to town.)

Nearest Towns

Dahlonega is fourteen miles southeast of Woody Gap. Suches is two miles northwest of Woody Gap.

Directions to the Trailheads

NORTHERN TRAILHEAD, WOODY GAP: GPS coordinates 34.67775, -83.99961. From Dahlonega, drive north on GA 60 and US 19. Stay on GA 60 as it splits to the left and US 19 splits to the right. You will reach Woody Gap in about four miles. There is parking on both sides of the road. The total trip is fourteen miles; allow fifteen minutes.

IN-BETWEEN TRAILHEAD FOR GEORGIA HIKES 3.1 AND 3.2, GOOCH GAP: GPS coordinates 34.65217, -84.03212. From Dahlonega, drive north on GA 60 and US 19. Stay on GA 60 when it splits to the left and US 19 splits to the right. Pass Woody Gap and drive another two miles to USFS 42 (Cooper Gap Road). Turn left onto USFS 42. Go south on USFS 42 about three miles until you see the parking area and the white blaze. This is Gooch Gap. The total trip is nineteen miles; allow thirty minutes.

SOUTHERN TRAILHEAD, HIGHTOWER GAP: GPS coordinates 34.66358, -84.12978. From Dahlonega, drive north on GA 60 and US 19. Stay on GA 60 when it splits to the left and US 19 splits to the right. Pass Woody Gap and turn left on Cooper Gap Road (USFS 42). Go south on USFS 42 for eight miles to Cooper Gap (USFS 42 and USFS 80). Go straight on USFS 42 for another three miles to Hightower Gap (USFS 42 and

USFS 69). There is parking on the side of the road. The total trip is twenty-seven miles; allow sixty minutes.

If you plan to shuttle using two cars, leave one car at Hightower Gap. Return to Woody Gap. The trip total from Dahlonega is forty miles; allow one hour and twenty minutes.

If you plan to shuttle using two cars for Georgia Hikes 3.1 or 3.2, leave one car at Gooch Gap for the end of the hike and then drive the other car to Hightower Gap or Woody Gap to begin the hike. For **Georgia Hike 3.1** (beginning at Hightower Gap), the total trip from Dahlonega to Gooch Gap to Hightower Gap is twenty-seven miles; allow sixty minutes. For **Georgia Hike 3.2** (beginning at Woody Gap), the trip total from Dahlonega to Gooch Gap and back to Woody Gap is twenty miles; allow forty minutes.

ALTERNATIVE TRANSPORTATION: For **Georgia Hike 3.0,** use a shuttle service to meet you at Hightower Gap where you will leave your car for the end of the hike and then drive you to Woody Gap to begin your hike. See the list of shuttle-service providers for Dahlonega, Suches, and Ellijay in the **Hiker Essentials** section.

For **Georgia Hikes 3.1 and 3.2,** use a shuttle service to meet you at Gooch Gap where you will leave your car and then drive you either to Hightower Gap or Woody Gap to begin your hike.

Fine Wine and Accommodations
Dahlonega

DAHLONEGA is an Appalachian Trail Community and welcomes thousands of hikers making their way to nearby Amicalola Falls State Park and Springer Mountain to begin their trek.

Dahlonega is the site of the country's first gold rush in 1828 and the US Branch Mint. The gold used on the dome of Georgia's capitol was mined in Dahlonega. The historic courthouse square has museums, shops, and restaurants. Every second Saturday from five thirty to eight p.m., Dahlonega hosts Gallery Walk Dahlonega. There are arts and music festivals throughout the year.

Lodging

Lodging Less than Ten miles from Woody Gap

BAREFOOT HILLS (A BOUTIQUE HOTEL), FORMERLY THE HIKER HOSTEL: ½ $ for a hiker hostel standard bunk with shared bath, $ for a deluxe or standard room, $$ for a private log cabin, an eco cabin, or a deluxe eco cabin, $$-$$$ + for a two, three, or four BR suite; free high-speed internet, kitchen, laundry facilities, and common area available for guests; 7693 US 19 North (six miles from Woody Gap), 404-736-9431, www.BarefootHills.com Note: In 2017, the Hiker Hostel was acquired by Barefoot Luxury, renovated, and upgraded.

The hotel provides shuttle service for a fee, and they have slackpacking packages. Well-mannered dogs are welcome in the eco cabins and the private log cabin but not in the main lodge. A cleaning fee is charged if you have a dog.

OUR EXPERIENCE: In 2007, Jim and I book this accommodation because they have a slackpacking package with shuttle service. Our friends Janice and John join us for one night.

Jim and I stay five nights, hike four days, and enjoy the relaxed atmosphere, the kitchen and laundry facilities, the hearty breakfasts, and the on-site shuttle services. We also enjoy the company of Leigh and Josh, the friendly, helpful, and caring owners.

When we return to the hostel after our first hike, we celebrate with pinot noir and brie in the common room downstairs and make dinner in the hiker kitchen. We heat up our almond chicken and rice with green beans that we'd prepared at home. Janice makes a salad from the vegetables she bought at the nearby store. We have chocolate cookies for dessert.

After dinner I say, "I don't think I have ever tasted such good food."

Janice laughs and says, "Me, either."

John says, "How about another glass of wine?"

After our second hike, we are eating dinner at the Corkscrew Café in Dahlonega when Leigh, the hostel owner, calls and asks, "Are you still on the trail?"

Jim smiles and says, "No, we are enjoying dinner here at the Corkscrew Café that you recommended. Thanks for checking on us." (Owners of small hostels are often very caring people and concerned about the well-being of hikers who are staying with them.)

As we are getting into the SUV to be shuttled for our hike on our third day, Leigh asks, "Where are your hiking poles?"

"I don't think I will need them today," I say.

Later, as we are walking over the wet slate outcroppings on the mountain, I say, "I wish I had my hiking poles."

CEDAR HOUSE INN AND YURTS: $$, includes full breakfast, food is prepared with seasonal vegetables and fruit from the inn garden when available and organic ingredients, vegetarian breakfasts are available, no children, no dogs, no smoking, 6463 US 19 North (eight miles from Woody Gap), 706-867-9446, www.georgiamountaininn.com.

This two-story cedar lodge with a passive solar design has guest rooms with private baths, queen-size beds, and mini refrigerators. (Passive-solar-designed buildings have windows, walls, and floors built to collect, store, and distribute solar heat in the winter and reject solar heat in the summer.)

Two large, comfortable-looking yurts are located in the woods behind the inn. (Yurts are dome-shaped tents with partial walls.) These have wooden floors and wooden wall supports. Each yurt has a queen-size bed, coffee maker, mini refrigerator, microwave, floor fan/heater, and composting toilet. The bathhouse for the yurts is located on the lower level of the lodge.

OUR EXPERIENCE IN JANUARY 2013: We take a short reprieve from city life and check out another lodging in Dahlonega.

Jim and I enjoy being the only guests at this eclectic inn.

As we pull into the parking space, I say, "Look at the blue bottle tree and the little windmills. I don't think I've seen anything like that in a long time."

We walk in and see that they have their Christmas tree up and Mary Beth, the owner, says, "We still have all of our decorations up because a couple just left who always spends New Year's with us, and we leave the decorations up for them."

We relax and enjoy glasses of wine, and I ask Mary Beth about local restaurants.

"We like the Corkscrew Café, Crimson Moon, and Gustavo's Pizza," she says.

That evening, we go back to the Corkscrew Café, we like and have tried before.

The next morning, Mary Beth fixes us some yummy breakfast strata with sausage and cheese topped with fresh tomatoes and says, "In the spring and summer, what we have for breakfast depends on what is growing in our garden."

MOUNTAIN LAUREL CREEK INN AND SPA: $$, includes a gourmet breakfast, queen or king beds with whirlpool and gas fireplace, 202 Talmer Grizzle Road (seven miles from Woody Gap), 706-867-8134, www.mountainlaurelcreek.com.

Lodging Ten to Twenty Miles from Woody Gap and Hightower Gap

LONG MOUNTAIN LODGE: $$ for rooms in the main lodge with full breakfast, wine and cheese in the afternoon; $$$ for the cabin or cottage, no breakfast; $$ for the Tree Top Room with deluxe continental breakfast; 144 Bull Creek Road (off of Wahsega Road, seventeen miles from Woody Gap and ten miles from Hightower Gap); 706-864-2337, www.longmountainlodge.net.

The main lodge is rustic and upscale and has rooms or suites with private baths, jetted garden tubs, flat-screen TVs, DVD players. The 3 BR, 2 BA cottage has a LR, DR, large kitchen, and wood-burning fireplace. The 2 BR, 2 BA cottage has a screened porch and fireplace. The Tree Top Room is in the top of the owner's lodge.

THE SMITH HOUSE: $$, historic hotel established in 1899, rooms and suites with private baths, swimming pool and restaurant on site, 84 South Chestatee Street (thirteen miles from Woody Gap), 800-852-9577, www.smithhouse.com.

THE PARK PLACE HOTEL ON THE SQUARE: $$, quaint hotel, rooms and suites with private baths, flat-screen TVs, high-speed internet, 27 South Park Street on the square in Dahlonega (thirteen miles from Woody Gap), 706-864-0021, www.parkplacedahlonega.

National Hotel Chains in Downtown Dahlonega (thirteen miles from Woody Gap)

HOLIDAY INN EXPRESS: $, free continental breakfast, outdoor pool, 835 South Chestatee Street, 706-867-7777, www.hiexpress.com.

QUALITY INN: $, mini refrigerators, coffee makers, microwaves, outdoor pool, 619 North Grove Street, 706-864-6191, www.choicehotels.com.

DAYS INN: $, free continental breakfast, microwaves, mini refrigerators, business center, outdoor pool, 833 South Chestatee Street, 706-864-2338, www.wyndhamhotels.com.

Selected Restaurants

CORKSCREW CAFÉ: $-$$, American, fine dining with a creative twist, full bar, 11:30 a.m. to 9 p.m. Sun through Thu, 11:30 a.m. to 10 p.m. Fri and Sat, 11:30 a.m. to 3 p.m. Sun, 51 West Main Street, 706-867-8551.

OUR EXPERIENCE: We have eaten here several times. This is a fine-dining experience. Waiters attend to your every need. The food is delicious and the wine smooth.

In March 2014 after the Dahlonega Literary Festival, where our friend Dennis talked about his new book, I say to Dennis and his wife, Peg, "Let's go to the Corkscrew Café for dinner. We have eaten there before, and the food is good."

While we wait to have a table set up for us, we look at the eclectic collection of local art on the wall, and Jim takes pictures. After they seat us, we order a bottle of merlot from a local vineyard. Jim and I order a filet mignon to share. Peg orders a pasta dish and Dennis selects pork tenderloin.

Soon our wine arrives, and Dennis says, "This is nice."

"Yes," I say, "and it's smooth."

While we are waiting, we talk about several new authors we heard and about Dennis's experience.

Dennis says, "We sold some books and exchanged some with other new authors."

I said, "I talked with April from University Press of North Georgia. They publish regional books and may be interested in publishing my book."

When the food is ready, the waiter brings it out; the food is artistically arranged on each plate.

Jim says, "Oh, they divided our entrée for us and the plates are hot."

Peg says, "The food is really good. I'm glad we came here."

BOURBON STREET GRILL: $-$$, Cajun and eclectic American, full bar, 11 a.m. to 10 p.m. Mon through Thu, 11 a.m. to 11 p.m. Fri, 9 a.m. to 11 p.m. Sat, 9 a.m. to 9 p.m. Sun, 90 Public Square North, 706-864-0086.

OUR EXPERIENCE: In June 2017 after Elizabeth, a friend, and I hike down from the Len Foote Hike Inn, we stop in Dahlonega on the way home for lunch. Elizabeth has eaten at the Bourbon Street Grill many times and enjoyed it.

They seat us on the porch overlooking the street. We talk about our hike and my slackpacking talk. (The Len Foote Hike Inn has nature programs in the evening and were delighted when I offered to give my talk about slackpacking the A.T.)

We share an order of fish tacos. They are spicy and delicious, just the different taste I was looking for. After lunch, we check out the bar and expanded seating downstairs.

"It looks like you can even bring your dog with you when you sit outside on this enclosed porch," Elizabeth says.

BACK PORCH OYSTER BAR: $-$$, seafood from North Carolina with a wide selection of cold-water oysters, full bar, 11:30 a.m. to 9 p.m. Mon through Thu, 11:30 a.m. to 10 p.m. Fri and Sat, 11:30 a.m. to 8 p.m. Sun, 19 North Chestatee Street, 706-864-8623, www.backporchoysterbar.net.

CRIMSON MOON: $, American with a creative bent, live music, full bar, 11 a.m. to 3 p.m. Mon, 11 a.m. to 9 p.m. Wed and Thu, 11 a.m. to 10:30 p.m. Fri, 9 a.m. to 10:30+ p.m. Sat, 9 a.m. to 9:30 p.m. Sun, 24 North Park Street in the 1858 Parker-Nix Storehouse—the second oldest building in Dahlonega, 706-864-3982, www.thecrimsonmoon.com.

THE LE VIGNE RESTAURANT AT MONTALUCE VINEYARDS: $$, contemporary American, fine dining, wine, 11 a.m. to 9 p.m. Wed through Sat, hours may vary with the season, 501 Hightower Church Road, 706-867-4060.

OUR EXPERIENCE: After a day of hiking on the A.T., Jim and I treat ourselves to the finest and go to Le Vigne. The restaurant is above the winery and has big windows, so we can look out over the vineyard while we dine. We ask our waiter to suggest one of their red wines.

The wine tastes fruity and smooth, "Um, just right," I say.

Then we enjoy local trout with fingerling potatoes and asparagus from the on-site garden. We finish with ice cream and amaretto.

I say, "Delicious. This was a great way to end the day."

YAHOOLA CREEK GRILL: $-$$, contemporary Southern, fine dining, full bar, 11 a.m. to 9 p.m. Wed through Sun, 1810 South Chestatee Street, 706-482-2200.

GUSTAVO'S PIZZA: $, NY pizzeria, beer and wine, 11:30 a.m. to 9 p.m. Sun and Mon, 11:30 a.m. to 10 p.m. Tue through Thu, 11:30 a.m. to 11 p.m. Fri and Sat, 16 South Public Square, 706-864-2366.

PUEBLOS MEXICAN RESTAURANT: $, Mexican, full bar, 11 a.m. to 9:30 p.m. Mon through Thu, 11 a.m. to 10 p.m. Fri and Sat, 11 a.m. to 9 p.m. Sun, 82 East Main Street, 706-867-7155.

SHENANIGAN'S RESTAURANT & IRISH PUB: $, Irish, full bar, 11 a.m. to 10 p.m. Mon and Tue, 11 a.m. to midnight Wed through Sat, 11 a.m. to 9 p.m. Sun, 87 North Chestatee Street, 706-482-0114.

THE SMITH HOUSE RESTAURANT AND COUNTRY STORE: $, Southern, family style, no beer or wine, 3:30 p.m. to 7:30 p.m. Tue through Thu, 3:30 p.m. to 8 p.m. Fri, 11 a.m. to 8 p.m. Sat, 11 a.m. to 7:30 p.m. Sun, 84 Chestatee Street, 706-867-7000.

OUR EXPERIENCE: In May 2007 after a short day of hiking, Jim and I treat ourselves to a real Southern meal at the historic Smith House. As we enter, I smell the aroma of delicious food. The hostess, dressed in an old-timey long gingham dress with a starched white apron, shows us to a table with four other diners. Then the waiters bring out platters and bowls of fried chicken, squash, sweet potatoes, green beans, okra, tomatoes, and cornbread. We eat to our hearts' content. For dessert, they bring peach cobbler.

"Oh, how delicious. This will fuel us for our long hike tomorrow," I say.

With a smile on his face, Jim nods in agreement.

Hiker Essentials, Splurges, and Emergency Stops

Shuttle-Service Providers

TOM BAZEMORE: 706-265-9454 and (865) 209-1827, Facebook: Appalachian Adventure Company.

THE FURTHER SHUTTLE APPALACHIAN: Donald (Grateful) Ballard, 772-321-0905, 706-400-9105.

MAMA'S TAXI: 706-482-8539.

PAT ROBERTS: 706-864-3229.

RON'S SHUTTLE SERVICE: 706-669-0919 (cell), 706-636-2825, hikershuttles@ outlook.com.

SUCHES HIKER SHUTTLES, MURRIS MILLER: 678-967-9510, 75¢ to $1.25 per mile. Murris says, "Shuttle drivers are volunteers, and you get better service with tips." Murris is the oldest volunteer.

Outfitters

WOODLANDS EDGE: 11 a.m. to 5 p.m. Mon through Sat, 36 North Park Street, 706-864-5358.

Groceries

WALMART SUPERCENTER: groceries, first-aid and hiking supplies, beer and wine, 24/7, 270 Walmart Way, 706-867-6912.

FRESH 'N FRUGAL: large variety of food, no beer or wine, 7 a.m. to 9 p.m. daily, 406 East Main Street, 706-864-3048.

Wine or Beer

HABERSHAM WINERY TASTING ROOM: 10 a.m. to 6 p.m. Mon through Fri, 10 a.m. to 8 p.m. Sat, 12:30 p.m. to midnight Sun, 16 North Park Street, 706 864-8275.

ATMs

WELLS FARGO ATM: 312 East Main Street.

BBT ATM: 60 West Main Street.

DIEBOLD INC. ATM: 270 Walmart Way.

Urgent Care and Emergency Services

NORTH GEORGIA PHYSICIANS GROUP: 8:15 a.m. to 5 p.m. Mon through Fri (same day appointments available), 90 Morrison Moore Parkway, 706 864-3323.

CHESTATEE REGIONAL HOSPITAL EMERGENCY ROOM: 24/7, 227 Mountain Drive, 706-864-6136.

Fun Places to Visit in or near Dahlonega

HALL HOUSE FINE ART GALLERY: 11 a.m. to 6 p.m. Sun through Thu, 11 a.m. to 8 p.m. Sat, 94 Public Square North, 706-867-5009.

BRAD WALKER POTTERY: Call to see when Brad is in. The business is never open past 2 p.m. Come watch the artist work. He makes products here and takes them home to glaze. 70 North Public Square, 706-864-7130.

CANVAS & CORK: 9 a.m. to 6:30 p.m. Mon through Fri, studio artists on site, wine tastings, 90 North Meaders Street, 706-525-1563.

BILL LAWSON ART STUDIO: Call to see his works, 28 William Lane (GA 52), 706-429-6844.

FOLKWAYS CRAFT GALLERY & COTTAGE VINEYARD TASTING ROOM: free tastings, 11:30 a.m. to 5:30 p.m. Wed through Sat, 12:30 to 5 p.m. Sun, 11 South Grove Street, Suite 300, 706-864-7132.

BOB OWENS ART GALLERY AT THE UNIVERSITY OF NORTH GEORGIA: 3 to 7 p.m. Sun, 8 a.m. to 8 p.m. Mon through Fri, 10 a.m. to 7 p.m. Sat, hosts six exhibitions annually, 315 Hoag Student Center (top floor), 678-717-3438.

THE GOLD MINE AND MUSEUM: adults, $6; seniors, $5.50; 9 a.m. to 5 p.m. Mon through Sat; 10 a.m. to 5 p.m. Sun; 1 Public Square in the historic 1863 Lumpkin County Courthouse.

CRISSON GOLD MINE: pan for gold, $9.96 per person (pp), 10 a.m. to 5 or 6 p.m. daily, 2736 Morrison Moore Parkway East, 706-864-6363.

CONSOLIDATED GOLD MINES: pan for gold; underground tours; adults, $16; children, $11; 185 Consolidated Gold Mine Road, 706-864-8473.

WOLF MOUNTAIN VINEYARDS AND WINERY: tasting room, $16-$20 pp; 11 a.m. to 5 p.m. Thu through Sat; 12:30 to 5 p.m. Sun; winemaker tour with a different theme every month, 2 p.m. Sat and Sun; café, ½$–$, 12 to 3 p.m. Thu through Sat; Sun brunch by reservation, $$$, 12:30 p.m. and 2:30 p.m.; days and hours vary by season; check their website; 180 Wolf Mountain Trail, 706-876-9862, www.wolfmountainvineyards.com.

THREE SISTERS VINEYARDS: Dahlonega's first family-farm winery; 100% Georgia-grown estate wine; tasting room, $10 to $20 pp; 11 a.m. to 5 p.m. Thu through Sat, 1 to 5 p.m. Sun; 439 Vineyard Way, 706-865-9463.

FROGTOWN CELLARS: tasting room: 12 to 5 p.m. Mon through Fri, 10:30 a.m. to 6 p.m. Sat, 12:30 to 5 p.m. Sun. panini bar: $, 12 to 3:30 p.m. Fri through Sun. Sunday brunch: $$, 12:30 to 2:30 p.m., 400 Ridge Point Drive, 706-865-0687.

MONTALUCE WINERY AND RESTAURANT: tasting flights, $18, 11 a.m. to 5 p.m. Mon and Tues, 11 a.m. to 7 p.m. Wed through Sat, 12:30 to 7 p.m. Sun; tours, free, 2 p.m. Mon through Fri, noon Sat and Sun; wine hike, $45 pp: 1.8-mile wine hike around vineyard ending with a tasting.

Fine Wine and Accommodations
Suches

SUCHES is a small community two miles north of Woody Gap. It has the highest elevation of any town in Georgia.

Suches is named for a Cherokee Chief, who lived in this valley in the early 1800s. When gold was discovered in nearby Lumpkin County, the state of Georgia began seizing the land of the Cherokees and Creeks, and the Cherokees were forced to leave Suches.

Lodging

TWO WHEELS OF SUCHES LODGE: $, rooms in lodge; $, cabins; ½ $, campground; lodging year round; restaurant open during riding season; 1915 Highway 60; 706-973-1671; www.twowheelsofsuches.com.

HIGH VALLEY RESORT CABINS AND CAMPGROUND: $$, cabins with two-night minimum, complete kitchens, TVs and VCRs, washers and dryers, linens, fireplaces, gas grills; $, bunkhouse; $15, camping, pavilion, and bathhouse; airplane landing strip; 3001 High Valley Road; 404-720-0087; highvalley@bellsouth.net.

WILDCAT LODGE AND CAMPGROUND: $$, lodge with two-night minimum; ½ $, bunkhouse and campground, shower house, laundry facilities; diner and store on site; diner serves breakfast food, hamburgers, hotdogs; store sells food, snacks, first-aid supplies, stove fuel, firewood; campground open year round; diner and store, 8 a.m. to 4 p.m. Thu, 8 a.m. to 6 p.m. Fri and Sat, open spring through fall and closed in winter, 7475 GA 60 (seven miles west of Woody Gap), 706-623-3422, www.wildcatsuches.com.

Restaurants

TWO WHEELS OF SUCHES RESTAURANT: American, no beer or wine, 6 to 9 p.m. Fri; 8 to 10:30 a.m., 11 a.m. to 3 p.m., 6 to 8 p.m. Sat; 8 to 10:30 a.m., 11 a.m. to 3 p.m. Sun; 8 to 10 a.m. Mon during riding season, March or April through Nov; 1915 Highway 60; 706-973-1671; www.twowheel-sofsuches.com.

Hiker Essentials, Splurges, and Emergency Stops

Shuttle-Service Providers

KELLY FIELDS: 706-635-6730.

RON'S SHUTTLE SERVICE: 706-669-0919 (cell), 706-636-2825, hikershuttles@outlook.com.

SUCHES HIKER SHUTTLES, MURRIS MILLER: 678-967-9510, 75¢ to $1.25 per mile. Murris says, "Shuttle drivers are volunteers, and you get better service with tips." Murris is the oldest volunteer.

SABIN "WES" WISSON: available year round, three miles from Woody Gap, 706-747-2671, dwisson@windstream.net.

Urgent Care and Emergency Services:

DR. PRUITT'S MEDICAL CLINIC: 9 a.m. to 5 p.m. Mon through Thu, 56 Firewater Lane, 706-747-1412.

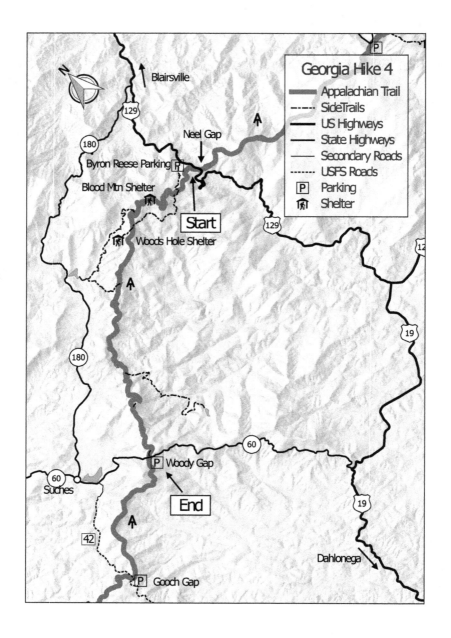

Georgia Hike 4

- Appalachian Trail
- Side Trails
- US Highways
- State Highways
- Secondary Roads
- USFS Roads
- P Parking
- 🏠 Shelter

Blairsville

129

180

Neel Gap

Byron Reese Parking P

Blood Mtn Shelter

Start

Woods Hole Shelter

129

P

180

19

60

P Woody Gap

End

60
Suches

19

42

P Gooch Gap

Dahlonega

Neel Gap to Woody Gap,
10.9 Miles, Challenging

GEORGIA HIKE 4

HIGHLIGHTS: Blood Mountain, which stands at 4,458 feet, is the highest point on the Appalachian Trail in Georgia. From there, you can see Brasstown Bald, the tallest peak in Georgia, the Nantahala Mountains, and Lake Burton.

Some say Blood Mountain and Slaughter Gap were named for the blood shed during battles between the Creek and Cherokee Indians; others say the names refer to battles between the Cherokees and the colonists.

Blood Mountain Shelter was built in the 1930s by the Civilian Conservation Corps from local stone and wood

DISTANCE: 10.9 miles.   **HIKE TIME:** 7–8 hours.

LEVEL OF EFFORT: Moderate to Challenging.

RECOMMENDED DIRECTION: North to south, from Neel Gap to Woody Gap.

DOWNHILL HIKE: 6.6 miles with an elevation loss of 2,650 feet. **UPHILL:** 4.3 miles with an elevation gain of 2,720 feet.

Me at Blood Mountain Shelter, May 2007

ALONG THE TRAIL: From Neel Gap, the trail up and down Blood Mountain and Cedar Mountain is rocky and steep and may be icy in the winter. There is a bypass trail around Blood Mountain for use in bad weather.

Switchbacks make going up and down these mountains easier and help control erosion.

The path at the lower elevations is earthen with some roots. In the fall and winter, it's covered with leaves. The A.T. goes through the Blood Mountain Wilderness area, where there is an abundance of hardwood trees and wildflowers.

SHELTERS: There are two shelters, Blood Mountain and Woods Hole. The Blood Mountain Shelter has a privy, but water is more than a mile away. The Woods Hole Shelter has a privy and nearby water source. Woods Hole Shelter was named for Roy and Tillie Wood, a Georgia couple who operated Wood's Hole Hostel in Virginia.

Follow the White Blazes

MILE 0.0: Neel Gap, 3,100 feet. Neel Gap was named for W.R. Neel, the engineer for the Blairsville Highway (US 129) that goes through the gap.

MILE 2.3: Blood Mountain Shelter, 4,450 feet.

MILE 3.3: Slaughter Creek Gap, 3,780 feet; Slaughter Creek Trail.

MILE 3.7: Bird Gap, 3,660 feet. Woods Hole Shelter is half a mile down the side trail.

MILE 5.1: Jarrard Gap, 3,310 feet. The blue-blazed Jarrard Gap Trail leads to Lake Winfield Scott.

MILE 5.5: Burnett Field Mountain, 3,410 feet.

MILE 7.6: Miller Gap, 2,870 feet.

MILE 9.7: Big Cedar Mountain, 3,700 feet.

MILE 10.9: Woody Gap, 3,170 feet. Woody Gap was named for the Woody family who has lived in this area for generations, including Georgia's first ranger, Arthur Woody, who replenished the forest with deer and the creeks with fish.

Peaks and Valleys

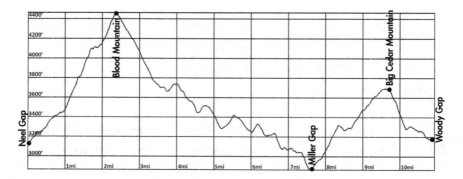

My Hiking Journal

MAY 2007: This is the third day of our five-day slackpacking adventure.

It is a sunny day with pink mountain laurels and fuchsia rhododendrons blooming. The views from Blood Mountain and Cedar Mountain are spectacular, but the treks up both the mountains are arduous.

This is a popular section of the A.T., and there are many hikers taking advantage of the beautiful weather. We pass a troop of Boy Scouts who have stopped to take a rest. With their sleeping pads rolled up on the tops of their backpacks, they look like they are out for an overnight.

When we reach the top of Blood Mountain, our shirts are wet with sweat and we are ready for a break. We take pictures and explore the historic mountain.

As we are exploring the Blood Mountain Shelter, I tell Jim a story about when I was hiking this section of the trail with our son, Harmon, and his friend Justin.

I remember it was late in the afternoon when all of a sudden it started pouring rain. We had planned to camp at Slaughter Creek, but decided to go another mile to Blood Mountain Shelter, hoping there would be room and that we could squeeze in.

Once we made it there, we used our headlights to glance around the sleeping loft in the back of the shelter. It was dark and filled with sleeping bodies from one side to the other with not an open space in sight. In the front room, we saw a little open area on the side, big enough for the three of us.

A guy was cooking in the open fireplace while he drank a beer. He had an old woolen blanket laid out on the stone floor and a small army pack.

Jim on Big Cedar Mountain, May 2007

I thought, "He does not look like a hiker; he must have just come up from the road."

I whispered to Harmon and Justin, "I am afraid. I want to sleep between the two of you."

Fortunately, we slept through the night with no disturbance. When we woke up in the morning, the guy was gone. This was the only time I felt afraid on that trip.

Me with the fuchsia rhododendrons, May 2007

Once I tell my story, Jim and I make our way on down the trail. We pass several young thru-hikers and stop to take their pictures. When we ask where they are going, they beam from ear to ear and reply, "Maine."

We stop to talk with a middle-aged, pudgy hiker with his pack off who is resting on a rock ledge. He is dressed in a cotton T shirt and knee-length shorts held up with suspenders. His face is red and his shirt wet.

Jim asks, "Where are you going?"

He replies, "Oh, I just hike up the trail a ways and then hike back to the car."

Jim inquires, "What do you do?"

He replies, "I'm a minister, but I like to get out on the trail when I can."

We have lunch on the ridgeline with a view of green valleys below and the Blue Ridge Mountains in the distance.

I say to Jim, "I feel a little hot spot on my heel. I'm going to take off my shoe to see what's going on."

I see a red spot that looks like the beginning of a blister.

I say, "It must be these new cotton socks that I decided to wear."

To try to prevent further abrasion, I apply a bandage. Unfortunately, I don't have moleskin, medical tape, or New-Skin.

Napping on top of Big Cedar Mountain: May 2007 on left, March 1992 on right

Near the end of the day, we come to Cedar Mountain and see the rock outcroppings.

I say to Jim, "This is the same place where Justin took a picture of me napping on the mountaintop. I think I had on these same shorts."

Jim says, "Let's retake that picture."

When we get back home and I look at both pictures, I say, "Oh, I'm surprised that I don't have on the same shorts. I was wearing blue shorts fifteen years ago and this time I was wearing black shorts. I had the blue shorts on this trip, but just wasn't wearing them that day."

Back at the Hiker Hostel, I check my heel because it is still hurting a little. I do have a small blister.

"Tomorrow, I will protect it better," I say.

Carol's Reminders

- **When hiking, wear synthetic wicking socks.** Cotton socks hold moisture, making your feet more susceptible to blisters.
- **When you first begin to feel a hot spot, examine it and protect it with moleskin, medical tape, or New-Skin.** Do not wait until a blister forms. Unfortunately, bandages will not protect the hot spot.
- **Air-dry your feet and change your socks at lunch or when they become damp.** Do not wear wet socks.
- **When possible, climb steep mountains first thing in the morning when you are fresh and full of energy.**
- **Be cognizant of any locals staying in shelters near major highway crossings.**

Nearest Towns

Blairsville is thirteen miles northwest of Neel Gap, the northern trailhead. Dahlonega is fifteen miles south of Woody Gap, the southern trailhead. Suches is two miles from Woody Gap.

Directions to the Trailheads

SOUTHERN TRAILHEAD, WOODY GAP: GPS coordinates 34.67775, -83.99961. From Blairsville, head south on US 19/129 for ten miles to GA 180. Turn right on GA 180 and go ten miles east to GA 60 at Suches. Turn left and drive two miles to Woody Gap. Total trip: twenty-two miles; allow thirty minutes.

NORTHERN TRAILHEAD, NEEL GAP: GPS coordinates, 34.73513, -83,91809. From Blairsville, drive thirteen miles south on US 19/129 to the parking area at the Byron Reece Memorial, then walk south a fraction of a mile (0.3) to Neel Gap. Do not park in front of the Mountain Crossings store. Total trip: thirteen miles; with the walk, allow fifteen minutes.

If you plan to shuttle using two cars, leave one car at Woody Gap. Drive the other car to the Byron Reece Memorial parking area, 0.3 miles north of Neel Gap. From Woody Gap, go north on GA 60 two miles to GA 180. Turn right and drive ten miles to US 19/129. Turn right and drive five miles to the Byron Reece Memorial parking area and walk 0.3 miles to Neel Gap. Trip total from Blairsville to Woody Gap to Neel Gap: thirty-nine miles, allow fifty minutes.

ALTERNATIVE TRANSPORTATION: Use a shuttle service to take you from Woody Gap, where you will leave your car for the end of the hike, to Neel Gap to begin your hike. See the list of shuttle-service providers in the **Hiker Essentials** sections for Blairsville, Dahlonega, Ellijay, and Suches.

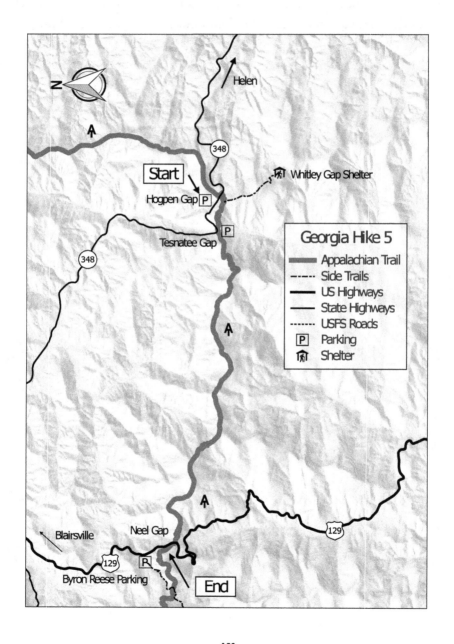

Helen

348

Start

Hogpen Gap P

Whitley Gap Shelter

P

Tesnatee Gap

348

Georgia Hike 5
━━━ Appalachian Trail
–·–·– Side Trails
━━ US Highways
─── State Highways
········ USFS Roads
P Parking
🏠 Shelter

Blairsville

Neel Gap

129

129

Byron Reese Parking

P

End

Hogpen Gap to Neel Gap,

6.7 Miles, Moderate

GEORGIA
HIKE
5

HIGHLIGHTS: The views from the open summits of Cowrock and Levelland Mountains are magnificent. At Neel Gap, the Appalachian Trail goes through the breezeway in the Walasi-Yi Center. This is the only place where the Appalachian Trail passes through a man-made structure.

The Walasi-yi Center is a stone building rebuilt by the Civilian Conservation Corps in the 1930s as a restaurant and an inn. The building now houses the Mountain Crossings outfitter store and hostel. It is on the National Register of Historic Places.

The Cherokee called Neel Gap Walasi-yi, meaning the place of Walasi, the Great Frog, chieftain of the animal council. According to legend, a hunter once spotted a frog as big as a house at this gap. Early white settlers called it

Me walking on the A.T. through the breezeway at the Walasi-Yi Center, May 2007.

Frogtown Gap. It was later named Neel Gap after W.R. Neel, the engineer of the highway that was built through the gap in 1925 from Lumpkin County, Georgia to Murphy, North Carolina.

DISTANCE: 6.7 miles.   **HIKE TIME:** 4–5 hours.   **LEVEL OF EFFORT:** Moderate.

RECOMMENDED DIRECTION: North to south, Hogpen Gap to Neel Gap.

DOWNHILL HIKE: 4 miles with an elevation loss of 2,180 feet. **UPHILL:** 2.7 miles with an elevation gain of 1,840 feet.

ALONG THE TRAIL: From Hogpen Gap , the A.T. goes quickly to the crest of Wildcat Mountain then down into Tesnatee Gap, then up the narrow, steep, rocky path to Cowrock Mountain and then Levelland Mountain. The path widens as you descend gently under the trees and walk through the breezeway of the Walasi-yi Center into Neel Gap.

SHELTER: Whitney Gap Shelter has a privy and nearby water source.

Follow the White Blazes

MILE 0.0: Hogpen Gap, GA 348, 3,450 feet.
MILE 0.2: Whitney Gap Shelter, 1.2 miles down the Whitney Gap side trail at the crest of Wildcat Mountain.
MILE 0.7: Tesnatee Gap, GA 348, 3,140 feet.
MILE 1.7: Cowrock Mountain, 3,840 feet, views .
MILE 2.4: Baggs Creek Gap, 3,510 feet.
MILE 3.0: Wolf Laurel Top, 3,760 feet.
MILE 4.5: Swaim Gap, 3,440 feet.
MILE 5.1: Levelland Mountain, 3,870 feet, views.
MILE 6.7: Neel Gap; 3,100 feet, Mountain Crossings Hostel and Outfitter.

Peaks and Valleys

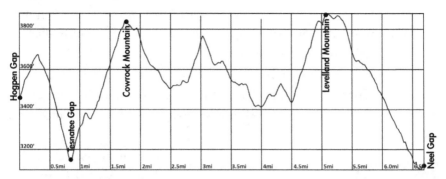

My Hiking Journal

MAY 2007: This is the fourth day of our hiking trip.

Jim and I get on the trail about ten o'clock. We are looking forward to this short hike.

Five minutes later, as we come to the Whitney Gap Trail, I yell, "Rattlesnake! What should I do?"

Jim surveys the situation and says, "I think we will just give this rattler room and walk in a wide circle around him through the underbrush." The rattler does not even move, rattle, or hiss.

When we get back on the trail, I say, "Whoo. That frightened me. I don't like snakes."

About noon, we stop on the rocky vista overlook at Cowrock Mountain, take pictures, and enjoy the views of the valley below.

"It is so beautiful. Let's eat lunch here," I say.

After lunch, Jim leads the way down one mountain and up another. He stops to take pictures of the fuchsia rhododendrons with bees buzzing about and getting nectar.

Rhododendron, May 2007

"What a beautiful sight. This bee is not even worrying about us," I say. We pass hikers with their dogs and ask them where they are going. "Oh, we are just out for a day on the trail," one of them replies. We detour around downed trees.

Jim says, "It must have been a bad storm because these are big trees."

I say, "These trees are probably still here because trail maintainers cannot use power tools in wilderness areas like this; they must use two-man crosscut saws."

"It's a beautiful day," I say. "This tree must have fallen when the hurricane came through." May 2007

We finish the hike about two thirty p.m. and stop to browse in the Mountain Crossings outfitter store. Jim says, "Look at all the boots hanging from the ceiling."

We go outside and are having beers on the veranda when I suddenly hear, "Carol!" I turn around to see Rene, a former public health colleague from Savannah. We chat and catch up on each other's lives.

I say, "I can't believe I'm seeing you here."

She replies, "Oh, we have a cabin near here."

I say, "This was a good hike and a great day."

We go back to the Hiker Hostel, where we are staying, for a hot shower before we go into Dahlonega for dinner. We plan to treat ourselves to dinner at the Smith House, a Southern inn known for their family-style dinners.

Mountain Crossings, May 2007

Carol's Reminders

- Sandwich an easy hiking day between any longer days you might have planned.
- Take time to enjoy the sights along the A.T.

Nearest Towns

Blairsville is thirteen miles northwest of Neel Gap on US 19/129. Cleveland is eighteen miles east on US 129. Helen is ten miles east of Hogpen Gap on GA 75.

Directions to the Trailheads

SOUTHERN TRAILHEAD, NEEL GAP: GPS coordinates 34.73513, -83.91809. From Blairsville, drive thirteen miles south on US 19/129 to the Byron Reece Memorial parking area; allow fifteen minutes. Neel Gap is 0.3 miles from the parking area. Do not park in front of the Mountain Crossings store.

NORTHERN TRAILHEAD, HOGPEN GAP: GPS coordinates 34.72589, --83.83985. From Blairsville, drive south on US 19/129 for eight miles, turn left onto GA 180 and travel for one mile, turn right onto GA 348 and go five miles to the large parking area on the left at Hogpen Gap. The total trip is fourteen miles; allow twenty minutes.

If you plan to shuttle using two cars, leave one car near Neel Gap in the Byron Reece Memorial parking area for the end of the hike. Drive the other car to Hogpen Gap by traveling north on US 19/129 for five miles, then turning right onto GA 180. Stay on 180 for one mile, then turn right onto GA 348, traveling five miles to Hogpen Gap. The trip total from Blairsville to Neel Gap and then to Hogpen Gap is twenty-five miles; allow thirty minutes.

ALTERNATIVE TRANSPORTATION: Use a shuttle service to meet you at Neel Gap, where you will leave a car, and take you to Hogpen Gap to begin your hike. See the list of shuttle-service providers in the **Hiker Essentials** sections for Blairsville, Dahlonega, Suches, and Ellijay.

Fine Wine and Accommodations
Blairsville

BLAIRSVILLE, a designated Appalachian Trail Community, is a small historic North Georgia town and the county seat of Union County. Nearly two-thirds of Union County is part of the Chattahoochee-Oconee National Forest and a natural outdoor haven.

The town hosts annual events such as the Downtown Spring Arts & Crafts Festival and the September Bluegrass Festival. Union County was dry until July 2010, and many restaurants still do not serve alcohol. Some let you bring it in; others do not. Ask before you go.

Lodging

Rustic Lodging Within Five Miles of Neel Gap

MOUNTAIN CROSSINGS HIKER HOSTEL, OUTFITTER, AND GIFT SHOP: ½ $, hostel is filled on a first-come-first-served basis, offering hot showers, bunks, and laundry facilities. The store has snacks and freeze-dried food. 9710 Gainesville Hwy at Neel Gap, 706-745-6095, www.mountaincrossings.com.

Mountain Crossings is housed in the historic Walasi-Yi Center and is an A.T. Community Supporter.

BLOOD MOUNTAIN CABINS AND COUNTRY STORE: $ (special hiker rate); cabins with kitchens and satellite TVs; all linens, toiletries, and paper products provided; no Wi-Fi except in the store for cabin guests; each cabin accommodates four to six adults; laundry free with stay.

The store has grocery and snack items, including frozen hot wings, pizza, and hamburgers, and it also carries video games. The store is open 8 a.m. to 5 p.m. Mon, Tue, and Thu through Sat; 8 a.m. to noon Sun; 12829 Gainesville Hwy (US 19/129); 0.4 miles south of Neel Gap. A trail from the A.T. leads to the store and cabins. 706-745-9454, www.bloodmountain.com. Blood Mountain Cabins is an A.T. Community Supporter.

VOGEL STATE PARK: $–$$ (two-night minimum), cabins for two to eight, furnished kitchens, TVs, linens provided, laundry facilities and telephone available in the park, $5 park entry fee, 405 Vogel State Park Road (three miles north of Neel Gap), 706-745-2628, www.gastateparks.org.

Lodging Four to Ten Miles from Neel Gap

ALPINE CABINS: $$; deluxe cabins with Jacuzzi tubs, fireplaces, fully equipped kitchens, TVs, radios and books; no Wi-Fi or VCRs in rooms, but free Wi-Fi available at the office; pet friendly; 77 Alpine Way (nine miles northwest of Neel Gap); 706-745-7589; www.alpinecabins.com.

MISTY MOUNTAIN INN AND COTTAGES: $, Inn rooms include breakfast, free Wi-Fi, TVs, fireplaces; six cottages have queen beds, baths, fully equipped kitchens, TVs, wood-burning fireplaces; cottages are pet-friendly, but not the Inn. Inn and cottages were updated in 2017. 55 Misty Mountain Lane (nine to ten miles from Neel Gap), 706-745-4786, www.mistymountaininn.com. Ask owner about shuttle service to the trailheads.

PARADISE CABINS RESORT AND SPA: $–$$–$$$ (two-night minimum); one-to-five-bedroom cabins with linens, fully equipped kitchens, TVs, and DVD players; cabins with dome-shaped roofs have hot tubs; massage and body treatments by appointment; vineyard and tasting room next to lodge; 366 Paradise Road (nine miles northwest of Neel Gap); 706-745-7483; www.paradisehillsga.com.

SUNRISE CABINS AND COTTAGES: $–$$ plus cleaning fee; 1, 2, and 3 BR, 1 BA; linens provided; fully equipped kitchens; satellite TVs, VCRs, and stone fireplaces; 7568 Gainesville Hwy (US 129/19, six miles north of Neel Gap); 706-745-5877.

YOUR HOME IN THE WOODS BED & BREAKFAST: $; full breakfast; guest rooms with private baths; guests may enjoy a living room, dining room, front and back porches, and garden; 143 Timber Lane (nine miles northwest of Neel Gap), 706-745-9337, www.yourhomeinthewoods.com.

OUR EXPERIENCE: Jim and I stay here in 2017 when we plan to attend Trail Days at Vogel State Park. Each suite has a theme and is tastefully decorated with guests' names on the door. The bed and breakfast is handicapped accessible throughout.

We have a lovely stay. In the evening, we relax on the screened-in porch, sipping wine, listening to music, and talking with another couple. The beds are comfortable and the rooms quiet.

The owners are friendly and accommodate our desire for an early breakfast so we could get to Vogel by nine o'clock for a Georgia Appalachian Trail maintenance trip. We will be refurbishing one of the trails. They fix a delicious full breakfast with an egg casserole, bacon, pancakes, homemade bread, fruit, juice, and coffee.

Lodging in Blairsville, Thirteen Miles North of Neel Gap

SEASONS INN: $ (special winter rates), family hotel, rooms with king or two doubles, TVs, free local calls, coffee in lobby, laundry service for guests, 94 Town Square, 706-7451631, www.seasons-inn.com.

BEST WESTERN MILTON INN: $ (hiker discount and winter special rates), complimentary full hot breakfast, pool, 201 Hwy 515 West, 706-745-6995, www.bestwestern.com/blairsville,ga.

Selected Restaurants in or near Blairsville
(thirteen miles north of Neel Gap)

JIM'S SMOKIN QUE: $–$$, American, no beer or wine, 11 a.m. to 8 p.m. Thu through Sat (closes when they sell out), 4971 Gainesville Hwy (US 19/129, ten miles north of Neel Gap), 706-835-7427, www.jimssmokinque.com.

Sign reads "Rated #6 nationwide. Don't go home hungry. No propane used. Has 'Butt Sauce' for Sale."

OUR EXPERIENCE: On a Friday evening in 2017, we are in Blairsville for Trail Days at Vogel State Park and decide we have to try this place we have heard about. We order short ribs with coleslaw and baked beans. The ribs are loaded with pork and are so tender they seem to fall off the bone into our mouths. It is mouth-watering good. We can not eat it all, and Jim enjoyed the ribs again the next day. If you are nearby, try them. Their portions are large, so you might want to split an entree.

AMERICAN CATCH SEAFOOD EXCHANGE: $–$$, American, website says "Fish is from American waters only," no beer or wine but you may bring it in, 4 to 8 p.m. Mon through Thu, 4 to 9 p.m. Fri and Sat, 94F Town Square, 706-745-3754.

ARMADILLO GRILL: $, Mexican-American, full bar, 11 a.m. to 8 p.m. Mon through Thu, 11 a.m. to 9 p.m. Fri and Sat, 24 Scott Drive, 706-745-4782.

DAN'S GRILL: $, authentic Cuban, menu advertises "pork fresh, cooked daily," no beer or wine but you may bring it in, 11 a.m. to 8 p.m. Tue through Sat, 305 Murphy Highway J (Union Station Mall), 706-745-0013.

MICHAELEE'S ITALIAN LIFE CAFFE: $–$$, no beer or wine but you may bring your own, 11 a.m. to 8 p.m. Mon through Thu, 11 a.m. to 9 p.m. Fri and Sat, 6C Town Square, 706-400-5603.

MONET'S ITALIAN GRILL & PIZZERIA: $, Italian, craft beer, 11 a.m. until close Tue through Fri, 5 p.m. until close Sat, 12 p.m. to 3 p.m. Sun, 130 Blue Ridge Street, 706-745-5305, www.2016MonetsItalianGrill.com, A.T. Community Supporter.

NANI'S DELI AND MORE, : ½ $, authentic Cuban, menu reads, "One of top 5 restaurants in Blairsville; have meals for vegetarians," no beer or wine but you may bring it in, 11 a.m. to 8 p.m. Tue through Sat, 51 D Earnest Street, 706-745-0010.

SICILY'S: $, Italian, no beer or wine, 11 a.m. to 8 p.m. Sun, 11 a.m. to 9 p.m. Mon through Sat, 305 H Murphy Highway (US 76, Union Station Mall), 706-745-0232.

THE BIG CHEESE: $, Pizza-American, no beer or wine, 11 a.m. to 7 p.m. Tue through Thu, 11 a.m. to 8 p.m. Fri, 4 to 8 p.m. Sat, 1735 Murphy Hwy (US76), 706-745-8686.

Hiker Essentials, Splurges, and Emergency Stops

Shuttle-Service Providers

ALPINE'S HIKER SHUTTLES: 970-903-1638.

MOUNTAIN CROSSINGS OUTFITTER: Call 706-745-6095 and they will help you find a driver.

Car Rental Agency

ENTERPRISE RENT-A-CAR: 8 a.m. to 6 p.m. Mon through Fri, 391 Blue Ridge Highway, 706-745-2816.

Outfitters

MOUNTAIN CROSSINGS AT NEEL GAP: premier outfitter on the Appalachian Trail in North Georgia with the expertise and gear that hikers need, 8:30 a.m. to 5 p.m. Mon through Thu, 8:30 a.m. to 6 p.m. Fri through Sun, 12471 Gainesville Highway (US 19/129), 706-745-6095, www.mountaincrossings.com, A.T. Community Supporter.

BIKES & HIKES: bike and hiking equipment and information, 10 a.m. to 5:30 p.m. Mon through Sat, 49 Blue Ridge Street, 706-745-5814.

SOUTHERN HIGHROADS OUTFITTERS: general gear, mostly for day hikers, 9 a.m. to 5 p.m. Mon through Sat, 253 GA 515, Building 1C, 706-781-1414.

Groceries

INGLES MARKET: groceries, beer, wine, 7 a.m. to 11 p.m. daily, 1070 GA 515, 706-745-9862.

FOOD CITY: groceries, beer, wine, 7 a.m. to 11 p.m. daily, 417 Blue Ridge Street, 706-835-2412.

FOODLAND: groceries, no beer or wine, 8 a.m. to 9 p.m. Mon through Sat, 12 to 9 p.m. Sun, 20 Young Harris Street, 706-745-2191.

SAVE-A-LOT: groceries, no beer or wine, 8 a.m. to 9 p.m. daily, 117 Murphy Highway (US 76), 706-745-1929.

SUNRISE GROCERY: snacks, drinks, fruits, vegetables, and products by local artisans; no beer or wine; 7:30 a.m. to 7 p.m. Mon through Sat; 9 a.m. to 6 p.m. Sun; 7586 Gainesville Hwy (US19/129, six miles north of Neel Gap); 706-745-5877; A.T. Community Supporter.

WALMART SUPERCENTER: groceries, camping supplies, beer and wine, 24/7, 2257 GA 515, 706-835-2881.

Beer or Wine Stores

THE WINE SHOPPE: 10 a.m. to 7 p.m. Mon through Sat, 6 Town Square, Suite A, 706-745-9463.

THE BEARDING BOTTLE SHOP: craft beer only, 1 to 8 p.m. Wed through Sat, 6 Town Square, Suite D, 706-745-2337.

ATMs

CARDTRONICS ATM: 458 GA 515.

CARDTRONICS ATM: 325 Cleveland Street.

CARDTRONICS ATM: 12 Murphy Highway (US 76).

COMMUNITY AND SOUTHERN BANK ATM: 271 GA 515.

UNITED COMMUNITY BANK ATM: 391 Brackett's Way.

UNITED COMMUNITY BANK ATM IN INGLES: 2070 GA 515 East.

Urgent Care and Emergency Services

THE CLINIC AT WALMART A SERVICE OF UNION GENERAL HOSPITAL: 9 a.m. to 6:30 p.m. Mon through Fri, 9 a.m. to 4:30 p.m. Sat, noon to 5:30 p.m. Sun, 2257 GA 515, 706-439-6860.

UNION GENERAL HOSPITAL EMERGENCY ROOM: 24/7, 35 Hospital Road, 706-745-2111.

Fun Places to Visit in Blairsville and Nearby

BYRON HERBERT REECE FARM AND HERITAGE CENTER (HOME OF THE APPALACHIAN POET AND NOVELIST): free, 10 a.m. to 4 p.m. Mon through Sat, 1 to 4 p.m. Sun, Apr through Nov, 8552 Gainesville Highway (US 19/129), 706-745-2034.

MOUNTAIN LIFE MUSEUM: Explore the 1906 Grapel Mock House, the 1861 John Payne Cabin, and historic farm buildings. 11 a.m. to 4 p.m. Thu through Sat, May through Dec, 25 Veterans Memorial Parkway (south of town), 706-745-5439.

OLIVE TREE ART CENTRE AND GALLERY: 10 a.m. 5 p.m. Tue through Sat, 563 Gainesville Highway (US 129/19), 706-835-1257.

UNION COUNTY COURTHOUSE MUSEUM: donations only, 10 a.m. to 4 p.m. Mon through Sat, 1 Town Square, 706-745-5493. The volunteer receptionist told me, "We have tours. Bill is the best tour guide. He is here 10 a.m. to 2 p.m., but not Wednesdays."

UNION COUNTY FARMERS MARKET: homegrown and handmade products, 2 to 6 p.m. Tue, 7 a.m. to 1 p.m. Sat, Jun through Oct, Trash and Treasure sale 7:30 a.m. to 2 p.m. Fri, 148 Old Smokey Road (turn off GA 515 at Home Depot).

BUTTERNUT CREEK GOLF COURSE: 18 holes over rolling hills with views of the mountains, rates vary with day of the week and tee time, daily Apr through Oct, grill and restaurant with full bar, 129 Union County Recreation Road, 706-459-6076.

ODOM SPRINGS VINEYARDS: 11 a.m. to 6 p.m. Wed through Sat, 1 to 5 p.m. Sun, 637 Odom Road, 706-745-3094, www.odomspringsvineyards.com.

PARADISE HILLS VINEYARD AND TASTING ROOM: tasting $5, 1 p.m. Mon through Wed, noon to 6 p.m. Thu through Sat, 366 Paradise Road, 706-745-7483, www.paradisehillsga.com/vineyard-winery/

BRASSTOWN BALD: the highest point in Georgia, where the views are spectacular. 10 a.m. to 5 p.m. daily Apr through Dec. From Neel Gap, go toward Blairsville on US 19/129, then right on GA 180 to GA 180 Spur. Turn left and go up the mountain. (sixteen miles from Neel Gap).

DESOTO FALLS: three waterfalls along Frogtown Creek with an overall height of 480 feet. From Neel Gap, go two miles southeast on US19/129 to Desoto Falls State Park. The falls are one mile from the parking area.

HELTON CREEK FALLS: two tall waterfalls cascading down through the trees with a small pool at the bottom and a wooden overlook. From Neel Gap, go toward Blairsville on US 19/129 one mile to USFS 118, then right. Follow signs. The trail leads 0.2 miles to the falls.

TRACK ROCK ARCHEOLOGICAL AREA: free, series of rock carvings, or petroglyphs, made by Native Americans on soapstone boulders, seen best in the low light of early mornings or late in the day. From Blairsville, take US 76 east about five miles to Track Rock Gap Road, turn right, and go about two miles to the gap, then go through the gap to parking on the right.

The beautiful Helton Creek Falls, May 2007

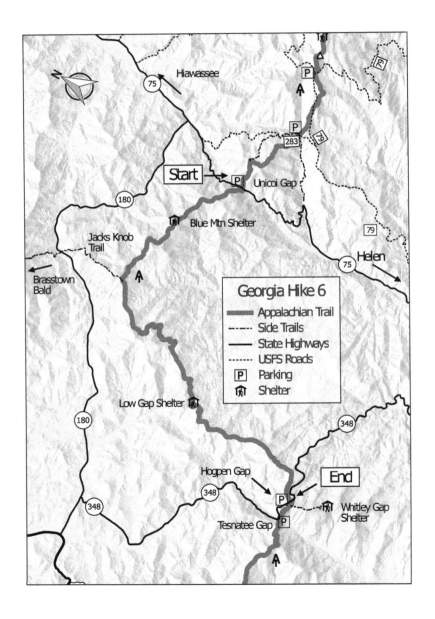

Unicoi Gap to Hogpen Gap,
14.2 miles, Challenging

GEORGIA HIKE 6

HIGHLIGHTS: The Mark Trail Wilderness Area is quiet and pristine with many wildflowers, birds, hardwood trees, and the headwaters of the Chattahoochee River. This wilderness area is named after naturalist Mark Trail, the comic-strip character created by Georgia cartoonist Ed Dodd.

DISTANCE: 14.2 miles.   **HIKE TIME:** 8–9 hours.

LEVEL OF EFFORT: Challenging, long with steep climbs.

RECOMMENDED DIRECTION: North to south, Unicoi Gap to Hogpen Gap.

DOWNHILL: 11.2 miles with an elevation loss of 2,770 feet. **UPHILL:** 3 miles with an elevation gain of 3,290 feet.

ALONG THE TRAIL: From Unicoi Gap, the A.T. climbs steeply up Blue Mountain on a narrow and rocky path before it widens and descends gently to Chattahoochee Gap, Poplar Gap, and Low Gap. The trail climbs up to Sheep Rock Top, goes over an old forest road and across stamps (large grassy areas) to Poor Mountain before it descends to Hogpen Gap.

The Mark Trail Wilderness, July 2011, Courtesy of Fran Laprade

Water is available for purifying down the blue-blazed trail at Chattahoochee Gap to Chattahoochee Spring, the headwaters of the Chattahoochee River. The Chattahoochee River flows 434 miles from Chattahoochee Spring to the Florida/Georgia border at Lake Seminole.

SHELTERS: There are two shelters, Blue Mountain and Low Gap. Stop at Blue Mountain Shelter to enjoy the views. I remember one night in particular when we were tenting near Blue Mountain Shelter. In the clear, crisp April air, I could read by the light of the full moon. It was amazing.

Follow the White Blazes

MILE 0.0: Unicoi Gap, 2,940 feet, northern boundary of the Mark Trail Wilderness. The word Unicoi comes from the Cherokee word for "white."

MILE 1.4: Blue Mountain, 4,010 feet.

MILE 2.3: Blue Mountain Shelter.

MILE 4.6: Chattahoochee Gap, 3,560 feet. Jacks Knob Trail to the west; blue-blazed trail to the east to Chattahoochee Spring, the headwaters of the Chattahoochee River.

MILE 5.6: Cold Spring Gap, 3,380 feet.

MILE 8.1: Poplar Stamp Gap, 3,340 feet.

MILE 9.5: Low Gap Shelter, 3,040 feet.

MILE 10.3: Sheep Rock Top, 3,530 feet.

MILE 11.5: Wide Gap, 3,190 feet.

MILE 12.2: Poor Mountain, 3,620 feet.

MILE 13.3: White Oak Stamp, 3,460 feet.

MILE 14.2: Hogpen Gap, 3,450 feet.

Peaks and Valleys

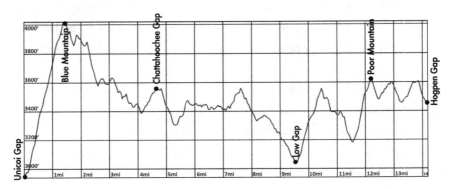

Alternative Hikes

Because this hike was challenging for us, we divide this 14.2-mile hike into two hikes.

GEORGIA HIKE 6.1:
Hogpen Gap to Chattahoochee Gap to Jacks Gap,
11.9 miles, Moderate

DISTANCE: 11.9 miles: 9.6 miles on the Appalachian Trail plus 2.3 miles on the blue-blazed Jacks Knob Trail to GA 180.

HIKE TIME: 6.5–7 hours.　**LEVEL OF EFFORT:** Moderate.

RECOMMENDED DIRECTION: South to north, Hogpen Gap to Chattahoochee Gap and then down the access trail to Jacks Gap.

JACKS KNOB TRAIL (ACCESS TRAIL): *Distance: 2.3 miles. Level of Effort:* Easy, but descends in a repetitive up-and-down pattern to Jacks Gap.

GEORGIA HIKE 6.2:

Unicoi Gap to Chattahoochee Gap to Jacks Gap, 6.9 miles, Challenging to Moderate

DISTANCE: 6.9 miles: 4.6 miles on the Appalachian Trail plus 2.3 miles on the Jacks Knob Trail.

HIKE TIME: 4 hours.

LEVEL OF EFFORT: Challenging to Moderate with steep climbs.

RECOMMENDED DIRECTION: North to south, Unicoi Gap to Chattahoochee Gap, and then down the access trail to Jacks Gap.

My Hiking Journal

MAY 2007: This is the fourth day of our day hiking trip.

As we leave the Hiker Hostel, I think, "This is going to be a long day. Before we can start our fourteen-mile hike, Josh, the hostel owner, has to shuttle us from Dahlonega to Unicoi Gap to leave a car and then drive us back to Hogpen Gap, a total of sixty miles. I wonder what time we'll get back."

As we are driving to Hogpen Gap, I tell Jim a story about my backpacking trip fifteen years earlier with Harmon and Justin (our son and his friend). We hiked twenty miles from Blood Mountain Shelter to Blue Mountain Shelter.

Harmon and Justin hopped from rock to rock up Blue Mountain. Blue Mountain Shelter was full, so they pitched our tent.

When I finally got to the top of the mountain, I dropped to the ground and began shivering. I was exhausted. Harmon told me to crawl into my sleeping bag and get warm while they cooked supper.

I took a nap. When I got up, supper was ready. After I ate, I felt better. It had been a long, hard hike.

With this memory fresh in my mind, I anticipate that today's hike will be arduous as well. Jim leads the way, walking quickly up the rocky trail to Poor Mountain. I scurry along behind, pausing to take frequent sips of water.

Jim notices that there are rock walls that support the trail along this section. He says, "I wonder how long these have been here."

"These walls could have been here since the Appalachian Trail was built eighty years ago," I say. "And through the years, the Georgia Appalachian Trail Club has built steps and walls to fight erosion."

We hike over the grassy stamps on an old logging road. There are beautiful orange flame azaleas blooming around us.

As we descend down the rocky path into Low Gap, I say, "Let's stop for lunch at the shelter. I need a break."

We pull out our peanut butter sandwiches, apples, and cookies. After lunch, I take off my shoes to check the blister that started forming on the hike two days ago.

"My blister looks okay," I say. "I protected it today with moleskin."

Feeling refreshed, we make the gradual climb over rolling hills to Chattahoochee Gap.

Jim says," Here's the blue-blazed trail. Let's go down to Chattahoochee Spring and see where the river starts."

We meet other day hikers who have come down to check out the spring as well.

As we climb up, up, up over the rocks toward Blue Mountain, Jim says, "I am really tired. I don't think we are ever going to get to the top."

"Lets stop, take a break, and eat an energy bar," I say.

I try to take a long sip from my water bladder and realize it is empty.

"I'm glad I threw an extra bottle of water into my pack," I say.

Finally, we get to the top.

"I want to take you down to Blue Mountain Shelter where Harmon, Justin, and I stayed on our hiking trip," I say. "We had wonderful views from the side of the mountain where the shelter is."

We pause briefly at the shelter to take pictures. We see a group of young women and begin talking with them.

Headwaters of the Chattahoochee River, May 2007

One of them tells us, "We're just out for a few days. I walk for stress reduction."

We walk rapidly down the grassy earthen trail to Unicoi Gap.

Jim looks at his watch and says, "It is only four thirty."

I say, "This is hard to believe—14.3 miles in seven and a half hours."

With our legs aching, we slowly climb into the car and head back to the Hiker Hostel.

"I'm going to have to soak my aching legs and feet in the tub tonight," I say.

After taking hot showers and soaking in the tub, we relax in our room.

We raise our glasses of champagne and Jim says, "We finished that hike."

I reply, "But I am so tired, I can barely move. I'm glad we bought boiled shrimp and potato salad for supper when we went to the store yesterday. I don't think I could have gotten dressed and gone into town to eat."

As we are eating, Jim says, "I'm too tired to hike another day. I need a break."

"Let's see how we feel tomorrow. I really want to finish the fifth hike to Dicks Creek," I say.

The next morning when we get up, Jim says, "My legs are hurting."

And I say, "I don't think my blister will take another day of hiking. Let's go over to Hiawassee and treat ourselves to the luxury hotel on the lake."

Jim smiles and gives me a hug.

Carol's Reminders

- **Stop and check out the shelters.** These are good places to take a break.
- **If a hike looks longer than you think you can comfortably walk, look for ways to divide it up into two or more hikes.** In this guide

Relaxing by Lake Chatuge on our day off, May 2007

I describe ways to do this by using short access trails that intersect the Appalachian Trail.

- **For long hikes, take an extra energy bar or energy drink to give you that added boost in the afternoon before your final ascents or descents.**
- **On long hikes, take extra water or take a water-purification device such as a water filter or ultraviolet light to treat water from the streams.** You do not want to need water and be without it.
- **Plan an easy evening meal after a long day of hiking.**
- **On a four- or five-day hiking trip, be willing to change your plans if you or your partner says, "I have had enough. I'm ready to take a day off."** When you are day hiking, you can always follow the planned route on another day. You are not on an epic journey from one end of the Appalachian Trail to the other.

Nearest Towns

Helen is nine miles south of Unicoi Gap and ten miles northeast of Hogpen Gap.

Directions to the Trailheads

SOUTHERN TRAILHEAD, HOGPEN GAP: GPS coordinates 34.72589, -83.83985. From Helen, drive south on GA 75 Alt. 3.5 miles. Turn right on GA 348, drive seven miles to the large parking lot on the right with a sign for Hogpen Gap. The trip total is eleven and one-half miles; allow fifteen minutes.

NORTHERN TRAILHEAD, UNICOI GAP: GPS coordinates 34.80151, -83.74280. From Helen, drive nine miles north on GA 75 to Unicoi Gap. The parking area is on the right.

TRAILHEAD AT JACKS GAP FOR GEORGIA HIKES 6.1 AND 6.2: GPS coordinates 34.8487, -83.7982. From Helen, go twelve miles north on GA 75. Turn left onto GA 180 and drive five miles until it intersects the GA 180 Spur at Jacks Gap. Parking is available at the Gap.

If you plan to shuttle using two cars:

GEORGIA HIKE 6.0: From Helen, drive to Hogpen Gap and leave a car. Drive the second car back to Helen and then travel north on GA 75 to Unicoi Gap. The total trip from Helen to Hogpen Gap to Unicoi Gap is thirty-two miles; allow forty minutes.

GEORGIA HIKE 6.1: From Helen, drive one car to Jacks Gap. Then drive the second car to Hogpen Gap by going south on GA 180 six miles to GA 348, then turn left on GA 348 and travel seven miles to the sign and parking area on the left for Hogpen Gap. The trip total from Helen to Jacks Gap to Hogpen Gap is thirty miles; allow forty minutes.

GEORGIA HIKE 6.2: From Helen, drive one car to Jacks Gap. Then drive the other car north on GA 180 five miles to GA 75. Turn right and drive three miles south to Unicoi Gap. Parking is on the left. The total trip from Helen to Jacks Gap and back to Unicoi Gap is twenty-five miles; allow thirty minutes.

ALTERNATIVE TRANSPORTATION: Use a shuttle service to pick you up at the trailhead where you plan to end your hike and take you to the trailhead where you plan to begin your hike. See the list of shuttle-service providers in the **Hiker Essentials** sections for Helen or for Blairsville.

Fine Wine and Accommodations
Helen

HELEN, a designated Appalachian Trail Community, was revitalized in 1969, when this small mountain town was turned into an alpine village with many shops, restaurants, and places to stay.

Lodging

B&Bs, Cabins, and Condos

ALPINE HILLTOP HAUS BED AND BREAKFAST: $$, desserts, tea and coffee on arrival and delicious breakfast in the morning, 362 Chattahoochee Strasse, 706-878-2388, www.alpinehiltop.com.

ALPINE MOUNTAIN CABINS: $–$$, queen-size beds, kitchenettes, TVs, VCRs, hot tubs, 7489 GA 75 Alt (one and a half miles south of Helen), 706-878-3111, www.amchelen.com.

BLACK FOREST B&B AND LUXURY CABINS: $$; rooms, suites, and cottages with queen-size beds, fireplaces, whirlpools, TVs, refrigerators, and coffee makers; 8902 North Main Street, 706-878-3995, www.blackforestva-cationrentals.com.

LORELEY RESORT: $$; nightly and weekly rentals of 1 or 2 BR fully furnished condominiums with outdoor and indoor pool, hot tub, outdoor games, game room, fitness center, and laundry facilities; 387 Brucken Strasse, 706 878-2238, www.loreleyresort.com.

UNICOI STATE PARK LODGE AND CONFERENCE CENTER: $ for lodge room; $$ for cabin; guests may enjoy lodge fireplace, beach, restaurant, and laundry facilities; 1788 GA 356 (two miles northeast of Helen on GA 356); 706-878-2201; www.gastateparks.org/Unicoi.

Selected Hotels

BEST WESTERN: $, complimentary breakfast, 8220 South Main Street, 706-878-3310, www.bestwestern.com/helen.

COUNTRY INN & SUITES: $, hot breakfast, indoor pool, guest laundry facilities, 8087 Edelweiss Strasse, 706-878-9000, www.countryinns.com/helen.

HAMPTON INN: $$, complimentary breakfast, outdoor pool, 147 Unicoi Street, 855-271-3622, www.hilton.com/hampton_inn/helen.

HEIDI MOTEL: ½ $, mini fridges, microwaves, 8820 North Main Street, 706-878-2689, www.heidimotel.com.

HELENDORF RIVER INN AND CONFERENCE CENTER: $–$$, suites with kitchenettes, free breakfast, outdoor pool, 33 Munich Strasse, 706-878-2271, www.helendorf.com.

QUALITY INN: $, free breakfast, microwaves, refrigerators, outdoor pool, 15 Yonah Street, 706-878-3310, www.choicehotels.com.

RIVERBEND MOTEL AND CABINS: $ for rooms, $$ for cabins, microwaves, refrigerators, 134 River Street, 706-878-2155, www.riverbendmotelandcabins.

Many other hotels and cabins are available. Go to the Alpine Helen/ White County Convention & Visitors Bureau, www.helenga.org.

Selected Restaurants

BODENSEE: $–$$, German fine dining, full bar, open 11 a.m., closing times vary daily, 64 Munich Strasse, 706-878-1026.

MULLY'S NACOOCHEE GRILL: $–$$, American, full bar, 11:30 a.m. to 9 p.m. Tue through Sun, 7277 South Main Street, 706-878-1020.

NACOOCHEE VILLAGE TAVERN & PIZZERIA: $, American, beer and wine, 12 to 9 p.m. Mon through Thu, 12 to 10 p.m. Fri and Sat, 7275 South Main Street, 706-878-0199.

NORTH GEORGIA BARBEQUE: ½ $–$; American; no beer or wine; 11 a.m. to 7 p.m. Mon, Tue, Thu through Sun; 663 Edelweiss Strasse; 706-878-5753.

SPICE 55: Thai fine dining and sushi, beer and wine, noon to 8 p.m. Sun, 11 a.m. to 9 p.m. Tue through Thu, 11 a.m. to 10 p.m. Fri, noon to 10 p.m. Sat, 705 Brucken Strasse, 706-878-1010.

There are many other restaurants in Helen. Go to www.helenga.org/ dining-restaurants.

Hiker Essentials, Splurges, and Emergency Stops

Shuttle-Service Providers

ALPINE TAXI: Doug Fortner, 706-969-5311.

WOODY'S BICYCLE SHOP: 706-878-3715.

Car Rental Agency

ENTERPRISE RENT-A-CAR: 7:30 a.m. to 6 p.m. Mon through Fri and 9:00 a.m. to noon Sat; 1847 Hwy 129, Suite B, Cleveland, GA (ten miles south of Helen); 706-348-818.

Outfitters

SMOKY MOUNTAIN TRADER: 9:30 a.m. to 5:30 p.m. Mon through Fri; 10 a.m. to 5 p.m. Sat; 18 East Jarrard Street, Cleveland (ten miles south of Helen on GA 75); 706-865-7296.

Groceries

BETTY'S COUNTRY STORE: groceries, souvenirs, books, beer, wine, 7 a.m. to 8 p.m. Mon through Thu, 7 a.m. to 9 p.m. Fri and Sat, 7 a.m. to 7 p.m. Sun, 18 Yonah Street, 766-878-2617.

INGLES: groceries, beer, and wine; 24/7; 55 Helen Highway (GA 75), Cleveland (ten miles south of Helen on GA 75); 706-219-4096.

Wine and Beer

ALPINE BREWS & BOTTLE HAUS: 8 a.m. to 10:30 p.m. Mon through Thu, 8 a.m. to12:30 a.m. Fri and Sat, 12:30 to 8 p.m. Sun, 8265 S Main St, 706-878-3196.

DISCOUNT SPIRITS OF HELEN: 9 a.m. to 9 p.m. Mon through Thu, 9 a.m. to 10 p.m. Fri and Sat, 50 Yonah Street, 706-878-7050.

HELEN CELLAR & PACKAGE STORE: 9 a.m. to 9 p.m. Mon through Thu, 9 a.m. to 10 p.m. Fri and Sat, 8065 South Main Street, 706-878-2651.

FROGTOWN CELLARS/HELEN VINEYARDS: 11 a.m. to 6 p.m. Fri and Sat, 12:30 to 5 p.m. Sun, 7601 South Main Street, 707-878-5000.

HABERSHAM WINERY TASTING ROOM: 10 a.m. to 6 p.m. Mon through Sat, 12:30 to 6 p.m. Sun, 705 South Main Street, 706-878-9463.

ATMs

UNITED COMMUNITY BANK ATM: 8460 Helen Hwy (GA 75).

KWIK SAK ATM: 8675 Main Street.

ATM: 705 Brucken Strasse.

Urgent Care and Emergency Services

NE GA PHYSICIANS GROUP URGENT CARE: 8 a.m. to 8 p.m. daily; 2578 Helen Highway (GA 75), Cleveland (ten miles south of Helen on GA 75); 706-348-4280.

Fun Places to Visit in and near Helen

There are many shops and galleries in downtown Helen.

FOLK POTTERY MUSEUM OF NORTHEAST GEORGIA: 283 GA 255 North, Sautee, GA (four miles east of Helen via GA 17).

MARK OF THE POTTER: oldest crafts shop in Georgia still in the original location, the old Grandpa Watts Gristmill; handcrafted pottery; potter working weekends; craft shop; 10 a.m. to 6 p.m. daily; 9982 GA 197, Clarkesville, GA (twelve miles northeast of Helen); 706-947-3440.

RAVEN CLIFF FALLS: : This unusual double cascading waterfall flows down through a fissure in a massive granite outcropping to Dodd Creek. The five-mile access trail is just off GA 348, four miles south of Hogpen Gap (thirteen miles west of Helen).

ANNA RUBY FALLS: : These twin waterfalls, created by Curtis Creek and York Creek, join at the base to form Smith Creek. Access through Unicoi State Park on a half-mile trail; $5 state park pass per vehicle and $3 per-person USFS visitor's pass; 1788 GA 356, Helen.

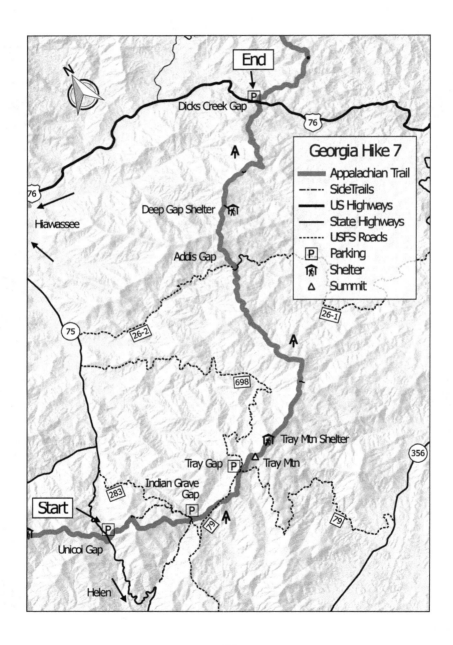

Georgia Hike 7

Legend:
- ▬▬ Appalachian Trail
- ·–·–· SideTrails
- ▬▬ US Highways
- ── State Highways
- ····· USFS Roads
- P Parking
- 🏠 Shelter
- △ Summit

End

Dicks Creek Gap

76

Deep Gap Shelter

Hiawassee

Addis Gap

76

75

26-2

26-1

698

Tray Mtn Shelter

Tray Gap P △ Tray Mtn

356

Indian Grave Gap

283

Start

P

79

79

Unicoi Gap

Helen

Unicoi Gap to Dicks Creek Gap,

16.5 miles, Challenging

GEORGIA
HIKE
7

HIGHLIGHTS: This hike is in the Tray Mountain Wilderness with beautiful hardwoods, rhododendrons, flame azaleas, and mountain laurels. There are three mountains at or above four thousand feet with views of Yonah Mountain with its granite dome; Brasstown Bald, the highest point in Georgia; Rabun Bald, the second highest point; the distant Nantahala Mountains; and Lake Chatuge. There is a gentle walk over rolling hills along the broad ridge crest, known as the Swag of the Blue Ridge. It is called the swag because it is the low point on the trail in this remote area.

DISTANCE: 16.5 miles.   **HIKE TIME:** 10 hours.   **LEVEL OF EFFORT:** Challenging.

RECOMMENDED DIRECTION: South to north, Unicoi Gap to Dicks Creek Gap.

DOWNHILL: 10.6 miles with an elevation loss of 5,100 feet. **UPHILL:** 4.9 miles with an elevation gain of 4,820 feet.

ALONG THE TRAIL: From Unicoi Gap, the A.T. goes up and down steep mountains with drop-offs on one side, but it is well maintained with stone steps and switchbacks. The path crosses gaps and knobs before rambling over the Swag of the Blue Ridge. Finally, it climbs another knob and mountain and drops into Dicks Creek Gap.

SHELTERS: There are two shelters, Tray Mountain and Deep Gap, with privies and water sources nearby. Have lunch at the Tray Mountain Shelter while you look out over the mountains.

Follow the White Blazes

MILE 0.0: Unicoi Gap, 2,949 feet.

MILE 1.3: Rocky Mountain, 4,010 feet.

MILE 2.5: Indian Grave Gap, 3,140 feet.

MILE 3.7: Cheese Factory site. Some say this was Georgia's first dairy.

MILE 4.4: Tray Gap, USFS 698 & USFS 79.

MILE 5.0: Tray Mountain, 4,430 feet.

MILE 5.5: Tray Mountain Shelter, east of A.T.

MILE 6.5: Wolfpen Gap, 3,590 feet.

MILE 7.6: Young Lick Knob, 3,750 feet.

MILE 8.8: Swag of the Blue Ridge, 3480 feet.

MILE 10.2: Sassafras Gap, 3,550 feet.

MILE 11.0: Addis Gap, 3,360 feet; fire road to Mill Creek Road, USFS 26-2.

MILE 12.1: Kelly Knob, 4,020 feet.

MILE 12.9: Deep Gap, 3,570 feet; Deep Gap Shelter, 0.3 miles east.

MILE 14.7: Powell Mountain, 3,600 feet.

MILE 16.5: Dicks Creek Gap, 2,670 feet.

Peaks and Valleys

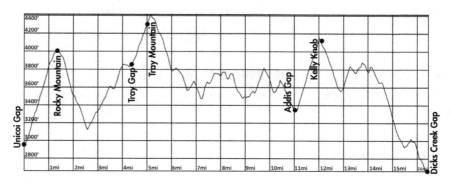

Alternative Hikes

This challenging hike was too long for us, so we divide the 16.5-mile hike into three shorter hikes.

GEORGIA HIKE 7.1:

Tray Gap to Unicoi Gap, 4.4 miles, Moderate

DISTANCE: 4.4 miles.   **HIKE TIME:** 3 hours.   **LEVEL OF EFFORT:** Moderate.

RECOMMENDED DIRECTION: North to south, Tray Gap to Unicoi Gap.

GEORGIA HIKE 7.2:

Tray Gap to Addis Gap, 7.6 miles, Moderate

DISTANCE: 6.6 miles on the A.T. plus 1.0 mile on Mills Creek access trail.

HIKE TIME: 4 hours.   **LEVEL OF EFFORT:** Moderate.

RECOMMENDED DIRECTION: South to north, from Tray Gap to Addis Gap.

GEORGIA HIKE 7.3:

Addis Gap to Dicks Creek Gap, 6.5 miles, Moderate

DISTANCE: 5.5 miles on the A.T. plus 1.0 mile on Mills Creek Road access trail.

HIKE TIME: 3–4 hours.   **LEVEL OF EFFORT:** Moderate.

RECOMMENDED DIRECTION: South to north, from Addis Gap to Dicks Creek Gap.

My Hiking Journal

JUNE 2007, Unicoi Gap to Dicks Creek Gap: On the last day of our vacation, as we are returning home from North Carolina, I say to Jim, "Let's go to Hiawassee and do that last hike we had planned to do in May when I got that blister and we were really tired. My blister has healed."

Jim says, "Well, I don't know."

I call the Hiawassee Inn and am told they have a room available and can shuttle us to the trail. We reach the Hiawassee Inn at 11:30 a.m.

Paul from the inn and his dog, Duke, are waiting for us in a van in front of the inn. We follow him to Dicks Creek, where we leave our car and then climb into his van to go to Unicoi Gap, where we will start our hike.

Paul turns his head and says to us, "This is long hike (16.5 miles). Are you sure you want to do it?"

"Yes," I reply.

But feeling rushed and a little apprehensive, I wonder, *"Can we really do this sixteen-mile hike before dark?"*

Jim leads the way, with his legs moving quickly up the stone steps to Rocky Mountain and then down rapidly to the gap. We switch places and I lead up Tray Mountain.

Enjoying the fuchsia rhododendrons blooming, we look down and see petals covering the trail.

"Aren't they beautiful?" I ask.

We stop for a break on the sunny, rocky overlook near Young Lick Knob. Jim takes pictures of me with my face red from exertion and my hair blowing in the wind.

As we go down the mountain into the trees, there are orange flame azaleas peeking through the bushes, and we see green ferns on the forest floor.

At the sign for the Swag of the Blue Ridge, we meet two college girls with their shoes off, resting. They tell us they're hiking the Georgia section of the Appalachian Trail.

Young Lick Knob, June 2007

Jim says, "We are too."

We walk easily over the next three miles of gentle, rolling hills through the remote forest. About seven p.m., with the light beginning to wane, we come to Addis Gap and see the sign for Dicks Creek Gap.

"We have 5.4 miles to go. We should be down by nine," I say. "Let's rest a minute and eat our energy bars. We will need them to go up and over these next two mountains."

As we are climbing through the woods up the steep trail to Kelly Knob, we see a father with two children and a dog. We saw the same group ten days ago during another hike. They were just north of Woody Gap at that time and planned to be out about three weeks.

We both say, "Hi."

The father says, "We only have a week to go."

Vista on Powell Mountain, June 2007

After crossing over the knob, we move quickly down the trail to Deep Gap. We see the sign to Deep Gap Shelter but don't go down to check it out. There is another mountain yet to climb. At the top of Powell Mountain, a sign says, *Vista*, but tall young trees and bushes cover the view.

As we head down the mountain through the rhododendron tunnels, the forest gets darker and darker.

I say, "We better get out our headlights."

We stop, take our headlights from the top of our packs and put them on.

About fifteen minutes later, I hear rustling in the bushes about three feet ahead and see the backside of a bear.

I yell, "Bear!"

Jim hurries to join me and asks, "Where???"

I reply, "He's gone down the mountain."

Jim responds, "I better take the lead."

I catch my breath and sigh with relief. This is the first bear we've seen on our day hiking trips in Georgia. He definitely did what authorities say most bears will do: turn and leave the scene. He did not want to hear or see me any more than I wanted to see him.

We see what looks like the road and parking lot through the trees and walk faster on this rocky, root-covered portion of the trail.

All of a sudden, I trip and fall to my knees. I feel pain and see blood coming from a gash on my leg just below my knee.

I call, "Jim, stop! I'm hurt."

He comes back and asks, "What happened?"

"I think I tripped over a root," I reply.

We look at my leg and get out our first-aid supplies. I clean the gash and apply a bandage.

Jim asks, "Can you make it out?"

"Sure. It cannot be much further," I reply.

With my leg aching, we walk slowly down the trail and get to the parking lot in about ten minutes.

It is nine p.m. when we reach the car. My leg is throbbing and I'm hungry.

"I wonder what is still open," I say.

As we drive into Hiawassee, we see that Zaxby's and Dairy Queen still have their lights on. These are both next to the Hiawassee Inn, where we are staying.

"Good. We better hurry before they close," Jim says. "And what do you want?"

"I want a vanilla cone from Dairy Queen and any kind of chicken from Zaxby's, but take me to the motel first. My leg is hurting," I say.

Jim unloads the car and gets a bucket of ice from the ice machine. I wash my leg, examine the gash, and take two Advil.

Jim asks, "Do you want to go to the emergency room?"

"No, I don't think so," I reply. "I don't know that I want to try the emergency room in this little town." (Later I learn that Hiawassee has a good emergency room and that doctors there treat many foot and knee problems.)

I lay down on the bed and put an ice pack on my leg.

Jim goes to get us something to eat. In about fifteen minutes, he returns with the food.

"They were just getting ready to close when I went in Zaxby's. I could only get chicken and potato salad," he says. "But I did stop at Dairy Queen and get you a small cone and me a sundae."

"Wonderful," I reply.

Jim says, "We really have stories to tell from this hike. I'm glad we made it back safely."

We eat our chicken, potato salad, and ice cream.

"I don't think anything has ever tasted so good," I say.

My Hiking Journal

AUGUST 2015, Tray Gap to Unicoi Gap: I make this short trek on a sunny day with the Georgia Appalachian Trail Club.

Don, our hike leader, tells us the history of this part of the A.T. He shows us where a cheese factory used to be. He tells us that they had to use a mule train to bring supplies up to the dairy and to make deliveries. I wonder why they put the cheese factory up on the mountain in the woods. Don has no answer for that.

Pointing to the campsites along the trail, Don says, "We are refurbishing these because we expect a flood of hikers in 2016 after the movie *A Walk in the Woods* comes out."

Near the top of Rocky Mountain, Don suggests we stop for lunch. We sit down on the rock slabs and enjoy the views.

Don points to the south. "That's Mount Yonah with the granite dome," he says.

After lunch we move quickly down the trail to Unicoi Gap, stopping to pick up litter at a campsite and an old wet sleeping bag along the creek.

Carol's Reminders

- **Plan your trips carefully so that you start day hikes in the mornings, not in the afternoons.** You do not want to risk being on the trail after dark when you are more vulnerable to accidents.
- **Always have your flash light readily available in your pack in case you find yourself on the trail after dark.**
- **Always have a fully equipped first-aid kit and know how to use it.**
- **Know where the nearest urgent-care center or emergency room is.** In this guidebook under **Hiker Essentials**, you will find urgent-care centers and emergency rooms near each section of the trail.
- **If you encounter a bear, stop, retreat slowly while facing the bear, and talk loudly.** Bears usually go the other way when they hear humans. Black bears rarely attack humans. (To read more, turn to the section entitled ***What should you do if you encounter a black bear or snake on the trail?*** in **Get Ready**)
- **Practice "Leave No Trace."** Leave only your footprints on the trail. Take out what you bring in and any other trash you find along the trail. (Read the **Leave No Trace** section in **Get Ready**)

Nearest Towns

Hiawassee is eleven miles west of Dicks Creek Gap and twelve miles north of Addis Gap. Helen is nine miles south of Unicoi Gap and seventeen miles southeast of Tray Gap.

Directions to the Trailheads

SOUTHERN TRAILHEAD, UNICOI GAP: GPS coordinates 34.80151, -83.74280. From Hiawassee, drive twelve miles south on GA 75 to Unicoi Gap; allow fifteen minutes. Parking is on the left side of GA 75. From Helen, drive nine miles north on GA 75 to Unicoi Gap; allow ten minutes. Parking is on the right.

NORTHERN TRAILHEAD, DICKS CREEK GAP: GPS coordinates 34.91222, -83.61883. From Hiawassee, take US 76 East for eleven miles; allow fifteen minutes. Look for the A.T. crossing sign and the parking area on the left.

From Helen, drive north on GA 75 for eighteen miles, turn right onto US 76, and drive eight miles; allow thirty minutes.

TRAILHEAD AT TRAY GAP: GPS coordinates 34.79928, -83.69098. From Helen, drive eleven miles north on GA 75, passing Unicoi Gap on the right. Continue to Milepost 2 and make a wide right turn onto USFS 283. Drive four miles to Indian Grave Gap and continue half a mile to the intersection with USFS 79. Turn left and go two miles to Tray Gap. The total trip is seventeen miles; allow forty minutes.

TRAILHEAD AT ADDIS GAP: GPS coordinates 34.8629, -83.6563.

From Hiawassee, drive east on US 76, then turn right onto GA 75/17 and go three miles. Turn left onto Mill Creek Road. At the turn you will see a concrete block building on the left and Owl Creek Road on your right. Drive one mile on the paved Mill Creek Road and turn left up the gravel USFS 26-2. The left turn is just after 3287 Mill Creek Road on the right. If you get to a gate and the end of the paved road, you have missed the gravel road to the left. Drive three miles on the gravel-and-dirt USFS 26-2 until you come to a dirt fire road on the left that goes uphill to a gate. Go straight at the fire road and park. Hike one mile up the fire road to the A.T. The trip total includes driving ten miles and hiking one mile; allow thirty-five minutes.

From Helen, drive fifteen miles north on GA 75/17. Pass Unicoi Gap. Turn right on Mill Creek Road. Follow the directions above. The trip total includes driving twenty miles and hiking one mile; allow fifty minutes.

If you plan to shuttle using two cars, leave one car at the trailhead where you plan to end your hike, then drive the other car to the trailhead where you plan to begin. Depending on where you are staying, Hiawassee or Helen, allow at least sixty minutes to position your cars at the beginning of the day before your hike. Also allow sixty minutes to go back to pick up your car at the beginning trailhead once your hike is over.

ALTERNATIVE TRANSPORTATION: Use a shuttle service to lead you to the trailhead where you will leave your car for the end of the hike and drive you to the trailhead where you plan to begin. Allow sixty minutes. See the list of shuttle service providers in the **Hiker Essentials** section for Hiawassee and Helen.

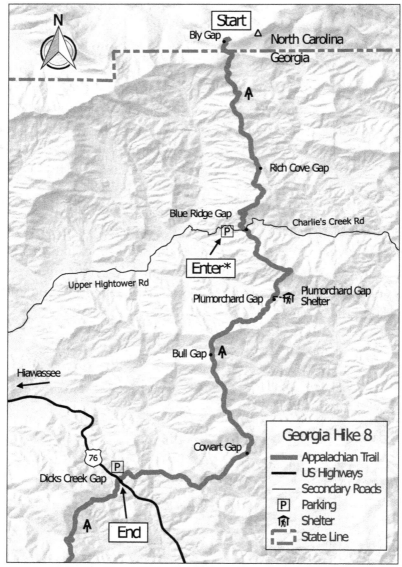

Start

Bly Gap

North Carolina
Georgia

Rich Cove Gap

Blue Ridge Gap

P

Charlie's Creek Rd

Enter*

Upper Hightower Rd

Plumorchard Gap

Plumorchard Gap
Shelter

Bull Gap

Hiawassee

Cowart Gap

76

P

Dicks Creek Gap

End

Georgia Hike 8

▬▬▬	Appalachian Trail
▬▬▬	US Highways
―	Secondary Roads
P	Parking
🛖	Shelter
▭	State Line

* Note: Begin the hike at "Enter" and hike to "Start" and down to "End."

Bly Gap to Dicks Creek Gap,
12.2 miles, Moderate

HIGHLIGHTS: For a thru-hiker whose adventure begins at Springer Mountain, the Georgia-North Carolina state line and Bly Gap are historic and exciting places, marking the completion of the first state on their trek to Maine. Day hikers also see such places as markers of achievement. Passing a famous gnarled tree near the state line means that you have

*This gnarled tree at Bly Gap has seen many hikers rejoicing and saying,
"We have finished the Appalachian Trail in Georgia." October 2008*

successfully slackpacked this last part in Georgia, which is no small accomplishment.

DISTANCE: 12.2 miles on the Appalachian Trail that includes 3.2 miles up the A.T. from Blue Ridge Gap to Bly Gap and then 3.2 miles back down the A.T. from Bly Gap to Blue Ridge Gap before continuing on the A.T. to Dicks Creek Gap. You will also have to hike 0.5-mile or so on Charlies Creek Road to access the A.T. at Blue Ridge Gap. Although the road crosses the A.T. at Blue Ridge Gap, you may not be able to drive to that crossing because the road is rough and rocky.

HIKE TIME: 7 hours.   **LEVEL OF EFFORT:** Moderate.

RECOMMENDED DIRECTION: South to north, Blue Ridge Gap to Bly Gap and then north to south, Bly Gap to Dicks Creek Gap.

DOWNHILL: 6.8 miles with an elevation loss of 3,320 feet. **UPHILL:** 5.4 miles with an elevation gain of 2,950 feet.

ALONG THE TRAIL: Near the ridgeline at the Georgia/North Carolina line, the path is rocky and narrow with sharp drop-offs on one side. It widens and becomes earthen as it goes down through the gaps.

Under the cover of tall, old hardwood trees, the trail is dimly lit, cool, and peaceful in the summer, then partially lit in the fall and winter as the trees lose their leaves. When the trees are bare, you have views from the ridgeline and Bly Gap. Have lunch on one of the rock outcroppings along the ridgeline.

SHELTERS: The Plumorchard Shelter is two tenths of a mile down the blue-blazed trail at Plumorchard Gap. It is tall and has three sleeping shelves, a picnic table, and a fire ring. There are a privy and spring nearby.

Follow the White Blazes

MILE 0.0: Blue Ridge Gap, 3,040 feet, Charlies Creek Road crosses the A.T.

MILE 3.2: Bly Gap, 3,840 feet.

MILE 3.3: Georgia-North Carolina state line, 3,830 feet.

MILE 6.4: Blue Ridge Gap, 3,040 feet, Charlies Creek Road crosses the A.T.

MILE 7.0: As Knob, 3,430 feet.

MILE 7.7: Plumorchard Gap, 3,090 feet, Plumorchard Gap Shelter, 0.2 mile east.

MILE 8.8: Bull Gap, 3,540 feet.

MILE 9.0: Buzzard Knob, 3660 feet.

MILE 10.4: Cowart Gap, 2,890 feet.

MILE 10.8: Little Bald Knob, 3,250 feet.

MILE 12.2: Dicks Creek Gap, 2,670 feet, US 76.

Peaks and Valleys

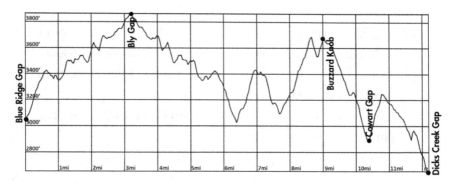

Alternate Hikes

GEORGIA HIKE 8.1:
Blue Ridge Gap to Dicks Creek Gap, 5.8 miles, Moderate
DISTANCE: 5.8 miles.   **HIKE TIME:** 3 hours.   **LEVEL OF EFFORT:** Moderate.
RECOMMENDED DIRECTION: North to south, Blue Ridge Gap to Dicks Creek Gap.

GEORGIA HIKE 8.2:
Blue Ridge Gap to Bly Gap to Blue Ridge Gap, 6.4 miles, Easy
DISTANCE: 6.4 miles.   **HIKE TIME:** 3.25 hours.   **LEVEL OF EFFORT:** Easy
RECOMMENDED DIRECTION: South to north to south
NOTE: Because there is no access to the A.T. at Bly Gap, **North Carolina Hike 1** goes south from Deep Gap, NC to Blue Ridge Gap, GA, passing Bly Gap and the GA/NC state line.

My Hiking Journal

OCTOBER 2008: This entry is from a portion of our 15.8-mile hike from Deep Gap, North Carolina, to Dicks Creek Gap, Georgia. As this was a long, tiring journey for us, we divided this hike into two hikes: Georgia Hike 8 and North Carolina Hike 1.

We hike from Deep Gap, North Carolina, in four hours and arrive at Bly Gap about one p.m.

Jim says, "Let me get a picture of the gnarled bent tree."

The gnarled bent tree is the picture that you see in Appalachian Trail guides describing Bly Gap. It is very unusual. According to legend, Native Americans marked a turn in the path by bending a tree limb parallel to the ground.

It is a perfect day, clear and cool. The trees are showing off their beautiful red and yellow colors, and leaves cover the path. We hike down the narrow pathway to the Georgia–North Carolina state line and take more pictures.

At Plumorchard Gap, I tell Jim I want to show him the shiny, new three–level shelter that Harmon, Justin, and I stayed at one rainy day during spring break fifteen years ago. (Harmon is our son and Justin, his friend.) We walk down to the shelter and see a group of trail maintainers there, so we don't climb up and check out the lofts.

Jim at the Georgia- North Carolina state line, October 2008.

I shrug and say, "The shelter looks old and worn."

As we come back to the trail, I utter quietly, "Maybe we should not have taken the time to go down to the shelter. It is almost four o'clock, and we have four and a half miles to go."

Jim leads the way, climbing briskly up the trail to Bull Gap then down into Cowart Gap, where we stop and put on our headlights. The sun has gone down and the light is dim in the forest.

As we go down the last knob, I warn Jim to be careful, because the trail is rocky and narrow as it goes down to Dicks Creek Gap. We walk slowly down the steep path, taking care to place each foot on steady ground before taking the next step.

It is now dark in the forest with only our headlights to guide us. When a car passes on US 76 below us, we look up and see our car through the trees.

I smile and say, "We're almost there."

When we reach Dicks Creek Gap about seven o'clock, we are exhausted. This 15.8-mile hike from Deep Gap, North Carolina to Dicks Creek Gap, Georgia has pushed our limits, but I am glad we did it.

Jim and I celebrate at Dicks Creek Gap.
October 2008.

We have completed the seventy-eight miles of the A.T. in Georgia in only seven day hikes over the last year and a half. I am beginning to believe that we can section hike the Appalachian Trail, one day at a time. Well, maybe not the entire 2,190 miles of the Appalachian Trail, but certainly a good portion of it.

We clown around and take selfies to record our accomplishment—finishing the Georgia portion of the Trail!

Finally, we head back to Franklin, North Carolina, where we are staying. It is only forty miles, but it seems as if we will never get there.

"I'm so tired; all I want to do is go back to the motel and jump into bed. Maybe we should just order pizza," I whine.

Jim replies, "I want a steak to celebrate finishing this hike!"

When we get back, I call Cody's Steak House and find they are open until ten o'clock. Jim pops the cork on the champagne bottle.

Raising a glass of champagne, he says, "We finished Georgia today!"

"Yes!" I exclaim.

We share the champagne, jump into the shower, dress, and rush to the restaurant. We celebrate with fine pinot noir and steak and salmon dinners.

I say, "I'm glad we came!"

Before driving back to Atlanta, we visit the Scottish Museum and the Gem Museum in Franklin. You can find a description of these museums in **Fine Wine and Accommodations: Franklin**, *Fun Places to Visit.*

Carol's Reminders

- **Stop and record visits to historic places (like Bly Gap) with pictures.**
- **Plan time to see *Fun Places to Visit.***

Nearest Town

Hiawassee is eleven miles west of Dicks Creek Gap and eleven miles southwest of Blue Ridge Gap.

Directions to the Trailheads

SOUTHERN TRAILHEAD AT DICKS CREEK GAP: GPS coordinates 34.91222, -83.61883. From Hiawassee, take US 76 East eleven miles. Just after you pass Mile Post 20, look for the A.T. crossing sign and the parking area on the left. The total trip is eleven miles; allow fifteen minutes.

NORTHERN TRAILHEAD AT BLUE RIDGE GAP: GPS coordinates 34.93888, -83.74673. From Hiawassee, drive east on US 76 for eight miles. Turn left on Upper Hightower Road (County Road 105) and drive three miles until the road is no longer paved just after the mailbox at 8440 Upper Hightower Road. Turn right on the rocky and rough Charlies Creek Road and drive one mile if you can. There are several pull-offs where you can park if the road becomes too rough. The total trip is twelve miles; allow thirty minutes.

If you plan to shuttle using two cars, leave one car at Dicks Creek Gap for the end of the hike, using the directions above. From Dicks Creek Gap, drive the other car west on US 76 about two and a half miles. Turn right on Upper Hightower Road. Follow the directions above from Upper Hightower Road to Blue Ridge Gap. The total trip from Hiawassee to Dicks Creek Gap and then to Blue Ridge Gap is almost eighteen miles; allow forty-five minutes.

ALTERNATIVE TRANSPORTATION: Use a shuttle service to take you from Dicks Creek Gap where you are leaving a car to Blue Ridge Gap to begin your hike. See the list of shuttle service providers in the **Hiker Essentials** section for Hiawassee.

Fine Wine and Accommodations
Hiawassee

HIAWASSEE is a designated Appalachian Trail Community and welcomes hikers. Hotels often give hikers a special rate, and some restaurants offer all-you-can-eat menus.

Hiawassee is the county seat of Towns County and the home of the Georgia Mountain Fair each summer. Towns County is in the Chattahoochee-Oconee National Forest with many creeks and waterfalls dotting the landscape. The Hiawassee River and Lake Chatuge add to the county's beauty. It is a great place to enjoy the outdoors whether you're hiking, biking, boating, or fishing.

Lodging

Lodging within Ten miles of Dicks Creek Gap

TOP OF GEORGIA HOSTEL: ½ $ for bunk beds in hostel and $ for cabins, free hearty breakfast; laundry, snacks, pizza, hot dogs, short-term re-supply items, shuttle service, hiking gear store, classes on hiking, A.T. Community Supporter, 7675 US 76 East, one half mile west of Dicks Creek Gap, 706-982-3252, www.topofgeorgiahostel.com.

HENSON COVE PLACE B&B: $–$$ with breakfast, comfortable guest rooms with private baths in main house; $$ for 3 BR, 1.5 BA cabin, not including breakfast, breakfast $8. A full gourmet breakfast is served at 8:30 and 9:15 a.m. in a peaceful dining room with pasture and mountain views. Shuttle service, parking for section hikers, laundry, 1137 Car Miles Road, seven miles from Dicks Creek Gap, 800-714-5542, www.henson-cove-place.com.

OUR EXPERIENCE: In June 2016, when we are doing some additional research for our book, we stay at Henson Cove. The owners are very friendly and helpful. They share a scrapbook with brochures from nearby restaurants and recommend two of their favorites. We decide to try the Chophouse in Hiawassee. Dave makes the reservations for us. It is nearby and gives a ten-percent discount to Henson Cove guests. (The Chophouse restaurant is now closed.)

Before we go to dinner, we sit on the front porch with a view of the mountains and sip red wine and nibble on chocolate chip cookies provided by the owners.

The next morning, we have a delicious breakfast of French toast, bacon, fruit, orange juice and coffee.

Lodging within Sixteen miles of Dicks Creek Gap

CHANCEY HILL INN: $$, luxurious B&B with beautiful views of the Blue Ridge Mountains and Lake Chatuge. The innkeepers' goal is to provide comfortable services to meet each guest's unique needs. 365 Chancey Drive, one mile from Hiawassee and twelve miles from Dicks Creek Gap, 706-896-8424, www.chanceyhillinn.com.

BED AND BREAKFAST ON SWAN LAKE: $$, guest suites for your wonderful nature getaway on Swan Lake with views of Eagle Mountain, cable TV, 2500 Hickory Nut Creek, five miles from Main Street in Hiawassee and sixteen miles from Dicks Creek Gap, 706-896-1582, www.bbswanlake.com.

HIDDEN VALLEY B & B: $$, hiker rate $, guest rooms and a spa in a quiet setting of rolling meadows. Owners pamper you with a delicious full breakfast on the deck and will arrange spa services for you. 441 Mull Road, three miles from Main Street and fourteen miles from Dicks Creek Gap, 706-781-9917, www.hiddenvalleybandb.com.

HOLIDAY INN EXPRESS: $–$$, rooms with refrigerators and coffee makers, complimentary hot breakfast, indoor pool with whirlpool, guest laundry, fitness room, hiker-friendly, nearby restaurants, 300 Big Sky Drive, eleven miles west of Dicks Creek Gap, 706-896-8884, www.ihg.com/holidayinnexpress.

LAKE CHATUGE LODGE: $ (varies seasonally), continental breakfast, weekend hot breakfast, guest laundry, lake views, close to a restaurant and the Georgia Mountain Fairgrounds, 653 US 76, twelve miles west of Dicks Creek Gap, 706-896-2252, www.lakechatugelodge.com.

THE RETREAT AT HIAWASSEE RIVER: $$, 2&3 BR cabins and cottages, whirlpools, 15 Cabin Drive (Just off GA 75/17, one and a half mile south of US 76), ten miles west of Dicks Creek Gap and two miles north of Mill Creek Road, (706) 896-7400.

THE RIDGES RESORT: $$–$$$ (prices vary seasonally), hotel on Lake Chatuge with rooms and suites, 2–5 BR villas, refrigerators, coffee makers, complimentary continental breakfast, freshly baked cookies served in the afternoon, casual dining on site, pool, Wi-Fi, 3499 US 76, five miles west of Main Street and sixteen miles from Dicks Creek Gap, 706-896-2262 or 888-834-4409, www.theridgesresort.com.

OUR EXPERIENCE: In May 2007, after hiking four days, we take a break and enjoy the luxury accommodations at The Ridges. We sip glasses of pinot noir outside as the sun sets on the lake and then take pleasure in an evening of fine dining. As our eyes begin to close, we snuggle in the comfy bed and dream of adventures to come.

BUDGET INN OF HIAWASSEE: ½ $, small hiker-friendly motel with guest laundry facilities, shuttle services, on-site outfitter, and nearby fast-food restaurants, 193 South Main Street, eleven miles west of Dicks Creek Gap, 706-896-4121, www.hiawasseebudgetinn.com.

OUR EXPERIENCE: In June 2007, we decide to try to do one more Georgia A.T. hike on the last day of our vacation. We call and make reservations for a room and shuttle service that day. When we arrive at noon, the shuttle is waiting. When we return that evening about nine thirty, the room is open and waiting for us. The accommodations are basic but clean.

MULL'S INN: ½ $, small motel that caters to fishermen and hikers, clean but basic, 213 North Main Street, twelve miles west of Dicks Creek Gap, 706-816-4195.

Selected Restaurants

THE BLUE OTTER RESTAURANT AND SPORTS BAR AT THE RIDGES RESORT: $, American casual dining on the water, full bar, 11 a.m. to 9 p.m. Sun through Thu, 11 a.m. to 10 p.m. Fri and Sat, 3379 US 76, 706-896-1919.

OUR EXPERIENCE: In May 2007 we take a break from hiking and treat ourselves to filet mignon dinners cooked just right, pinot noir wine, and ice cream with amaretto for dessert.

ASIANO: $, Chinese-Japanese-Mongolian delights, beer and wine, 11 a.m. to 9 p.m. daily, 1382 US 76, 706-896-0508, www.Asianorestaurant.com.

BIG AL'S PIZZA: $, Italian, dough made daily from fresh ingredients, no beer or wine, 11:30 a.m. to 8 p.m. Tue through Sun, 757 Bell Creek Road, 706-896-1970.

DANIEL'S STEAK HOUSE: $, Southern buffet or menu, no beer or wine, 11 a.m. to 8:30 p.m. daily, 273 Big Sky Drive, 706-896-8008.

HAWG WILD BBQ AND CATFISH HOUSE: $, great barbecue, beer and wine, 11 a.m. to 9 p.m. Mon through Sat, 11 a.m. to 7 p.m. Sun, 625 US 76, 706-896-3200.

MONTE ALBAN RESTAURANT: $, Mexican, beer and wine, 11 a.m. to 9 p.m. daily, 581 North Main Street, 706-896-6698, www.montealbargrill.com.

Restaurant in Nearby Young Harris

BROTHERS AT WILLOW RANCH: $, American, beer and wine, 11 a.m. to 8:30 p.m. Sun through Thu, 11 a.m. to 9:30 p.m. Fri and Sat, 6223 US 76, 706-379-1272.

Restaurant in Nearby Hayesville, NC

THE COPPER DOOR: $$, American fine dining, full bar, 5 p.m. to 10 p.m. Mon through Sat, 2 Sullivan Street, 828-389-8460.

Hiker Essentials, Splurges, and Emergency Stops

Shuttle-Service Providers

BILL'S WHEELS OF GEORGIA: 865-202-1041, BillsWheelsOfGeorgia@yahoo.com.

BUDGET INN OF HIAWASSEE: 706-896-4121, www.ronhavenhikerservices.com.

TOP OF GEORGIA HOSTEL: 706-982-3252, www.topofgeorgiahostel.com, A.T. Community Supporter.

Car Rental Agency

ENTERPRISE RENT-A-CAR: 8 a.m. to 6 p.m. Mon through Fri; 391 Blue Ridge Highway, Blairsville; fifteen miles west of Hiawassee; 706-745-2816.

Outfitters

TOP OF GEORGIA HOSTEL & OUTFITTERS: 7 a.m. to 7 p.m. daily, A.T. Community Supporter, 7675 US 76 East, 706-982-3252.

Groceries

INGLES MARKET: groceries, beer and wine except Sun, 7 a.m. to 10 p.m. daily, 94 North Main Street, 706-896-8312.

SAVE-A-LOT: groceries, no beer or wine, 8 a.m. to 8 p.m. Mon through Fri, 8 a.m. to 10 p.m. Sat, 10 a.m. to 7 p.m. Sun, 236 North Main Street, 706-896-4871.

Wine and Beer

BACCHUS WINE SHOPPE & BACCHUS BEER AND GROWLERS (SEPARATE SHOPS AND ENTRANCES): 11 a.m. to 6 p.m. Mon through Thu, 11 a.m. to 7 p.m. Fri and Sat, A.T. Community Supporter, 355 North Main Street, 706-896-9947, www. bacchuswineshoppe.com and www.bacchusbeerandgrowlers.com.

ATMs

CARDTRONICS ATM: Circle M Food, 20 South Main Street.

CARDTRONICS ATM: 830 North Main Street.

UNITED COMMUNITY BANK ATM: 214 North Main Street.

Urgent Care and Emergency Services

SERENDIPITY CLINIC: Cash or credit card, (they do not file insurance claims.) By appointment, 9 a.m. to 5 p.m. Mon, 9 a.m. to 3 p.m. Tue, and 9 a.m. to 5 p.m. Wed; walk-in day Fri, 10 a.m. to 6 p.m. Walk-ins will be worked in on appointment days. 620 Suite B Bell Creek Road (across from car wash), 706-970-1154.

CHATUGE REGIONAL HOSPITAL & NURSING HOME, EMERGENCY RM: 24/7, 110 South Main Street, 706-896-2222.

Fun Places to Visit

THE TOWN OF HIAWASSEE: hosts concerts in the square in the summer.

GEORGIA MOUNTAIN FAIR: hosts fairs and festivals. Go to www.georgiamountainfairgrounds.com to view upcoming events.

HAMILTON GARDENS ON LAKE CHATUGE: largest collection of rhododendrons in Georgia, $3, 8 a.m. to 3 p.m. daily, 1311 Music Hall Road, 706-896-4191.

DEB COLLINS SIGNATURE GALLERY: awesome studio and shop, 10 a.m. to 5 p.m. Mon through Sat, 347 North Main Street, 706-896-1294.

ARTWORKS ARTISAN CENTRE: operated by Mountain Regional Arts & Crafts Guild, 308 Big Sky Drive, 706-896-0932.

HIGHTOWER CREEK VINEYARDS: wine tours, check website for upcoming events, 12 to 5 p.m. Mon through Sat, 12 to 5:30 p.m. Sun, 7150 Canaan Drive (just off US 76, two miles west of Dicks Creek Gap), 706-896-8963, www.hightowercreekvineyards.com.

CRANE CREEK VINEYARDS: tasting room, special events, 11 a.m. to 6 p.m. Tue through Sat, 1 to 5 p.m. Sun, food served 6 to 8 p.m. Fri and Sat, 916 Crane Creek Road, 706- 379-1236.

THE RIDGES MARINA: rental boats; canoes; pontoon boats; kayaks; prices vary per boat type and hours of usage; 8:30 a.m. to 5 p.m. Mon through Fri; 3379 US 76, 706-896-2112.

BOUNDARY WATERS RESORT AND MARINA: rentals, prices vary per boat type and hours of usage, 9 a.m. to 5 p.m. Tue through Sat, 107 Boundary Waters Drive, 706-896-2530, www.bioboating.com.

MILLCREEK FALLS: Ground Hog Branch combines with Mill Creek, forming a waterfall as it cascades down into Mill Creek Gorge. From Hiawassee, go east on US 76 East, turn right on GA 75/17, drive south three and a half miles, turn left on Mill Creek Road, drive one mile, then turn left on USFS 26-2, and drive about two and a half miles to parking for campsites and the falls. Hike one half mile through the camping area to Mill Creek.

BRASSTOWN BALD: the highest point in Georgia, where the views are spectacular. The visitors center is open 10 a.m. to 5 p.m. daily Apr through Dec. From Hiawassee, go east on US 76 East, turn right on GA 75/17 and travel for six miles, turn right on GA 180 and go nine miles, turn right on the GA 180 Spur, then go three miles up the mountain to the parking lot.

Young Harris *(eight miles west of Hiawassee on US 76)*

BRASSTOWN VALLEY RESORT & SPA: hosts events like the state fiddlers' convention and the Mountain Storytelling Retreat, golfing available, 6321 US 76, 706-379-9900.

YOUNG HARRIS COLLEGE: hosts music, theater, and fine-art events, 1 College Street, 1-800-241-3754.

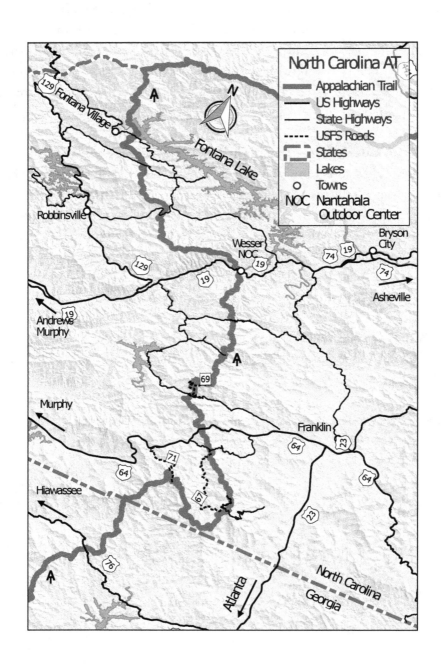

The Appalachian Trail in Southwestern North Carolina

We never tire of stopping on the mountaintops or rocky ledges to view the mountains and valleys as the Appalachian Trail winds eighty-eight miles through the remote, rugged Nantahala National Forest from the Georgia–North Carolina state line to the southern boundary of the Great Smoky Mountains National Park. Most of the A.T. in this section is at or above thirty-five hundred feet with six five-thousand-foot mountaintops.

There are striking natural and man-made creations along the trail. Stop in the Nantahala River Gorge and watch rafters plunging over the rapids. Pause at Fontana Lake and enjoy the beauty and serenity. Check out the legendary Fontana "Hilton" Shelter. Visit the Fontana Dam Museum and learn how this dam was built in thirty-six months by five thousand workers in the 1940s.

These Southern Appalachian Mountains, with a mild climate and abundant rainfall, are rich and diverse in fauna and flora. Stop and examine the delicate wildflowers and watch tiny creatures scurry across the trail and through the bushes. Use your camera to capture this hike of beauty and discovery so you can share it with your friends.

Look at the NC Hikes 1 through 9 on the adjoining page and see which ones you want to explore.

Southwestern North Carolina, April 2008

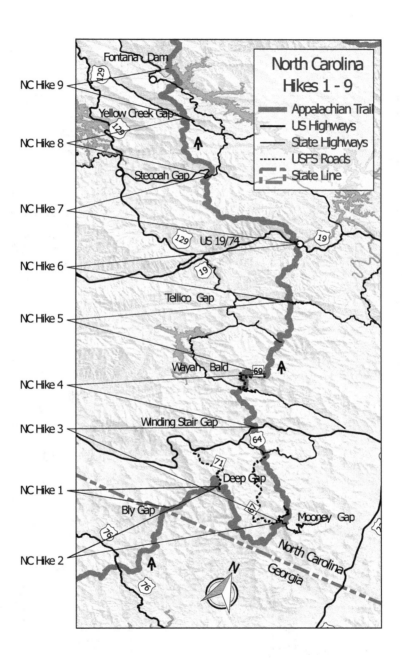

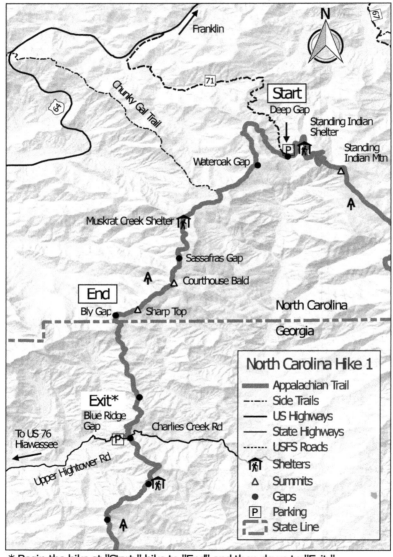

* Begin the hike at "Start," hike to "End" and then down to "Exit."

Deep Gap to Bly Gap to Blue Ridge Gap,
10.0 miles, Easy to Moderate

NC
HIKE
1

HIGHLIGHTS: Enjoy the beautiful views of the Blue Ridge Mountains and Lake Chatuge from the mountain ridges. Take pictures at Bly Gap, traditionally considered to be the end of the A.T. in Georgia and the beginning of the A.T. in North Carolina. The actual Georgia-North Carolina state line is one tenth of a mile south of Bly Gap.

DISTANCE: 6.8 miles from Deep Gap to Bly Gap, plus 3.2 miles south on the A.T. to Blue Ridge Gap, and west on Charlies Creek Road 0.5 miles to parking. Total hike: 10.5 miles.

HIKE TIME: 5 hours.   **LEVEL OF EFFORT:** Easy to Moderate.

RECOMMENDED DIRECTION: North to south.

DOWNHILL: 6.5 miles with an elevation loss of 1,700 feet. **UPHILL:** 3.5 miles with an elevation gain of 1,600 feet.

Views, October 2008

Rhododendron tunnels, October 2008

ALONG THE TRAIL: From Deep Gap the A.T. goes through the hardwood forest with moss, fern, and wildflowers covering the forest floor. The path is covered with leaves.

As the trail goes up along the ridge crests and through the rhododendron and mountain laurel tunnels, it becomes narrow and rocky. On the hillsides, the A.T. passes large rock outcroppings before it widens and flows downhill through the gaps.

SHELTERS: Stop for lunch at Muskrat Shelter, which has a large covered porch, a table, benches, and a privy.

Follow the White Blazes

MILE 0.0: Deep Gap, 4,340 feet, water.

MILE 2.1: Wateroak Gap, 4,460 feet.

MILE 3.2: Chunky Gal Trail, 4,570 feet.

MILE 3.4: Whiteoak Stamp, 4,550 feet, water. Whiteoak Stamp is the northernmost grassy stamp along the Appalachian Trail. Cattle were once herded here after a summer in the forest.

MILE 4.0: Muskrat Creek Shelter, water.

MILE 4.9: Sassafras Gap, 4,230 feet.

MILE 5.5: Courthouse Bald, 4,650.

MILE 6.3: Sharp Top, 4,000 feet.

MILE 6.7: Bly Gap, 3,840 feet, water.

MILE 6.8: Georgia-North Carolina state line, 4,170 feet.

MILE 10.0: Blue Ridge Gap.

Peaks and Valleys

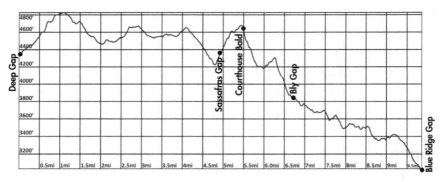

My Hiking Journal

OCTOBER 2008: We combined Georgia Hike 8 and North Carolina Hike 1 for a sixteen-mile day hike. This entry from **My Hiking Journal** is only about North Carolina Hike 1.

On this clear, crisp day with smiles on our faces, we hike along, taking pictures of the mountain ranges, the changing leaves, and the rhododendron tunnels.

"Let's stop here at Muskrat Shelter and eat lunch. I need to use the privy too," I say.

Jim looks at the hiker register and says, "*Why Not* was here last week." (Hikers sign in with trail names that are either given to them or that they select.)

As we go down toward the gap, we see hunters with guns and dogs. Jim asks, "What are you hunting?"

"Bear," one of them says.

Jim asks, "Have you seen any?"

"No," the hunter replies.

The dogs are pulling on the leashes, so they move on.

We haven't seen hunters on the trail before, and it makes me a little nervous. If I had known it was hunting season, I would have worn an orange shirt and hat. When I look it up later, I find that bear-hunting season in North Carolina is about six weeks each year during October, November, and December.

When we get to Bly Gap and the Georgia-North Carolina state line, we take pictures of these historic places.

Me at the GA/NC state line, October 2008

Jim at Bly Gap, October 2008

Carol's Reminders

- Enjoy the sights along the trail and document them with pictures.

Nearest Towns

Franklin, North Carolina, is twenty miles from Deep Gap, the northern trailhead. Hiawassee, Georgia, is eleven miles west of Blue Ridge Gap, the southern trailhead.

Directions to the Trailheads

SOUTHERN TRAILHEAD AT BLUE RIDGE GAP: GPS coordinates 34.93888, -85.74673. From Franklin, drive west on US 64, going twenty-eight miles to NC 175. Turn left and drive eight miles to US 76 in Hiawassee. Turn left onto US 76 and drive east for eight miles. Turn left on the paved Upper Hightower Road (County 105) and drive three miles until the pavement ends (just after the mailbox at 8440 Upper Hightower Road). Turn right on the rough and rocky Charlies Creek Road and drive one mile or as far as you can go. There are several pull-offs that you can use for parking if the road becomes too rough. The total trip is forty-eight miles; allow seventy minutes.

NORTHERN TRAILHEAD AT DEEP GAP: GPS coordinates 35.03956, -83.55271. From Franklin, drive west on US 64 fourteen miles. Turn left on USFS 71, just past the Macon-Clay County line. Drive six miles on the single-lane gravel road to Deep Gap and parking. The total trip is twenty miles; allow forty-five minutes.

If you plan to shuttle using two cars, leave one car near Blue Ridge Gap for the end of the hike. Drive the other car to Deep Gap to start your hike. From Franklin, follow the directions above to Blue Ridge Gap then backtrack to NC 175 and US 64. Drive fourteen miles east to USFS 71. Turn right and drive six miles on the single-lane gravel road to parking for Deep Gap. The total trip is eighty-eight miles; allow seventy-five minutes.

ALTERNATIVE TRANSPORTATION: Arrange for a shuttle service to meet you in Hiawassee and lead you to Blue Ridge Gap, where you will leave your car and then drive you to Deep Gap. See the list of shuttle-service providers in the **Hiker Essentials** sections for Hiawassee and Franklin.

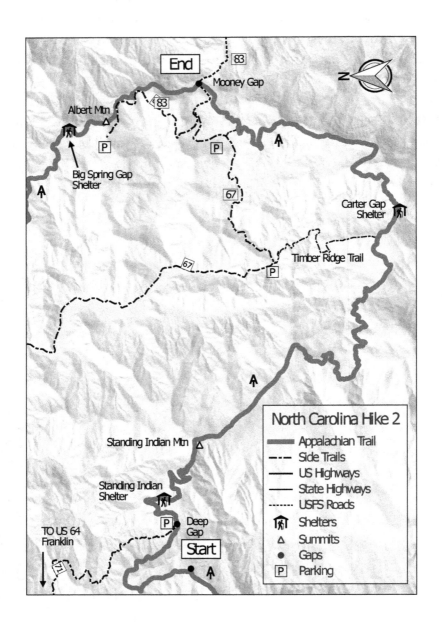

Deep Gap to Mooney Gap,

13.0 miles, Moderate

NC HIKE 2

HIGHLIGHTS: Just north of Deep Gap, you enter the pristine Southern Nantahala Wilderness, trampled only by hikers and God's wild creatures. Enjoy the views of Tallulah Gorge and the Georgia mountains from Standing Indian Mountain, the tallest mountain south of the Smoky Mountains.

DISTANCE: 13.0 miles. **HIKE TIME:** 7 to 8 hours. **LEVEL OF EFFORT:** Moderate.

RECOMMENDED DIRECTION:
South to north.

DOWNHILL: 7.3 miles with an elevation loss of 2,365 feet. **UPHILL:** 5.7 miles with an elevation gain of 2,520 feet.

ALONG THE TRAIL: From Deep Gap, the A.T. leads through

April 2008

the hardwood forest on a well-worn earthen path with only some rocks and tree roots. Switchbacks go up and down Standing Indian Mountain to ease the climb and stop erosion.

SHELTERS: There are two main shelters, both built in the Nantahala style: one as you are going up Standing Indian Mountain, and the other at Carter Gap. Both have privies and nearby water sources. At Carter Gap, the old shelter is still standing and available for overflow hikers when the main Carter Gap Shelter is full. The old shelter is a little wobbly-looking with its tin roof and sleeping floor.

Follow the White Blazes

MILE 0.0: Deep Gap, 4,340 feet, water.

MILE 0.9: Standing Indian Shelter, water, privy.

MILE 2.4: Standing Indian Mountain, 5,425 feet, Lower Trail, Ridge Trail. A rock formation near the summit gives the mountain its name. According to Cherokee legend, this rock formation was created when a warrior standing guard on the mountain fled his post and was turned to stone by the Great Spirit.

MILE 5.3: Beech Gap, 4,450 feet, Beech Gap Trail, water.

MILE 7.0: Coleman Gap, 4,290 feet.

MILE 8.1: Timber Ridge Trail, 4,680 feet.

MILE 8.3: Carter Gap Shelter, water, privy.

MILE 9.4: Ridgepole Mountain, 4,950 feet.

MILE 12.0: Betty Creek Gap, 4,300 feet, water.

MILE 13.0: Mooney Gap, 4,480 feet, USFS 83. This gap is named for James Mooney a historian who wrote *Myths of the Cherokee* in 1898.

Peaks and Valleys

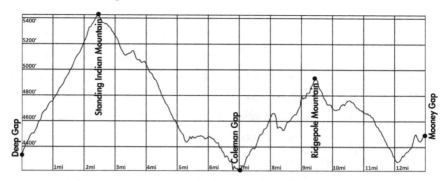

Alternate Hikes

Because this is a long hike, we divide it into two shorter hikes.

NC HIKE 2.1:

Deep Gap to Timber Ridge Trail, 10.2 miles, Moderate

DISTANCE: 8.1 miles on the A.T. and 2.1 miles on Timber Ridge Trail for a total of 10.2 miles.

HIKE TIME: 5 to 6 hours.   **LEVEL OF EFFORT:** Moderate.

RECOMMENDED DIRECTION: South to north, Deep Gap to Timber Ridge Trail.

NC HIKE 2.2:

Timber Ridge Trail to Mooney Gap, 7.0 miles, Challenging to Moderate

DISTANCE: 4.9 miles on the A.T. plus 2.1 miles on Timber Ridge Trail for a total of 7.0 miles.

HIKE TIME: 4 to 5 hours.   **LEVEL OF EFFORT:** Challenging to Moderate.

RECOMMENDED DIRECTION: South to north, Timber Ridge Trail to Mooney Gap.

My Hiking Journal

APRIL 2008: This is the fifth day of our five-day North Carolina hiking trip.

This cool day is perfect for hiking. It starts off cloudy and then the sun comes out and the sky is pristine and clear. We climb easily to the summit of Standing Indian Mountain and have lunch looking out over the valley with views of Brasstown Bald, Blood Mountain, and Rabun Bald in Georgia. After our relaxing lunch, we are ready for the ten-mile walk downhill into Mooney Gap.

We stop for a break at Carter Gap Shelter and read the hiker register. We notice that "Shamrock Game 08" is hoping to get a shuttle from Mooney Gap. "DahWahtte" writes, "Hurtin' Today."

Thru-hikers often leave messages in the register anticipating that another hiker or a Trail Angel might see them and respond. Deep in the wilderness like this, it is unlikely that their cell phones will work so that they can call a shuttle service. Because Mooney Gap is on a forest service road, it is also doubtful that someone will just come along and offer them a ride.

As we are going down the mountain, we see a group of backpackers; one is limping. Jim asks, "Do you want a ride from Mooney Gap? We have a car there and can give you a lift to Franklin."

They smile and nod in agreement.

When we get to the gap about five o'clock, there are several thru-hikers eager to hitch a ride into town. We load our SUV with five grimy hikers and their packs. We roll the windows down so the breeze will carry their sweaty, musty smell outside.

The hikers talk excitedly about how much food they will eat tonight. We drop each off at his hotel and then head back out about 6 p.m. to pick up our second car at Deep Gap.

On the way back to town, we pick up a white-haired, tired-looking hiker waiting at Winding Stair Gap on US 64. He missed the free shuttle that comes at 5 p.m. and said he was hoping someone would pick him up. Franklin is a hiker-friendly place, and drivers often give hikers a lift into town. Jim drops him at his motel.

We leave our second car at our motel and head to the store for shrimp and potato salad. We celebrate the completion of the North Carolina section from Deep Gap to the Nantahala River with champagne and shrimp. The next day we drive to Greystone Inn on Lake Toxaway to enjoy a weekend of relaxation.

Carol's Reminders

- **Give Trail Magic to other hikers**. In addition to rides, Trail Magic can be unexpected food, water, first-aid supplies, or a place to sleep—things a hiker will appreciate.
- **Celebrate your slackpacking successes**. Share your good news and pictures with your friends on Facebook.

Nearest Town

Franklin is twenty miles from Deep Gap, the southern trailhead and twenty-four miles from Mooney Gap, the northern trailhead.

Directions to the Trailheads

SOUTHERN TRAILHEAD AT DEEP GAP: GPS coordinates 35.03956, -83.55271. From Franklin, drive west on US 64 for fourteen miles. Turn left on USFS 71 just past the Macon-Clay County line. Drive six miles on the single-lane gravel road to parking at Deep Gap. The total trip is twenty miles; allow forty-five minutes.

MIDDLE TRAILHEAD AT TIMBER RIDGE TRAIL AND USFS 67: From Franklin, take US 64 west for twelve miles. Turn left on Allison Creek Road at the sign saying, "Standing Indian Campground" and "Appalachian Trail." Drive about one and a half miles to USFS 67 where you will see a sign saying, "Standing Indian Campground." Turn right and continue 4.7 miles past parking for the Backcountry Information Center on USFS 67 to the joint trailhead for Big Laurel Falls Trail and Timber Ridge Trail. The trip total is eighteen miles; allow forty-five minutes.

NORTHERN TRAILHEAD AT MOONEY GAP: GPS coordinates 35.03287, -83.467656. From Franklin, take US 64 west about twelve miles. Turn left on Allison Creek Road at the sign that says, "Standing Indian Campground" and "Appalachian Trail." Drive about one and a half miles to USFS 67 where you will see a sign saying "Standing Indian Campground" and turn right on the paved USFS 67. Continue past Standing Indian Campground as the road becomes gravel. Follow this road nine miles to the junction with USFS 83. Turn right on USFS 83 and go less than a mile to Mooney Gap. There is limited parking on the side of the road at the campsite. The total trip is twenty-four miles; allow sixty minutes.

ALTERNATIVE ROUTE TO MOONEY GAP: From US 441/US 23 near Otto, turn at the sign that says "Coweeta Hydrological Laboratory." Drive west on Coweeta Lab Road to the Coweeta Experiment Station. Continue on Ball Creek Road, USFS 83, as it angles to the left up the mountain. This road is rough and steep. Drive ten miles to Mooney Gap. The total trip is twenty miles; allow fifty minutes from Otto.

If you plan to shuttle using two cars, drive to Mooney Gap and leave one car. Then backtrack to US 64 and turn left. Drive two miles to USFS 71. Turn left and drive six miles to Deep Gap. The total trip is forty-four miles; allow two hours.

ALTERNATIVE TRANSPORTATION: Arrange for a shuttle service to lead you from Franklin to Mooney Gap, where you will leave your car. Then have the shuttle driver take you to Deep Gap to begin your hike. See the list of shuttle-service providers in the **Hiker Essentials** section for Franklin.

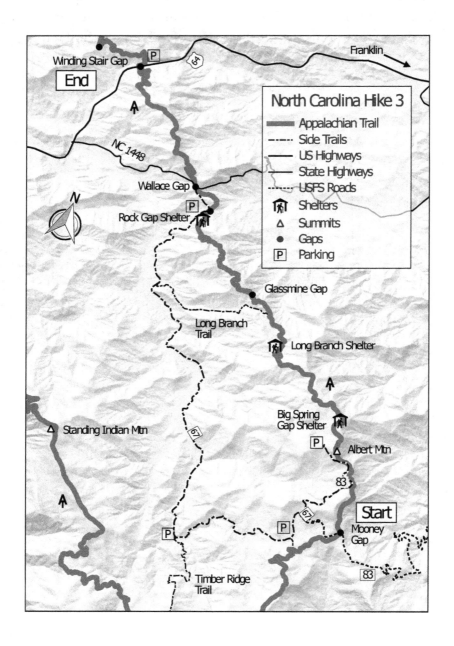

North Carolina Hike 3

Appalachian Trail
Side Trails
US Highways
State Highways
USFS Roads
Shelters
Summits
Gaps
Parking

Franklin

Winding Stair Gap
End

NC 1448

Wallace Gap
Rock Gap Shelter

Glassmine Gap

Long Branch Trail

Long Branch Shelter

Standing Indian Mtn

Big Spring Gap Shelter

Albert Mtn

Start
Mooney Gap

Timber Ridge Trail

Mooney Gap to Winding Stair Gap,
11.2 miles, Challenging to Moderate

NC HIKE 3

HIGHLIGHTS: From the fire lookout tower on top of mile-high Albert Mountain, you have magnificent views of the Blue Ridge Mountains to the east, the Smoky Mountains to the northwest, and Rabun Bald to the southeast. Fire lookout towers originated in the early 1900s so that lookouts could warn nearby towns of forest fires, significant weather changes, and lightning strikes. With technology changes and budget cuts in the 1960s, fire lookout towers were left unmanned and began to deteriorate. The USFS and volunteers continue to maintain historic and essential fire lookout towers, such as the one on Albert Mountain.

DISTANCE: 11.2 miles.   **HIKE TIME:** 7 hours.

LEVEL OF EFFORT: Challenging to Moderate.

RECOMMENDED DIRECTION: South to north.

DOWNHILL MILES: 7.1 miles with an elevation loss of 2,790 feet. **UPHILL:** 4.1 miles with an elevation gain of 1,980 feet.

ALONG THE TRAIL: From Mooney Gap, the A.T. ascends mile-high Albert Mountain gradually on log steps and then steeply over rock boulders. The trail then descends gently down the mountain on a wide, leaf-covered earthen path under a canopy of hardwood trees and rhododendrons.

SHELTERS: There are two shelters. The Long Branch Shelter, built in the Nantahala style, has two sleeping shelves, a table, and benches. The overused Rock Gap Shelter, near USFS 67, is an old lean-to with a side porch, a table, and a bench. Both shelters have privies and nearby water sources.

The fire lookout tower on top of Albert Mountain, April 2008

Follow the White Blazes

MILE 0.0: Mooney Gap, 4,490 feet.

MILE 0.9: Bearpen Gap, 4,730 feet.

MILE 1.5: USFS 87 and Bearpen Trail, 4,790 feet.

MILE 1.6: Albert Mountain, at 5,250 feet, is the most difficult rock scramble on the southeastern section of the A.T. (A rock scramble is where you have to use your hands to climb up steep rocky terrain.) If there are lightning storms or if there is ice, do not go up Albert Mountain. Go around the mountain on the bypass trail. Albert Mountain was named for Albert

Siler, grandfather of A. Rufus Morgan, founder of the Nantahala Hiking Club. The club maintains the A.T. in southwestern North Carolina.

MILE 2.2: Big Spring Gap, 4,955 feet.

MILE 4.1: Long Branch Shelter, water, privy.

MILE 5.2: Glassmine Gap, 4,160 feet, Long Branch Trail. Glassmine was the name of a nearby mica mine.

MILE 7.5: Rock Gap Shelter, 3,760 feet, water, privy.

MILE 7.6: Rock Gap, USFS 67. Standing Indian Campground is just half a mile down the road on USFS 67. It has drinking water, flush toilets, showers, a phone, and a general store that is open from Apr 1 to Oct 30.

MILE 8.1: Wallace Gap, 3,740 feet, Allison Creek Road (old US 64).

MILE 11.2: Winding Stair Gap, 3,690 feet, water. This gap was named for its steep switchbacks.

Peaks and Valleys

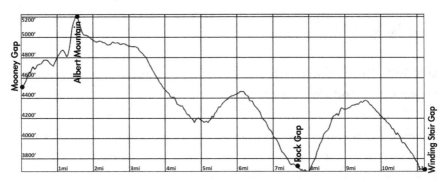

Alternate Hikes

Since this hike is over ten miles and there is good road access, we have divided it into two hikes.

NC HIKE 3.1:

Mooney Gap to Rock Gap, 7.6 miles, Challenging to Moderate
DISTANCE: 7.6 miles.   **HIKE TIME:** 5 hours.
LEVEL OF EFFORT: Challenging to Moderate.
RECOMMENDED DIRECTION: South to north, Mooney Gap to Rock Gap.

NC HIKE 3.2:

Winding Stair Gap to Rock Gap, 3.6 miles, Moderate
DISTANCE: 3.6 miles.   **HIKE TIME:** 2 to 3 hours.   **LEVEL OF EFFORT:** Moderate.
RECOMMENDED DIRECTION: North to south, Winding Stair Gap to Rock Gap.

My Hiking Journal

APRIL 2008: This is the fourth day of a five-day hiking trip. The forecast calls for cool and clear weather.

We climb out of Mooney Gap on log steps with gradual elevation increases; this seems easy. But soon, we are climbing hand over hand over boulders. I have to stop frequently to catch my breath. I wonder if I will ever get to the top of Albert Mountain.

Then through the leafless trees I see the fire lookout tower. "We are almost there," I say.

After another thirty minutes, we are at the top.

"Let's relax and have lunch," I say.

We sit down with another hiker and enjoy cheese, crackers, sardines, dried apples, and chocolate chip cookies. Now we have the energy to climb the stairs up to the fire lookout station. From the station we take pictures of the panoramic views. We can see forever from here.

In the afternoon, we enjoy the gentle ups and downs of the trail as it goes down to Wallace Gap.

"I need a break before we go over the next ridge," I say.

We drink water and eat energy bars.

"Now, I think I'm ready," I say.

When we finally get to Winding Stair Gap, Jim leans against the sign and says, "I can't go another step."

As we are loading our car, Ron Haven's shuttle service comes up and other hikers, who have been sitting around waiting, rush to get on the bus. Ron, a motel owner and Community A.T. Supporter, provides free shuttle service from Winding Stair Gap to Franklin several times a day during the peak thru-hiker season in March and April.

Winding Stair Gap, April 2008

I hear one hiker say, "This is the first time I have taken a day off since I started on March first." It is now April twentieth.

How amazing, I think. It is a hundred and ten miles from Springer Mountain to Winding Stair Gap. This hiker has been on the trail for seven weeks, a very long time without a break.

Carol's Reminders

- **If you have a steep climb, do it at the beginning of the day when you are fresh if it is possible.**
- **Take one step at a time and enjoy the views.**
- **Take pictures to record the memories of your trip.**

Nearest Town

Franklin is twenty-four miles from Mooney Gap, the southern trailhead and ten miles from Winding Stair Gap, the northern trailhead.

Directions to the Trailheads

SOUTHERN TRAILHEAD AT MOONEY GAP: GPS coordinates 35.03287, -83.467656. From Franklin, take US 64 West about twelve miles. Turn left on Allison Creek Road at the sign that says, "Standing Indian Campground" and "Appalachian Trail." Drive about one and a half miles to USFS 67 where you will see a sign saying "Standing Indian Campground." Turn right on the paved USFS 67. Drive past Standing Indian Campground and continue as the road changes to gravel. Follow the road nine miles to the junction with USFS 83. Turn right on USFS 83 and go less than a mile to Mooney Gap. Limited parking is available on the side of the road near the campsite. The total trip is twenty-four miles; allow sixty minutes.

MIDDLE TRAILHEAD AT ROCK GAP: GPS coordinates 35.09405, -83.52241. Use the directions above to the sign for Standing Indian Campground. Continue on USFS 67 for half a mile to Rock Gap.

NORTHERN TRAILHEAD AT WINDING STAIR GAP: GPS coordinates 35.11974, -83.54810. From Franklin at the intersection of US 64 and US 441/US 23, drive west on US 64 for ten miles. As you come up the big hill, there is a parking lot on the left with an A.T. marker. This is Winding Stair Gap. The total trip is ten miles; allow fifteen minutes.

If you plan to shuttle using two cars, leave one car for the end of the hike at Winding Stair Gap, using the directions above, and then drive to Mooney Gap to begin your hike. The total trip is twenty-four miles; allow sixty minutes.

ALTERNATIVE TRANSPORTATION: Have a shuttle service meet you at Winding Stair Gap, where you will leave your car for the end of the hike, and take you to Mooney Gap. See the list of shuttle- service providers in the **Hiker Essentials** section for Franklin.

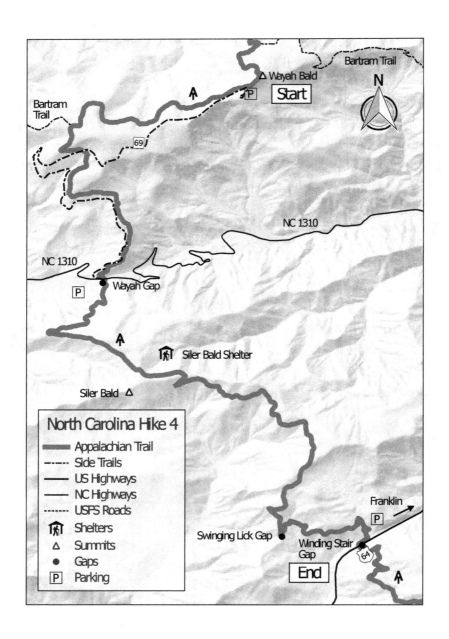

Bartram Trail

△ Wayah Bald

Bartram Trail

Start

N

69

NC 1310

NC 1310

P Wayah Gap

Siler Bald Shelter

Siler Bald △

North Carolina Hike 4

— Appalachian Trail
—·—· Side Trails
— US Highways
— NC Highways
····· USFS Roads
Shelters
△ Summits
● Gaps
P Parking

Franklin

P

Swinging Lick Gap

Winding Stair Gap

64

End

Wayah Bald to Winding Stair Gap,
10.0 miles, Moderate to Easy

NC
HIKE
4

HIGHLIGHTS: Partake of the panoramic views from historic Wayah Bald Fire Lookout Tower. It was built by the Civilian Conservation Corps in 1937. The tower was damaged by the wildfires of 2016. In the spring, delight in wildflowers covering grassy Siler Bald and Wayah Bald. Enjoy picturesque Moore Creek as it cascades over the rocks through the rhododendrons.

DISTANCE: 10.0 miles.   **HIKE TIME:** 5 hours.

LEVEL OF EFFORT: Moderate to Easy.

RECOMMENDED DIRECTION: North to south, from Wayah Bald to Winding Stair Gap.

DOWNHILL MILES: 6.4 miles with an elevation loss of 3,115 feet. **UPHILL:** 3.6 miles with an elevation gain of 1,460 feet.

ALONG THE TRAIL: The wide and leafy path from Wayah Bald to Wayah Gap winds down through the hardwood Nantahala National Forest and up a grassy slope to Siler Bald. Then it makes its way through the hardwood trees, crossing several creeks to Panther and Winding Stair Gaps. Siler Bald is to the west of the trail.

SHELTERS: The Nantahala-style Siler Bald Shelter has a privy and water source nearby.

Moore Creek, just north of Winding Stair Gap, April 2008

Follow the White Blazes

MILE 0.0: Wayah Bald, 5,340 feet, water and latrines.

MILE 1.7: Bartram Trail, 5,330 feet, spring located to the west. The yellow-blazed Bartram Trail runs from Cheoh Bald to the South Carolina border.

MILE 2.3: USFS 69, 5,025 feet, water.

MILE 4.1: Wayah Gap, 4,170 feet. Wayah is the Cherokee word for "wolf." For the Cherokees, this was the main route west over the mountains. Wayah Gap was the site of a decisive battle between the North Carolina militia and the Cherokees in 1776. After this battle and warring with the people of North Carolina for eighteen years, the Cherokee Nation moved to southeastern Tennessee near what is now Chattanooga.

MILE 5.8: Siler Bald Shelter, half a mile east, 4,700 feet, water, privy.

MILE 7.9: Panther Gap, 4,445 feet.

MILE 8.9: Swinging Lick Gap, 4,060 feet.

MILE 10.0: Winding Stair Gap, 3,680 feet, water.

Peaks and Valleys

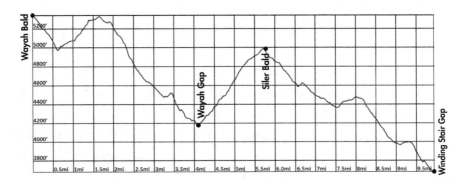

My Hiking Journal

APRIL 2008: This is the third day of our five-day hiking trip.

We awaken to the sound of raindrops on the roof and decide to sleep in. We arrive at the trailhead about noontime and have lunch on one of the picnic tables.

From the Wayah Bald Fire Lookout Tower, we look north toward Wesser Bald and the Smokies. It is cloudy and a little chilly, but the sun is peeking around the clouds.

As we hike down the mountain, we meet several groups of hikers. Most are coming up the hill to Wayah Bald with their backpacks loaded, looking a little weary.

My knees are aching as we go down the hill. But we hike four miles to Wayah Gap in just two hours. We often plan to hike two miles per hour, but don't usually reach this goal. There are too many scenes to explore and treasures to find.

As we come to a forest service road, I notice a truck parked along the road with a camper and a grill. I wonder if this is a Trail Angel or someone preying on hikers. I have a strange feeling, but there is no one around to ask. I tell Jim, "I want to report this to the forest rangers."

The sun comes out as we hike up grassy Siler Bald. We take a break and look out over the Blue Ridge Mountains. We hear hikers at the Siler Bald Shelter talking and laughing. As we turn to walk downhill, we see a tree bent over as if it is directing our way. According to legend, Native Americans bent young saplings to mark turns along trails. We saw this on another hike at Bly Gap as well.

We stop at Moore Creek and watch the rapidly moving water fall over the rocks and rush through the rhododendrons. Later, I decide to use a picture of the scenic creek to introduce this hike.

Finally, we come to Winding Stair Gap. Jim looks at his watch, "It's 6:30 p.m.; we'd better hurry," he says. "It will take us about an hour to get our other car and drive back to Franklin."

Bent tree, April 2008

We barely make it to the Motor Company Grill for dinner before it closes at nine. When we get back to the motel, Jim says, "My steam is running out."

"These first three days were hard because the trailheads were a long way from Franklin," I reply. "The hikes weren't bad, but we had to hurry because of the lengthy shuttles. The next two days, the trailheads will be closer. It should be better, even though the hikes will be longer."

Update: We did get a good night's sleep and did indeed finish the last two hikes. At the end of the trip, we stopped at the ranger station and reported the camper parked at the side of the forest service road. The ranger told Jim that anyone could camp on forest service land but that they would check out the camper. This made me feel better.

Carol's Reminders

- Give yourselves a break when it is raining.
- Take time to enjoy the views.

Nearest Town

Franklin is ten miles east of Winding Stair Gap, the southern trailhead and seventeen miles east of Wayah Bald, the northern trailhead.

Directions to the Trailheads

SOUTHERN TRAILHEAD AT WINDING STAIR GAP: GPS coordinates 35.11974, -83.54810. From Franklin, at the intersection of US 64 and US 441/US 23, drive west on US 64 about ten miles. As you come up a big hill, there is a parking lot on the left with an A.T. marker. This is Winding Stair Gap. The total trip is ten miles; allow fifteen minutes.

NORTHERN TRAILHEAD AT WAYAH BALD: GPS coordinates 35.174949, -83.556456. From Franklin, at the intersection of US 64 and US 441/23, drive three miles west. Turn right at the signs for Wayah Bald. After a short distance, turn left on Wayah Road (NC 1310). Follow this road for nine miles to the top of a hill where you will see signs for Wayah Bald on the right and Wayah Crest on the left. Turn right and follow the gravel road for five miles. The parking area will be just around a sharp right turn. The total trip is seventeen miles; allow forty-five minutes.

Park and walk up the paved path to Wayah Bald. A few feet up the path, you will see the white A.T. blazes. If you are headed south to Winding Stair Gap, make a sharp left turn just before the latrines and follow the blazes downhill.

If you plan using two cars, leave one car at Winding Stair Gap for the end of the trip. Then drive east about six miles to the sign that says "Wayah Bald." Follow the directions above to Wayah Bald to start the hike. The total trip is twenty miles; allow fifty minutes.

ALTERNATIVE TRANSPORTATION: Ask a shuttle driver to meet you at Winding Stair Gap, where will you leave your car, and drive you to Wayah Bald. See the list of shuttle-service providers in the **Hiker Essentials** section for Franklin.

Fine Wine and Accommodations
Franklin

FRANKLIN is a small community surrounded by the mountains of southwestern North Carolina. Visitors enjoy its streams, waterfalls, trails, and gem mines. It is a designated Appalachian Trail Community and embraces Appalachian Trail hikers with its friendliness, services, and festivals.

Lodging in Downtown Franklin

Hostels

"BALTIMORE JACK'S PLACE" HIKER HOSTEL: open seasonally, March and April; ½ $; bunk room, some single rooms; kitchenette w/microwave and refrigerator; coin laundry; $2 for washer, $2 for dryer; bike rentals; small hiker store with drinks and snacks; 7 East Palmer Street; 828-524-4403.

GOODER GROVE ADVENTURE HOSTEL: ½ $; home in private woods; one private room with queen bed, and two rooms with single beds; 1.5 shared bathrooms; bunk room for groups; common area with couch, kitchen, washer, and dryer; internet; heating and air conditioning; family friendly; dog friendly with fenced lot for dogs to run; shuttle service available, served by the local transit company (MCT) during season; walking distance from downtown shops; offers hiking and white water rafting adventures; 130 Hays Circle (one block from Main Street); 828-332-0228; A.T. Passport stamped here.

B&Bs

THE BLAINE HOUSE: $–$$ with complimentary English breakfast, historic hundred-year-old house with three suites and a cottage, flat-screen TV, high-speed broadband internet with free Wi-Fi, vacation homestay experience, outdoor concerts Saturdays in May, 661 Harrison Avenue, 828-371-1844 or 828-332-0743, www.blainehouse.com.

OAKHILL COUNTRY INN: $–$$ with complimentary breakfast; historic hundred-year-old home on a hilltop encircled by century- old oak trees; five suites; cottage with 1 BR, 1BA, kitchen, and laundry room; breakfast prepared by Connie, the owner and a Le-Cordon-Bleu-trained chef; 689 Old Murphy Road; 828-349-9194; www.oakhillcountryinn.com.

Hotels and Motels

HAVEN'S BUDGET INN: ½ $; hiker rate; pets $10; hiker and biker friendly refurbished motel located in downtown Franklin near restaurants, grocery stores, and medical facilities; rooms have microwaves, refrigerators, and cable TV; free high-speed internet in lobby; on-site laundry facilities, $2 for washer and $2 for dryer; owner Ron Haven provides shuttle service for motel guests, free to trailhead Mar through May at specified times; 433 East Palmer Street; 828-524-4403; www.havensbudgetinn.com; A.T. Passport stamped here.

OUR EXPERIENCE: Ron is an amiable, hiker friendly host who provides guests with basic, clean accommodations. He puts us in his best room away from the noise of traffic. When we get back late from our first hike, he recommends an excellent restaurant nearby. He arranges the shuttle for our long hike from Deep Gap to Dicks Creek Gap and answers all our questions about forest service roads and the A.T. around Franklin.

KNIGHTS INN: $, recently renovated rooms with heated floors in bathrooms, pet friendly, free breakfast, free Wi-Fi, 1320 East Main Street, 828-349-0600, www.knightsinn.com.

SAPPHIRE INN: $, updated king and queen rooms with mini refrigerators and microwaves, Wi-Fi, computer, pool, no washer or dryer, biker friendly, pet friendly, near fast-food restaurants and shops, 761 East Main Street, 828-524-4406, www.thesapphireinn.com, AT Passport stamped here.

Lodging near or South of the Intersection of US 64 and US 441/US 23

Cabins

BIG BEAR LOG CABINS: $$ with two-night minimum, four 2BR/1BA and one 3BR/1.5 BA log-cabin homes with fully furnished kitchens, linens provided, located on wooded acreage, pet friendly (fee), within walking distance of restaurants and shops, located at Georgia Road (US 441) & US 64, 357 Wide Horizon Drive (off US 441S), 866-349-0099, www.bigbearfranklin.com.

Hotels & Motels

CAROLINA MOTEL: $ with free continental breakfast; refurbished rooms with flat screen TVs, free Wi-Fi; some rooms with microwaves and refrigerators; log cabins with full kitchens; outdoor pool; 2601 Georgia Road (US 441/

US 23), south of the intersection of US 64 and US 441; 828-524-3380, www.carolinamotel.com.

COMFORT INN: $$ with free hot breakfast; king and queen rooms with microwaves, refrigerators, TVs; business center; exercise room; indoor heated pool; laundry room; $2 for washer, $2 for dryer; 313 Cunningham Road, 828-369-9200, www.comfortinn.com.

HAMPTON INN: $-$$ with free hot-breakfast buffet, king and queen rooms, Wi-Fi, business center, fitness center, outdoor pool, no pets, 244 Cunningham Road, 828-369-0600, www.hamptoninn3.hilton.com.

MICROTEL INN & SUITES BY WYNDHAM: $ with free continental breakfast, queen rooms and suites with refrigerators, microwaves, smoking and non-smoking rooms, pool, 81 Allman Drive, 1-800-337-0050, https://www.wyndhamhotels.com/microtel/franklin-north-carolina/microtel-inn-franklin/.

Lodging West of Franklin near Nantahala National Forest

WAYAH CREEK COTTAGES AND GARDENS: $–$$, two-night minimum, seven 1-2BR/1BA rustic mountain cabins with kitchens, creek-side rentals with fireplaces, smoke free, no pets, linens provided, located on Wayah Creek in the midst of large rhododendron bushes and dogwood trees and in the shadow of the Nantahala National Forest, 26 Wayah Way, 828-524-2034, www.wayahcreekcottages.blogspot.com.

Selected Restaurants in Downtown Franklin

CAFFÉ REL: $, bistro with upscale food (hamburgers, steaks), wine. Don't let the gas-station location scare you off. 11 a.m. to 8:30 p.m. Tue through Sat, 459 East Main Street, 828-369-9446, www.facebook.com/cafferel.

ELEVATIONS PIZZA & EATS: $, American, beer and wine, 11 a.m. to 8 p.m. Mon through Thu, 11 a.m. to 9 p.m. Fri and Sat, 228 NE Main Street, 828-369-1359, www.facebook.com/ElevationsPizzaEats, A.T. Community Supporter.

JAXON'S DOWNTOWN: $, American (pizza, subs, hamburgers), beer and wine, 11 a.m. to 9 p.m. Tue through Sat (hours vary in winter), great patio, dog friendly, 381 Depot Street, 828-369-1302, www.jaxonsdowntown.com.

LUCIO'S ITALIAN RESTAURANT: $, authentic Italian with romantic atmosphere, beer and wine, 5 p.m. until (closing time varies) Wed through Sat, 313 Highlands Road (Bella Vista Square), 828-369-6670, www.lucionc.com.

MI CASA: $, Mexican, wine and beer, special every day, 11 a.m. to 9 p.m. Sun through Thu, 11 a.m. to 10 p.m. Fri and Sat, 788 East Main Street, 828-369-1580, www.facebook.com/micasa.

MS. LOIS' RESTAURANT: $ (cash only), American, no alcohol, diner, 7 a.m. to 8 p.m. Mon through Sat, 145 Highlands Road, 828-369-8628.

    OUR EXPERIENCE: We have breakfast here the last morning of our hiking trip. Ms. Lois serves us our usual Southern fare of eggs, ham, bacon, and grits.

We have a fun conversation with a couple that we meet.

Jim says, "What do you do?"

"Oh, we retired to Franklin. I worked as the safety engineer for the Georgia Department of Transportation," says the man, whose name was Paul.

Jim says, "Are you that fellow that I used to call when I found a safety problem?"

"Yes," Paul replies.

Jim says, "I can't find anyone to call now when I have a problem. I am really glad to meet you."

MOTOR COMPANY GRILL: $; American; short-order menu with hamburgers, hot dogs, and meat-and-vegetable plates; local craft beer and wine; 1950s atmosphere; 11 a.m. to 3 p.m. Sun and Mon; 11 a.m. to 8 p.m. Tue through Thu; 11 a.m. to 9 p.m. Fri and Sat; 86 West Main Street, 828-524-0099, www.motorcogrill.com.

OUR EXPERIENCE IN APRIL 2008: Tonight we decide to try a new restaurant after our long hike. Motor Company Grill is the only one that fits the bill; it's in downtown Franklin, still open, and serves beer and wine.

We arrive about thirty minutes before closing and are the only ones in the restaurant. They take our order immediately. We relax, have some wine, and talk about our beautiful hike. We enjoy broiled chicken and vegetables; it's plain but satisfying. We finish with a bowl of ice cream.

A FRIEND WEIGHS IN: Pam says, "Best burgers around and good local beer too."

ROOT & BARREL KITCHEN: $–$$, American (steak, seafood, sandwiches), full bar, 11 a.m. to 2:30 p.m. and 5 to 9:30 p.m. daily, 77 East Main Street, 828-369-3663.

SUNSET RESTAURANT: $, family-style diner, hiker friendly (10% off), 7 a.m. to 8 p.m. Mon through Sat, 498 Harrison Avenue, 828-524-4842, www. sunsetrestaurantfranklin.com.

A FRIEND WEIGHS IN: Lee says, "Great local place."

Selected Restaurants South of Downtown Franklin near US 64 and US 441

THE BOILER ROOM STEAKHOUSE: $–$$, Appalachian cuisine, no beer or wine, children's play area, 11 a.m. to 8 p.m. Mon through Thu, 11 a.m. to 9 p.m. Fri and Sat, 1024 Georgia Road, 828-349-5555, www.boilerroom-steakhouse.com.

FAT BUDDIES RIBS AND BBQ: $–$$, American, beer and wine, 11 a.m. to 9 p.m. Mon through Sat, 311 Westgate Plaza Shopping Center, 828-349-4743, www.fatbuddiesribsandbbq.com.

FATZ CAFÉ: $, American, full bar, 11 a.m. to 9 p.m. Sun, 11 a.m. to 10 p.m. Mon through Thu, 11 a.m. to 11 p.m. Fri and Sat, 107 Sawmill Village Lane, 828-524-5265.

THAI PARADISE: $; Asian; beer, wine, and sake; 4:30 to 8:30 p.m. Sun through Thu; 4:30 to 9 p.m. Fri and Sat; 3078 Georgia Road (US 441 South); 828-349-0973.

Hiker Essentials, Splurges, and Emergency Stops

Shuttle-Service Providers

COLIN GOODER, GOODER GROVE ADVENTURE HOSTEL: 828-332-0228.

RON HAVEN'S HOSTEL AND HIKER SERVICES, HAVEN'S BUDGET INN: 828-524-4403, www.ronhavenhikerservices.com.

LARRY JACOBS TAXI: 828-421-4987.

JUDY LAKE TAXI: 8:30 a.m. to 6 p.m. Mon through Sat, 828-369-5042.

MACON COUNTY TRANSIT (MCT): $3, provides transit services to Winding Stair Gap and Rock Gap during hiker season, three runs a day, call for reservations, 7:30 a.m. to 5 p.m. Mon through Fri, 828-349-2222.

OUTDOOR 76 OUTFITTER: 10 a.m. to 7 p.m. Mon through Sat, 828-349-7676, during thru-hiker season, shuttles three times a day, A.T. Community Supporter, A.T. Passport stamped here.

ROADRUNNER DRIVING SERVICE, DARLENE SWOFFORD: 828-524-3265, answering service, leave number for service, 706-201-7719 (cell), dswofford@gmail.com.

THREE EAGLES: 10 a.m. to 6 p.m. Mon through Sat, 12 to 5 p.m. Sun, 828-524-9061. Call for a list of local shuttle-service providers. A.T. Community Supporter, A.T. Passport stamped here.

Car Rental Agency

ENTERPRISE RENT-A-CAR: 8:30 am to 5:30 p.m. Mon through Fri, 9 a.m. to noon Sat, 71 West Palmer Street, 828-349-0078.

Outfitters

OUTDOOR 76 OUTFITTER: full service outfitter, 10 a.m. to 7 p.m. Mon through Sat, 35 East Main Street in downtown Franklin, 828-349-7676, www. outdoor76.com., A.T. Community Supporter, A.T. Passport stamped here.

THREE EAGLES: full-service outfitter, Mon through Sat 9:30 a.m. to 6 p.m., 12 to 4 p.m. Sun (seasonal hours), 78 Siler Road. (near intersection of US 441 and US 64), 828-524-9061, www.threeeaglesoutfitters.net., A.T. Community Supporter, A.T. Passport stamped here.

Groceries

BI-LO GROCERY: 7 a.m. to 11 p.m. daily, groceries, beer and wine, 245 Macon Plaza Drive (Off Highlands Road near US 441), 828-369-2970.

INGLES MARKET: 7 a.m. to 11 p.m. daily, groceries, beer and wine, 152 West Palmer Street in downtown Franklin, 828-524-5616.

INGLES MARKET: 7 a.m. to 11 p.m. daily, groceries, beer and wine, 398 Westgate Plaza (south of the intersection of US 441 & US 64), 828-524-9321.

INGLES MARKET: 7 a.m. to 11 p.m. daily, groceries, beer and wine, 4501 Highway 441 Bypass, 828-524-5011.

WALMART SUPERCENTER: 24/7, groceries, outdoor gear, beer and wine, 273 Commons Drive, 828-524-9111.

Wine or Beer Shops

CURRAHEE BREWING COMPANY: 12 to 9 p.m. Mon through Thu, 12 to 10 p.m. Fri and Sat. The Mountain Fresh Food Trailer has fare to complement beer and wine offerings. 100 Lakeside Drive, 828-634-0078, A.T. Community Supporter, A.T. Passport stamped here.

FRANKLIN ABC LIQUOR STORE: 9 a.m. to 9 p.m. Mon through Sat, 175 Macon Plaza Drive, 828-369-9274.

LAZY HIKER BREWING COMPANY: 12 to 9 p.m. Mon through Thu, 12 to 11 p.m. Fri and Sat, 12 to 8 p.m. Sun. Food truck serves burgers and sandwiches. 188 West Main Street, 828-349-2337, www.lazyhikingbrewing.com., A.T. Community Supporter, A.T. Passport stamped here.

ROCK HOUSE LODGE INSIDE OUTDOOR 76: craft beer and wine, 10 a.m. to 9 p.m. Mon through Sat, 35 East Main Street, 828-349-7676, www.outdoor76.com.

ATMs

There are more than twenty ATMs located in downtown Franklin, Westgate Plaza, and Franklin Plaza. These include:

ATM (PNC): 100 West Main Street.

ATM (TD): 55 East Main Street.

ATM: 1281 Georgia Road.

ATM (FIRST CITIZENS BANK): 114 Westgate Plaza.

ATM: 344 Westgate Plaza.

CARDTRONICS ATM: 61 Franklin Plaza.

WELLS FARGO BANKS: 55 East Main Street and 28 East Palmer Street.

Urgent Care and Emergency Services

ANGEL URGENT CARE: 8:30 a.m. to 5 p.m. Mon through Fri, 10 a.m. to 2 p.m. Sat and Sun, 195 Franklin Plaza, 828-369-4427.

ANGEL MEDICAL CENTER, EMERGENCY DEPARTMENT: 24/7, 120 Riverview Street, 828-369-4211.

Fun Places to Visit in or Near Franklin

FRANKLIN GEM & MINERAL MUSEUM: free (staffed by volunteers), 12 to 4 p.m. Mon through Sat May–Oct, 12 to 4 p.m. Sat Nov–April, thousands of specimens from forty-nine states, Canada and Australia, classes & field trips available, 25 Phillips Street in downtown Franklin (located in the Old Jail, built in 1850), 828-369-7831.

OUR EXPERIENCE: After our last day hike near Franklin, we take a day to explore the town and find the gem museum. This is a fascinating place. There are gems of all shapes, colors, and sizes. They are from all over the world and are separated into collections by state and country so that you can identify the gems that come from your state.

MACON COUNTY HISTORICAL MUSEUM: $5 donation; 10 a.m. to 4 p.m. Mon, Tue, and Thu; 10 a.m. to 1 p.m. Wed and Sat; 36 West Main Street.

RUBY CITY GEMS MUSEUM: free, seasonal hours—check website, 130 East Main Street, 828-524-3967, www.rubycity.com, A.T. Passport stamped here.

SCOTTISH TARTANS MUSEUM: $2 for adults, $1 for children, 10 a.m. to 5 p.m. Tue through Sat April–Nov, 11 a.m. to 4 p.m. Tue through Sat Dec--Mar, 86 East Main Street, 828-524-7472.

OUR EXPERIENCE: We go to the Scottish Tartans Museum because my great-grandfather was from Scotland. I enjoy looking at the different tartan patterns and period clothing. We look up the tartan for my great-grandfather's clan, the Leslies, and actually find a tie to buy.

THE SMOKY MOUNTAIN CENTER FOR PERFORMING ARTS: performances on the weekends during the summer. For upcoming events, go to www.discoverfranklinnc. com, 1028 Georgia Road, 828-524-1528.

GEM MINING: available at many nearby mines, including the Cherokee Ruby and Sapphire Mine, Cowee Mountain Ruby Mine, Mason's Ruby and Sapphire Mine, Rocky Face Gem Mine, Rose Creek Mine, and Sheffield Mine. Check their websites for more information.

FLY-FISHING: on the Nantahala River, Cullasaja River, Little Tennessee River, and Tuckasseegee River. For more information, go to www. WesternNCFlyFishingGuide.com and www.EndlessRiverAdventures.com.

FRANKLIN GOLF COURSE: nine-hole course founded in 1920, pro shop, 255 First Fairway Drive, 828-524-2288, www.franklingolfcourse.com.

MILL CREEK COUNTRY CLUB: eighteen-hole golf course open to the public, fees vary with season, 341 Country Club Drive, 828-524-6458, www.mill-creekcountryclub.com.

WATERFALLS: ten to twenty miles east of Franklin on US 64 in the Cullasaja Gorge, see **Cullasaja Falls** cascading 250 feet down the mountainside, walk behind the 75-foot **Dry Falls** and drive behind the 120-foot **Bridal Veil Falls**.

   Rufus Morgan Falls, Big Laurel Falls and **Mooney Falls** are west of Franklin, off forest service roads. Go to www.VisitFranklinNC.com for directions.

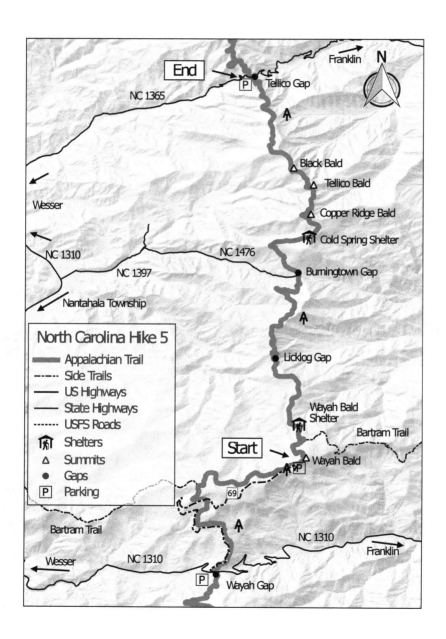

Franklin

N

End

P   Tellico Gap

NC 1365

Black Bald

△ Tellico Bald

Wesser

△ Copper Ridge Bald

Cold Spring Shelter

NC 1310

NC 1476

NC 1397

Burningtown Gap

Nantahala Township

North Carolina Hike 5

━━━ Appalachian Trail
–·–·– Side Trails
──── US Highways
──── State Highways
······ USFS Roads
🏠 Shelters
△ Summits
● Gaps
P Parking

Licklog Gap

Wayah Bald
Shelter

Bartram Trail

Start

Wayah Bald

P

69

Bartram Trail

NC 1310

Wesser

NC 1310

Franklin

P   Wayah Gap

266

Wayah Bald to Tellico Gap,

9.3 miles, Easy to Moderate

NC HIKE 5

HIGHLIGHTS: The Wayah Bald Fire Lookout Tower, built by the Civilian Conservation Corps (CCC) in 1935, sits majestically on Wayah Bald. From Wayah Bald, you have a panoramic view of the Smokies to the north, the North Carolina Highlands to the east, and the Georgia mountains to the south.

DISTANCE: 9.3 miles.   **HIKE TIME:** 5 hours.

LEVEL OF EFFORT: Easy to Moderate.

RECOMMENDED DIRECTION: South to north, Wayah Bald to Tellico Gap.

DOWNHILL: 6.2 miles with an elevation loss of 2,100 feet. **UPHILL:** 3.1 miles with an elevation gain of 800 feet.

ALONG THE TRAIL: From Wayah Bald, the earthen, leaf-covered path winds under hardwood trees, over hills, and through gaps. It climbs gradually on switchbacks to the ridge below Copper Ridge Bald and Rocky Bald and descends through the rhododendrons to Tellico Gap. Only one small section of the path is rocky, just before Burningtown Gap.

Wayah Bald Fire Lookout Tower, April 2008

SHELTERS: Wayah Shelter was constructed in the Nantahala design. Cold Spring Shelter is a historic log shelter built by the CCC in the 1930s. Each one has a privy and water source nearby.

Follow the White Blazes

MILE 0.0: Wayah Bald, 5,340 feet. Wayah is the Cherokee word for "wolf."

MILE 0.9: Wayah Shelter, water, privy.

MILE 2.3: Licklog Gap, 4,410 feet. Licklog is a log that farmers notched and put salt in for their stock.

MILE 4.5: Burningtown Gap and NC 1397, 4,220 feet. In 1776, the Cherokees retreated to the mountains west of the gap as the Carolina militia burned thirty-six of their towns.

MILE 5.7: Cold Spring Shelter, 4,920 feet, water, privy.

MILE 6.4: Copper Ridge Bald Lookout, 5,050 feet.

MILE 7.6: Side trail to Rocky Bald Lookout, 5,010 feet.

MILE 9.3: Tellico Gap, 3,860 feet, NC 1365 (Otter Creek Road). Tellico Gap was named for the Cherokee town of Great Tellico, which was located just over the Nantahala Mountains.

Peaks and Valleys

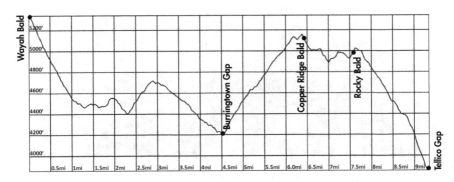

My Hiking Journal

APRIL 2008: This is the second day of our five-day hiking trip.

It is a beautiful spring day. We explore the historic Wayah Bald Fire Lookout Tower and read the poster that tells about the history of the bald. We look out over the horizon and watch clouds swirl through the sky and the haze rise from the Smoky Mountains.

We walk down a paved road from the tower to what we think is the A.T. going north.

Jim says, "This sign says *A.T. S.* I think we are going the wrong way."

We retrace our steps about fifty feet, find the *A.T. N* sign on the opposite side of the tower, and begin our hike. We walk down the trail less than a mile to the Wayah Shelter.

The shelter was built in 2007 by the Nantahala Hiking Club in memory of Larry and Ann McDuff. The McDuffs were avid hikers and had hiked the A.T. as well as the John Muir and Pacific Coast Trails. When Ann was killed in a bicycle accident in 2003, her husband raised

Views from Wayah Bald, April 2008

money to build a shelter and worked with the Nantahala Hiking Club to select a site. Before it could be built, he was killed in a bicycle accident as well.

We continue under the trees on the well-worn path as it winds down through Licklog Gap. Then we follow the rocky path down to Burningtown Gap. At the gap, we meet Bob, a trail maintainer.

"What are you doing?" Jim asks.

"Restoring this rocky path, and I brought an ice chest with sodas," says Bob.

Sam, a hiker, is resting and drinking a coke.

Jim asks his usual question: "Where are you going?"

Sam smiles and replies, "Maine. This is my second thru-hike."

From the gap, we climb gradually up the ridge trail and stop to rest and explore the small log Cold Spring Shelter, located just beside the trail. The shelter was built by the CCC in 1933.

We take pictures from Copper Ridge Bald and Rocky Bald. The views across the hazy mountain ridges remind me of why we treasure the

Copper Ridge Bald Lookout, April 2008

A.T. and the national forests. There are no houses on the mountaintops, just nature at its finest.

When we come down the hill to our car at Tellico Gap, we meet several thru-hikers.

Jim asks, "Would you like cold Cokes or water? I have some in my ice chest."

"Sure," they say.

This tall lean thru-hiker, in the picture, tells us that he has support bands around his knees because they have been giving him problems. I can only imagine that they have, because he must be at least seven feet tall. He towers over Jim, who is five foot, ten inches tall.

As we climb into the car, I say, "It feels good being Trail Angels. This has been a wonderful day, but my knees are aching a little."

Jim and one of the thru-hikers, April 2008

Jim says, "My calves are hurting."

We go back to the motel to enjoy hot-tub baths, and then we're off to Codys Original Roadhouse for dinner. (Codys has closed since we were there.) All the tables at the restaurant are full, so we sit at the corner of the bar. Jim makes friends with a man named Ken who is sitting to his right, and I talk to a real estate developer who is sitting to my left.

On the way back to the motel, Jim beams and says, "You will not believe this. Ken, the fellow I was talking to, is an engineer who worked at Cape Canaveral in the early sixties. He wrote some computer programs that I later modified." We lived at Cape Canaveral from 1966 to 1969. Jim was a computer programmer.

Carol's Reminders

- **Take time to see what you can see, savor the mystique of the A.T., and take pictures to share with your friends.**
- **Be a Trail Angel.**

Nearest Towns

Franklin is seventeen miles east of Wayah Bald, the southern trailhead. Wesser is seventeen miles north of Tellico Gap, the northern trailhead. Nantahala Township is nine miles west of Tellico Gap and seventeen miles west of Wayah Bald.

Directions to the Trailheads

SOUTHERN TRAILHEAD AT WAYAH BALD: GPS coordinates 35.174949, -83.556456. From Franklin, at the intersection of US 64 and US 441/23, drive three miles west. Turn right at the signs for Wayah Bald. After traveling a short distance, turn left on Wayah Road (NC 1310). Follow this road for nine miles to the top of a hill where you will see signs for Wayah Bald to the right and Wayah Crest to the left. Turn right and follow the gravel road for five miles. The parking area is around a sharp turn to the right. Park and follow the white A.T. blazes up the paved path to the Wayah Bald Fire Lookout Tower. The trailhead is on the northeast side of the tower. The total trip is seventeen miles; allow thirty minutes.

NORTHERN TRAILHEAD AT TELLICO GAP: GPS coordinates 35.180321, -83.560654. From Franklin, at the intersection of US 64 and US 441/US 23, go west on US 64 for three miles. Turn right at the sign saying "Wayah Bald." After traveling a short distance, turn left on Wayah Road (NC 1130). Follow NC 1130 nine miles, pass the road to Wayah Bald, and go another fourteen miles to the sign for Tellico Gap. Turn right on Otter Creek Road (NC 1365), and drive four miles to the top of the hill. Parking is on the right. The total trip is thirty miles; allow fifty minutes.

From Wesser at the Nantahala Outdoor Center, drive west on US 74/19 about eight miles to Wayah Road (NC 1310). Turn left and drive south five miles to Otter Creek Road (NC 1365). Turn left and drive four miles to Tellico Gap. The total trip is seventeen miles; allow thirty minutes.

If you plan to shuttle using two cars, drive one car to Tellico Gap for the end of the hike, then drive eighteen miles to Wayah Bald to begin the hike.

ALTERNATIVE TRANSPORTATION: Have the shuttle driver take you to Tellico Gap to leave your car and then to Wayah Bald to begin your hike. See the list of shuttle-service providers in the **Hiker Essentials** sections for Franklin and Wesser.

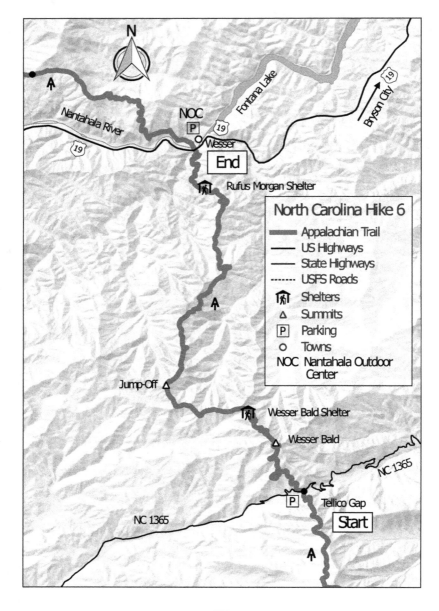

Tellico Gap to the Nantahala River,

7.9 miles, Challenging

NC HIKE 6

HIGHLIGHTS: In the spring, the beautiful wildflowers are just beginning to bloom. From the Wesser Bald observation tower, delight in the panoramic views of the Smokies, Fontana Lake, Nantahala Gorge, Cheoah Bald, and Wayah Bald. As you finish your hike, watch the paddlers try to avoid the rocks as they raft down the Nantahala River. Then check out the legendary Nantahala Outdoor Center (NOC). See Wesser: **Fun Places to Visit**.

DISTANCE: 7.9 miles.　　**HIKE TIME:** 5 to 6 hours.　　**LEVEL OF EFFORT:** Challenging.

Star chickweed, April 2008

Trillium, April 2008

RECOMMENDED DIRECTION: South to north, Tellico Gap to the Nantahala River.

DOWNHILL: 6.5 miles downhill and along the ridge with an elevation loss of 3,430 feet. **UPHILL:** 1.4 miles with an elevation gain of 1,300 feet.

ALONG THE TRAIL: From Tellico Gap the A.T. is rocky as it goes up and down Wesser Bald, across the ridgeline, and turns down suddenly toward Nantahala Gorge. The path becomes earthen as you walk under the young hardwood trees in the gorge.

Enjoy lunch from one of the overlooks, or if the weather turns bad, take a break at one of the shelters.

At the end of the hike, the trail passes through the five-hundred-acre Nantahala Outdoor Center (NOC) complex and crosses the Nantahala River at Wesser. The NOC was started as a river outpost by outdoor enthusiasts and paddlers. It has grown to become a training center for national paddling competitors, champions, and Olympians as well as a fun place for recreational rafting.

Nantahala Outdoor Center, April 2008

SHELTERS: Wesser Bald Shelter is a Nantahala-style shelter. The A. Rufus Morgan Shelter is a log shelter built in memory of the man who started the Nantahala Hiking Club and maintained this section of the trail. Each shelter has a privy and water source nearby.

Follow the White Blazes

MILE 0.0: Tellico Gap, 3,860 feet, Otter Creek Road (NC 1365). Tellico Gap was named for the Cherokee town of Great Tellico, which was located just over the Nantahala Mountains.

MILE 1.4: Wesser Bald observation tower, 4,610 feet.

MILE 2.2: Wesser Bald Shelter, Wesser Creek Trail, 4,115 feet, water, privy.

MILE 3.8: Jump-up Lookout, 3,640 feet. This is a rocky outcrop that you have to scramble to reach with good views of Cheoah Bald and the Nantahala River Gorge. (Scramble is to climb hand-over-hand up a rocky cliff.)

MILE 7.1: A. Rufus Morgan Shelter, water, privy.

MILE 7.9: Nantahala River, US 19/US 74, Nantahala Outdoor Center, 2,300 feet, water, restrooms, hostel, restaurants, outfitter, and nearby hotels and motels. Nantahala means "midday sun" in Cherokee. The steep gorges in the Nantahala River basin block the sun until noon.

Peaks and Valleys

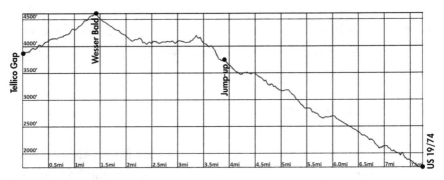

My Hiking Journal

APRIL 2008: This is the first day of our five-day hiking trip.

The air is clear and crisp, and the trees are still bare—just the right day for a hike.

When we reach Wesser Bald, we have lunch on the platform of the observation tower.

I say, "The trail is a bit more challenging than I thought."

On the profile, the trail looks like a moderate downhill hike, but in real life, we are forever stepping up and over rocks and boulders and going up and down. Luckily, we are rewarded with beautiful views of the mountains and valleys.

When we stop at the Jump-up Lookout, we find an anxious-looking hiker with his dog.

"Where are you going?" Jim asks.

"Maine, and I am out of water," the hiker replies.

"We have extra," Jim says. We fill the dog's bowl and the hiker's water bottle from our water bladders.

The hiker smiles and says, "Thanks. This should get us to the river." He offers to take our picture.

The view from Wesser Bald observation tower, April 2008

Jump-up, April 2008

After five hours of hiking on rocky ground, we are happy to see the Nantahala Outdoor Center.

"Let's go to River's End Restaurant for a snack before we head back," I say. We relax, split a calzone, and have some beer.

Jim says, "This is just what we needed."

We are staying in Franklin, but must go back by Tellico Gap to pick up our other car before we wind back through the mountains to Ron Haven's Budget Inn. When we finally get there, we fall into bed and take a long nap before dinner.

River's End Restaurant, Wesser, April 2008

Carol's Reminders

- **Be a Trail Angel.**
- **Always be prepared for the worst with extra water and food.**

Nearest Towns

Wesser is on the Nantahala River at the northern trailhead and seventeen miles north of the southern trailhead. Bryson City is thirteen miles east of the northern trailhead. Nantahala Township is nine miles west of Tellico Gap, the southern trailhead. Franklin is seventeen miles southwest of the southern trailhead.

Directions to the Trailheads

SOUTHERN TRAILHEAD AT TELLICO GAP: GPS coordinates 35.180321, -83.560654. From the Nantahala Outdoor Center (NOC) in Wesser, drive west on US 19/74 eight miles to Wayah Road (NC 1310). Turn left and drive south five miles to Otter Creek Road (NC 1365). Turn left and drive four miles to the parking area at Tellico Gap. The total trip is about seventeen miles; allow thirty minutes.

NORTHERN TRAILHEAD AT US 19/74, THE NANTAHALA RIVER, AND NOC: GPS coordinates 35.198613, -83.355006. Parking is just east of the trailhead and north of US 19/74. Look for the A.T. hiker parking signs.

If you plan to shuttle using two cars, leave one car at the hiker parking lot on the Nantahala Outdoor Center campus for the end of the hike, and drive the other car to Tellico Gap, using the directions above. The total trip is seventeen miles; allow thirty minutes.

ALTERNATIVE TRANSPORTATION: Ask the shuttle driver to take you from the Nantahala Outdoor Center parking lot to Tellico Gap. See the list of shuttle-service providers in the **Hiker Essentials** section for Wesser, Bryson City, the Nantahala Township, or Franklin.

Fine Wine and Accommodations
Wesser, Bryson City, and
the Nantahala Township

WESSER is a remote community along the Appalachian Trail on the banks of the Nantahala River. The Nantahala Outdoor Center is here with its outfitter, restaurants, lodging, and general store. You will also find a food market and gas station one mile to the east. As Wesser does not have a post office, businesses here have Bryson City addresses.

BRYSON CITY is thirteen miles east of the A.T. at Wesser and the Nantahala Outdoor Center. It is a small Appalachian town in the Tuskegee River Valley, surrounded by the Smoky Mountains to the north and the Cowee Mountains to the south. Bryson City is known as a place to enjoy hunting, fishing, and other outdoor activities. It is also known for its rich Cherokee history. It has lodging, restaurants, grocery stores, a post office, and health care facilities.

NANTAHALA TOWNSHIP is a group of small communities in Macon County, near Lake Nantahala. It is west of the A.T. and Wayah Road, midway between Franklin and Wesser. Postal addresses here can be either Topton or Nantahala. The township has a hiker lodge, rental cabins, rental homes, a restaurant, a market, and a marina for vacationers and outdoors enthusiasts.

Lodging and Restaurants in or near Wesser and within Seven Miles of the A.T. Trailhead as it Crosses US 74/US 19

Lodging

THE NANTAHALA OUTDOOR CENTER BASECAMP: ½ $ (special prices for thru-hikers); handicap accessible; bunkhouses accommodating two to eighteen per unit with twin beds; heating and air conditioning; shared community building with kitchen, dining hall, charcoal grill, individual shower stalls, and wireless internet; men's and women's community bathhouses; selected bunkhouses are pet friendly; linens, dishes, and cookware are not provided; 13077 West Highway 19, 828-785-4837. Get your A.T. Passport stamped here.

NANTAHALA OUTDOOR CENTER DOGWOOD MOTEL (RENOVATED, 2016): $–$$, four double and twin bunk rooms with shared bath and shower across the hall; four rooms with in-room baths, showers, and flat-screen TVs; common area with refrigerator, microwave, coffee pot, flat-screen TV, washer, dryer and wireless internet access; no dogs; 13077 West Highway 19; 828-785-4845, https://noc.com/stay-at-noc/dogwood-motel.

NANTAHALA OUTDOOR CENTER DELUXE CABINS: $$–$$$; 2BR/1BA, 3BR/1BA, 2BR/2BA, and 6BR/3BA cabins; fully equipped kitchens; satellite TVs; DVD players; charcoal grills; linens and towels; 13077 West Highway 19; 828-785-4845; https://noc.com/stay-at-noc/deluxe-cabins.

NANTAHALA VILLAGE HISTORIC LODGE ROOMS AND SUITES, CABINS, TREEHOUSE COTTAGES, AND HISTORIC TABOR HOUSE: $$–$$$; 1BR/1BA or 2BR/2BA suites; 2BR/2B mountain suites with kitchens, pool tables, and fireplaces. Some have hot tubs. 1BR/1BA, 2BR/1BA cabins, some with hot tubs, some with kitchens, choice of king or queen beds; 1BR/1BA, 2BR/1BA cottages with kitchens and TVs. Tabor House is a 4BR/1.5BA 1800s farmhouse with kitchen, LR, DR. All are within walking distance of the Village Bistro, swimming pool, fitness room, game room, tennis and basketball courts, horseback riding stables, hiking and biking trails, 9400 Highway 19 West, four miles east of Wesser, 828-488-9000, http://nantahalavillage.com.

LAKEVIEW AT FONTANA: $$ with continental breakfast, afternoon wine & cheese, boutique mountain inn and spa with views of Fontana Lake, queen and king rooms, suites with kitchens, pet friendly, 171 Lakeview Lodge Drive, seven miles east of Wesser, 1-800-742-6492, www.lakeviewatfontana.com.

Selected Restaurants

NOC RIVER'S END RESTAURANT: $, American, sandwiches, pizza, seafood, beef and chicken entrees, beer and wine, seating with river views, 8 a.m. to 7 p.m. Sun through Thu, 8 a.m. to 8 p.m. Fri and Sat (hours vary seasonally), next to the Appalachian Trail, 828-488-7172.

OUR EXPERIENCE: We have eaten here several times. After our hike from Stecoah Gap south to the Nantahala River, we scurry down the hill about six thirty, hoping the restaurant will still be open. The hostess welcomes us, even in our sweat-soaked clothes. We sit outside on the porch and relax with glasses of pinot noir. We watch the river flow over the rocks as the daylight wanes and the crickets begin their chorus. I have a delicious trout dinner and Jim has steak.

I say, "This was a challenging hike. What a peaceful way to end the day."

NOC BIG WESSER BBQ & BREW: $, American, beer, live music on weekends, 11 a.m. to 9 p.m. Sun through Wed, 11 a.m. to 10 p.m. Thu through Sat, Memorial Day through Labor Day, next to the A.T., 828-488-7174.

VILLAGE BISTRO: $, American, beer and wine, casual but elegant setting, outdoor seating with views of the Smoky Mountains, 5 to 9 p.m. Fri and Sat, not open in winter months, Nantahala Village, 9400 Highway 19 West, four miles east of the A.T., 828-488-9000.

VILLAGE GRILL: $, American, full bar, casual patio setting, 11 a.m. to 10 p.m. Fri and Sat, not open in winter, Nantahala Village, 9400 Highway 19 West, four miles east of the A.T., 828-488-9000.

Lodging and Restaurants in Bryson City

Lodging

CALHOUN HOUSE INN AND SUITES B&B (UPDATED 2016): $$ with continental breakfast, historic inn, four suites with kitchens, hot tubs, fireplaces, child friendly, pet friendly, 110 Bryson Avenue, 828-788-0505, www.calhounhouse.com.

THE EVERETT HOTEL AND BISTRO (UPDATED 2017): $$–$$$ with complimentary breakfast, luxury boutique hotel with seven suites, full-service restaurant, 16 Everett Street, 828-488-1976, www.theeveretthotel.com.

FRYEMONT INN B&B: $$–$$$ with breakfast and family-style dinner included during the season; historic inn with queen and king rooms, suites, cottages, cabins, pool, billiards, and bar; cottages and cabins open year round, inn and restaurant during the season; 245 Fremont Street; 828-488-2159; www.fryemontinn.com.

RIDGE TOP MOTEL & CAMPGROUND (UPDATED 2017): $; old-style motel and campground; rooms with TVs, refrigerators, and microwaves; outdoor pool, guest laundry, and free Wi-Fi; pet friendly, 390 Arlington Avenue, 828-488-6335, www.ridgetopmotel.com.

ROSEWOOD INN: $ (prices vary by season), hiker discount, rooms on upper level have balconies overlooking the river, pool, free Wi-Fi, coffee makers, 265 Main Street in downtown Bryson City, 828-488-2194.

SLEEP INN: $$ with continental and hot breakfast (prices vary by season), microwaves and mini refrigerators, outdoor pool, 500 Veterans Boulevard, 828-488-0326.

Selected Restaurants

ANTHONY'S: $, Italian, full bar, covered outdoor seating, free Wi-Fi, 11 a.m. to 9 p.m. Sun through Thu, 11 a.m. to 10 p.m. Fri and Sat, 15 Depot Street, 828-488-8898.

THE EVERETT HOTEL CORK & BEAN BISTRO: $$; American; fine dining in rustic setting, daily chef specials, full bar; 4:30 to 8:30 p.m. Tue through Thu; 11 a.m. to 9:30 p.m. Fri; brunch 9 a.m. to 3:30 p.m., dinner 4:30 to 9:30 p.m. Sat; brunch 9 a.m. to 3 p.m., dinner 4:30 to 9 p.m. Sun; 16 Everett Street; 828-488-1976.

FRYEMONT INN: $–$$; American; fine dining with full bar; 6 to 8 p.m. Sun through Thu, 6 to 9 p.m. Fri and Sat during season; 245 Fryemont Street; 828-488-2159.

GREAT SMOKY MOUNTAINS WINERY: $; American; wine; located in rustic, restored 1911 building; 4 to 9 p.m. Mon through Sat; 70 Veterans Boulevard; 828-788-1346.

GUAYABITO'S MEXICAN RESTAURANT: $–$$ (cash only), authentic Mexican, menu includes vegetarian meals, full bar, dine in or take out, no reservations, no delivery, 11 a.m. to 9:30 p.m. Mon through Fri, noon to 9:30 p.m. Sat, noon to 8:30 p.m. Sun, 236 Highway 19 South, 828-488-1336.

NATE AND NICK'S: $–$$; American; bar; casual; outdoor seating available; 11 a.m. to 9 p.m. Mon, Wed and Thu; 11 a.m. to 9:30 p.m. Fri and Sat; noon to 8 p.m. Sun; 225 Everett Street; 828-488-0500.

PASQUALINO'S: $–$$, classic Italian, full bar, 11:30 a.m. to 10 p.m. daily, 25 Everett Street, 828-488-9555, www.greatsmokies.com/pasqualinos.

Lodging and Restaurants in Nantahala Township

Lodging

THE NANTAHALA MOUNTAIN LODGE: ½ $–$$, March 1 to June 1, single beds in two mixed dormitory rooms with shared baths, two private en-suite rooms for two, bed linens provided, $6 for breakfast, $12.50 for three-course dinner, $10 for pizza, $5 per person per laundry load, resupply and snack shop open in a.m. and p.m., shuttle and slackpacking services, 63 Britanna Drive, Topton (seventeen miles west of Wesser, nine miles west of Tellico Gap, six miles west of Burningtown Road, and seventeen miles west of Wayah Bald), 828-321-2340, www.northcarolinalogcabin. rentals, A.T. Passport stamped here.

AQUONE CABIN RENTALS: *Adohi Lodge:* $$, luxury 2BR/1BA with fireplace, hot tub, pool table, full kitchen, and four-thousand-foot views of the Appalachian Mountains. *White Oak View:* call for rate, 6BR/4BA, full kitchen, outside decks with hot tub. *Blueberry Hill:* $$, 2BR/1BA with queen beds, full kitchen, and hot tub. *Laurel Ridge:* $$, 1BR/1BA, full kitchen, hot tub, and pool table. Near Nantahala Lake, 828-321-9949, www.northcarolinalogcabin.rentals

Restaurants

LAKES END CAFÉ AND GRILL: $; outside seating overlooking marina on Lake Nantahala; 8 a.m. to 4 p.m. Sun, 11:30 a.m. to 2 p.m. Tue and Wed, 7:30 a.m. to 8 p.m. Thu through Sat during the season; 17838 Wayah Road; Topton, 828-321-3000.

Hiker Essentials, Splurges, and Emergency Stops in Wesser, Bryson City, and the Nantahala Township

Shuttle-Service Providers

NANTAHALA OUTDOOR CENTER OUTFITTERS STORE: posts a list of local people who provide shuttle service. Store personnel do not post the list on the website or provide the information over the phone.

PATRICE PRICE: Wesser, NC, 828-538-1236, pdkprice@frontier.com.

Car Rental Agencies *(closest)*

ENTERPRISE RENT-A-CAR: special weekend rates, 8 a.m. to 5:30 p.m. Mon through Fri, 9 a.m. to noon Sat, 1188 West Main Street, Sylva, 828-631-0142.

ENTERPRISE RENT-A-CAR: 8:30 am to 5:30 p.m. Mon through Fri, 9 a.m. to noon Sat, 71 West Palmer Street, Franklin, 828-349-0078.

Outfitters

NANTAHALA OUTDOOR CENTER OUTFITTERS STORE: 8 a.m. to 8 p.m. daily, at the Nantahala River and the US 19/74 trailhead, 13077 West Highway 19, Wesser, 828-488-7230, A.T. Passport stamped here.

BRYSON CITY OUTDOORS: 10 a.m. to 5 p.m. Mon through Thu, 10 a.m. to 6 p.m. Fri and Sat, 10 a.m. to 4 p.m. Sun, 169 Main Street, Bryson City, 828-342-6444, www.brysoncityoutdoors.com.

LAKES END ADVENTURE STORE ON LAKE NANTAHALA: boating, camping, and water-sports supplies; snacks; canned foods; 8 a.m. to 4 p.m. Sun, 7:30 a.m. to 2 p.m. Mon through Wed, 7:30 a.m. to 8 p.m. Thu through Sat during season; 17839 Wayah Road, Topton; 828-321-3001.

Groceries

NOC WESSER GENERAL STORE: snacks, beer, wine, 8 a.m. to 8 p.m. daily Mar through Nov, 13077 West Highway 19 (beside the A.T.), 828-488-7226.

IGA: groceries, beer and wine, 8 a.m. to 8 p.m. Mon through Sat, 10 a.m. to 7 p.m. Sun, beer and wine from noon to 6 p.m. on Sun, 345 Main Street, Bryson City, 828-488-2584, A.T. Passport stamped here.

INGLES MARKET: groceries, beer, wine, 7 a.m. to 10 p.m. daily, 76 Hughes Branch Road, Bryson City, 828-488-6600.

LAKES END RUSTIC MARKET ON LAKE NANTAHALA: fresh baked goods, local honey and grocery items, local art and handmade items, gifts, 10 a.m. to 6 p.m. Wed through Sun during season, 18420 Wayah Road, Topton, 828-321-1337, www.lakesend.com.

Wine or Beer Shops

ABC LIQUOR STORE: 9 a.m. to 9 p.m. Mon through Sat, 254 Veteran's Boulevard, Bryson City, 828-468-682.

THE COTTAGE CRAFTSMAN WINE SHOP: North Carolina wines; wide variety of pottery, food, coffee, soaps, jewelry, and art; 10:30 a.m. to 5 p.m. Mon through Sat; noon to 5 p.m. Sun; 44 Fry Street, Bryson City; 828-488-6207, www.thecottagecraftsman.com.

NANTAHALA BREWING COMPANY: noon to 10 p.m. Sun through Thu, noon to 11 p.m. Fri and Sat (hours vary by season), brews and craft beer, 61 Depot St., Bryson City, 828-488-2337, www.nantahalabrewing.com.

ATMs

ATM: 110 South US 19, Bryson City.

CARDTRONICS ATMS: 610 Main Street and 1245 Main Street, Bryson City.

UNITED COMMUNITY BANK ATM: 145 Slope Street, Bryson City.

Urgent Care and Emergency Services

SMOKY MOUNTAIN URGENT CARE AND FAMILY MEDICINE CENTER: 9 a.m. to 7 p.m. Mon through Fri, 9 a.m. to 5 p.m. Sat and Sun, 80 Veterans Boulevard, Bryson City, 828-538-4546.

SWAIN COUNTY HOSPITAL AND MEDICAL CENTER, EMERGENCY SERVICES: 24/7, 45 Plateau Street, Bryson City, 828-488-2155.

Fun Places to Visit

NANTAHALA OUTDOOR CENTER (NOC): was started by outdoor enthusiasts and paddlers Payson and Aurelia Kennedy and Horace Holden Sr. The NOC has grown from a river outpost to a river legacy, where national paddling competitors, champions, and Olympians work during the peak season and train in the off- season.

NOC brings together a community of paddlers who work and play together. It is a fun place to experience, whether you are just walking through on your hike, need hiking supplies, or want to go white water rafting or fly-fishing. You can rub elbows with champions as you paddle.

NOC operates white water rafting trips and a paddling school and offers kayak rentals and zip lining. The center provides guides, services, and lodging. Restaurants and an outfitter are part of the center as well. 13077 West Highway 19 (US Highway 19/US 74 at the A.T. Nantahala River trailhead), 828-488-2175.

ENDLESS RIVER ADVENTURES: white water rafting, kayaking, fly- fishing, international trips, kayak store, and fly-fishing loft; 9 a.m. to 5 p.m. daily; 14157 US Hwy 19/US 74 West (east of the Nantahala River A.T. trailhead); 828-488-6199.

LAKES END BOAT RENTALS AND MARINA ON LAKE NANTAHALA: 8 a.m. to 9 p.m. daily during season, 17838 Wayah Road, Topton, 828-321-3001.

FISHING: www.Greatsmokiesfishing.com.

GREAT SMOKY MOUNTAINS RAILROAD AND MUSEUM: $9 for adults, $5 for children for museum admission; $51–$95 for half-day and full-day train excursions; scenic jeep excursions; 9 a.m. to 4:15 p.m. Tue through Sat; 45 Mitchell Street, Bryson City; 1-800-872-4681.

SWAIN COUNTY HERITAGE MUSEUM: displays the early history of the area, children's area, fishing pond, free, 9 a.m. to 6 p.m. daily, 210 Main Street, Bryson City, 1-800-867-9246.

THE STORYTELLING CENTER OF SOUTHERN APPALACHIA: preserves and promotes the musical and oral heritage of the Southern Highlands, 255 Everett Street, Bryson City, 828-488-5705.

Shops and Galleries in Downtown Bryson City

BUTTERMILK FARMS ANTIQUE MARKET: antique and vintage items; 10 a.m. to 6 p.m. Mon, Tue, and Thu through Sat, noon to 6 p.m. Wed and Sun; 147A Main Street; 828-736-5529.

CHARLES HEATH STUDIO GALLERY: 10 a.m. to 5 p.m. Mon through Thu, 10 a.m. to 7 p.m. Fri and Sat, 175 Everett Street, 828-538-2054, www.charlesheath.com.

CHARLESTON STATION: baskets, pottery, jewelry, antiques, 10 a.m. to 5 p.m. Mon through Sat during season, 105 Main Street, 828-488-2534.

CALBY'S ANTIQUES & GIFTS: 10 a.m. to 5:30 p.m. Mon through Sat during season, days and hours vary off season, 108 Everett Street, 828-538-4830.

THE COTTAGE CRAFTSMAN: wine shop, gallery, and market; 10 a.m. to 5:30 p.m. Mon through Sat; 15 Everett Street, Bryson City; 828-488-6207; www.thecottagecraftsman.com.

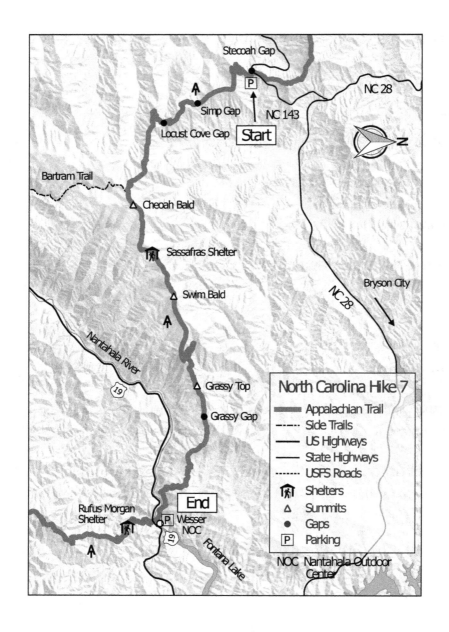

Stecoah Gap

P

NC 28

NC 143

Simp Gap

Locust Cove Gap

Start

N

Bartram Trail

Cheoah Bald

Sassafras Shelter

Bryson City

NC 28

Swim Bald

Nantahala River

Grassy Top

19

Grassy Gap

North Carolina Hike 7

▬▬▬	Appalachian Trail
·–·–·	Side Trails
———	US Highways
———	State Highways
··········	USFS Roads
🏠	Shelters
△	Summits
●	Gaps
P	Parking

Rufus Morgan
Shelter

End

P Wesser
NOC

19

Fontana Lake

NOC Nantahala Outdoor
Center

Stecoah Gap to the Nantahala River,
13.4 miles, Challenging

NC HIKE 7

HIGHLIGHTS: The views of never-ending, tree-covered mountain ranges are unbelievable. You can see the Nantahala Mountains, Snowbird Mountains, Cheoah Mountains, and the Smoky Mountains from Cheoah Bald. The brilliant colors of the blooming mountain laurel and flame azalea scrubs burst forth as you walk under an umbrella of hardwood and evergreen trees.

Mountain Laurel, May 2009

DISTANCE: 13.4 miles.
HIKE TIME: 9 to 10 hours.

LEVEL OF EFFORT: Challenging because of the big changes in elevation and the length of the hike.

Flame Azalea, May 2009

The Nantahala and Smoky Mountains from Cheoah Bald, May 2009

RECOMMENDED DIRECTION: North to south, from Stecoah Gap to the Nantahala River.

DOWNHILL: 7.9 miles with an elevation loss of 4,660 feet. **UPHILL:** 5.5 miles with an elevation gain of 3,250 feet.

ALONG THE TRAIL: From Stecoah Gap, the well-trodden earthen path winds up, up, and up the mountain, passing large rhododendron scrubs before it plateaus on Cheoah Bald. The path then turns, and goes down and up, crossing gaps and climbing over balds and knobs with views of the mountains and the Nantahala River Gorge. Finally, the path narrows and drops steeply down the mountainside.

SHELTERS: The Nantahala-designed Sassafras Gap Shelter is one mile south of Cheoah Bald. It has two sleeping shelves, and there is a privy and spring water nearby.

Follow the White Blazes

MILE 0.0: Stecoah Gap, 3,135 feet, NC 143 (Sweet Water Creek Road), water.

MILE 2.0: Simp Gap, 3,560 feet.

MILE 3.1: Locust Cove Gap, 3,670 feet, water.

MILE 5.1: Bartram Trail, 4,830 feet. From here, the Bartram Trail goes east to South Carolina.

MILE 5.5: Cheoah Bald, 5,060 feet.

MILE 6.7: Sassafras Gap Shelter, water.

MILE 7.5: Swim Bald, 4,685 feet.

MILE 8.6: The Jump-up, 3,980 feet, views. This spot got the name jump-up because of the steep hand-over-hand climb to that high point, but now there are switchbacks around the steep part.

MILE 10.5: Grassy Gap, 3,050 feet.

MILE 11.1: Tyre Knob, 2,980 feet.

MILE 12.0: Wright Gap, 2,410 feet.

MILE 13.4: The Nantahala River, 1,730 feet, US 19/74, the Nantahala Outdoor Center, outfitter, restaurants, lodging.

Peaks and Valleys

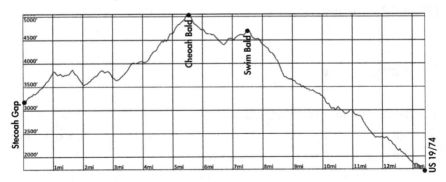

Alternate Hikes

Because this is a long and challenging hike, it has been divided into two hikes, both of which use the Bartram Trail to access the A.T. from USFS 259. Be aware that USFS 259 is not always open to the public. The road is gated in the winter. Call Nantahala National Forest, Cheoah Ranger District, at 828-479-6431 to see if USFS 259 will be open to the public when you plan to hike.

NC HIKE 7.1:
Bartram Trail to the Nantahala River, 8.8 miles, Challenging
DISTANCE: 8.3 miles on the A.T., plus 0.5 miles on the Bartram Trail.
HIKE TIME: 5 to 6 hours.
LEVEL OF EFFORT: Challenging to moderate.
RECOMMENDED DIRECTION: North to south, from Bartram Trail to the Nantahala River.

NC HIKE 7.2:
Bartram Trail to Stecoah Gap, 5.6 miles, Moderate
DISTANCE: 5.1 miles on the A.T., plus 0.5 miles on the Bartram Trail.
HIKE TIME: 3 to 4 hours.
LEVEL OF EFFORT: Moderate.
RECOMMENDED DIRECTION: South to north, from Bartram Trail to Stecoah Gap.

My Hiking Journal

MAY 2009: Knowing that this will be a long and challenging hike, we hit the trail early on this beautiful, cool, and windy day. From Stecoah Gap, we climb up and down hills and around knobs.

When we reach Cheoah Bald about noon, we are exhausted. I say, "Let's take a long lunch break here."

Jim takes pictures and explores the bald, but I sit down on the log near the fire pit and unwrap my lunch. Another hiker is also having lunch here.

"Where are you going?" I ask.

"I'm section hiking to Fontana Dam," he replies. "I'm waiting for my partner. It was a steep climb up from the Nantahala River."

After resting and enjoying the views, we begin the eight-mile hike down the ridge, passing delicate pink mountain laurel and orange flame azalea.

"These are beautiful," I say.

In late afternoon, as we descend the narrow path to the river, we meet backpacker after backpacker hiking at a rapid pace up the steep trail.

"Where are you going?" Jim asks each of them.

Many of them say, "Sassafras Gap Shelter." They are all smiles and tell us they are just out for the weekend and began their hike at the Nantahala River about 30 minutes ago.

I'm glad I'm not just beginning my hike at five o'clock, I think, and going uphill seven miles to the shelter.

About six o'clock, we reach our car at the Nantahala River Gorge. We put our packs in the car and rush to River End's Restaurant, hoping to make it before it closes.

When the hostess comes to seat us, Jim asks, "When do you close?"

"Seven o'clock," she replies.

I sigh with relief as she seats us on the veranda. We relax with glasses of pinot noir and watch the river flowing swiftly around the rocks.

"Let's celebrate our long hike with a steak dinner," I suggest.

"That sounds great," Jim replies.

After our delicious meal, Jim drives us up winding North Carolina 28 to the Hike Inn. We mark the end of this three-day hiking trip with a champagne toast and fall into bed about eight thirty. The next day we explore the museums and shops of the sleepy little town of Robbinsville before we head home.

Carol's Reminders

- Get an early start for a long slackpacking hike.
- Celebrate your successes.

Nearest Towns

Fontana Dam is thirteen miles north of Stecoah Gap, the northern trailhead. Robbinsville is eight miles west of Stecoah Gap. Wesser is at the Nantahala River, the southern trailhead and about sixteen miles from Stecoah Gap, the northern trailhead.

Directions to the Trailheads

SOUTHERN TRAILHEAD AT THE NANTAHALA RIVER: GPS coordinates 35.198613, -83.3500. From the town of Fontana Dam, drive south on NC 28 twenty-one miles to US 19/74. Turn right and drive four miles to the Nantahala Outdoor Center (NOC) hiker parking area on the right by the railroad tracks. The total trip is twenty-five miles; allow thirty minutes.

MIDDLE TRAILHEAD AT BARTRAM TRAIL AND USFS 259 FOR ALTERNATE HIKES: From the town of Fontana Dam, drive ten miles south on NC 28. Turn right on NC 143 and drive nine miles. Turn left on US 129 and drive about ten miles to Ledbetter Road (SR 1200). Turn left and drive about one mile to Nolton Ridge Road (USFS 259). Turn left and drive about five miles up the gravel USFS 259. Bartram Trail, marked with yellow rectangular blazes, crosses the road here. Follow the Bartram Trail one half mile to the A.T. (When you are planning your hiking trip, you will need to call Nantahala National Forest, Cheoah Ranger District, 828-479-6431 to see if USFS 259 is open to Bartram Trail. Ask about road conditions and more detailed directions.) The total trip is about thirty-five miles; allow one hour.

NORTHERN TRAILHEAD AT STECOAH GAP: GPS coordinates 35.35838, -83.717484. From the town of Fontana Dam, drive eleven miles on NC 28 South. Turn right on Sweetwater Road (NC 143) and drive two miles. Parking is on the left. The total trip is thirteen miles; allow fifteen minutes.

If you plan to shuttle using two cars, leave one car at the Nantahala Outdoor Center hiker parking area in Wesser for the end of the hike. Drive east on US 19/74 four miles to NC 28. Turn left on NC 28 and drive twelve miles to Sweetwater Road (NC 143). Turn left on NC 143 and drive two miles to Stecoah Gap. Parking is available on the south side of the gap. The total trip is eighteen miles; allow twenty minutes.

ALTERNATIVE TRANSPORTATION: Ask the shuttle service to meet you in the hiker parking lot at NOC, where you will leave your car for the end of the hike. Ask the driver to take you to Stecoah Gap. See the list of shuttle-service providers in the **Hiker Essentials** section for Bryson City, Robbinsville, and Fontana Village.

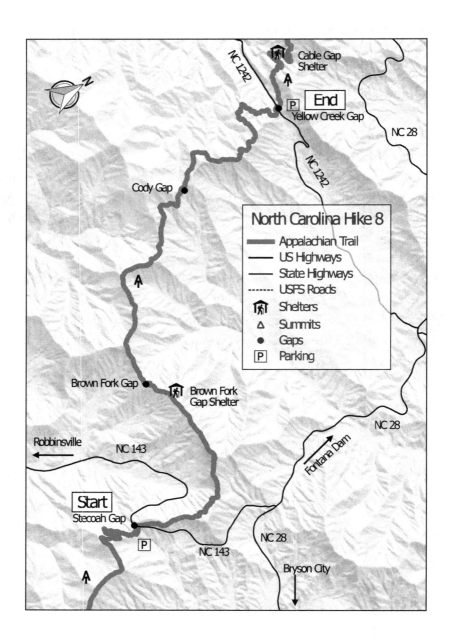

North Carolina Hike 8

Legend:
- Appalachian Trail
- US Highways
- State Highways
- USFS Roads
- Shelters
- Summits
- Gaps
- P Parking

Cable Gap Shelter

End
Yellow Creek Gap

NC 1242

NC 28

Cody Gap

Brown Fork Gap

Brown Fork Gap Shelter

Robbinsville

NC 143

Fontana Dam

NC 28

Start
Stecoah Gap

P

NC 143

NC 28

Bryson City

Stecoah Gap to Yellow Creek Gap,
7.6 miles, Moderate

HIGHLIGHTS: This hike winds through the solitude and beauty of the Nantahala National Forest in the Cheoah Mountains. Congress protected this remote forest from clear-cutting in 1920.

DISTANCE: 7.6 miles.   **HIKE TIME:** 5 to 6 hours.   **LEVEL OF EFFORT:** Moderate.

RECOMMENDED DIRECTION: South to north, Stecoah Gap to Yellow Creek Gap.

DOWNHILL: 4.0 miles with an elevation loss of 2,205 feet. **UPHILL:** 3.6 miles with an elevation gain of 2,015 feet.

ALONG THE TRAIL: From Stecoah Gap, the A.T. rises gently on an earthen path to Sweetwater Gap, then you will make a steep climb past the rock outcroppings to the ridge. Before reaching the ridge, there is a side trail to the cliffs with splendid views of the Snowbird Mountains to the west. This would be a great place to rest and have lunch.

On the open ridges, there are mountain laurel and blueberry bushes. From the ridges, the trail descends around knobs to Brown Fork Gap, Hogback Gap, Cody Gap, and finally to Yellow Creek Gap.

SHELTER: Brown Fork Gap Shelter is about two hundred feet down the blue-blazed side trail at Brown Fork Gap. The Smoky Mountains Hiking Club and the US Forest Service built this log shelter in 1994 from tulip-poplar and locust trees that had been blown down during storms. A privy and spring are located nearby.

A tree knotted with burls in the Nantahala National Forest, May 2009

Follow the White Blazes

MILE 0.0: Stecoah Gap, 3,135 feet, water.

MILE 1.0: Sweetwater Gap, 3,280 feet.

MILE 2.7: Brown Fork Gap Shelter, water.

MILE 4.4: Hogback Gap, 3,480 feet.

MILE 5.2: Cody Gap, 3,600 feet, water.

MILE 7.2: Yellow Creek Gap, 3,560 feet, stream.

MILE 7.6: Yellow Creek Mountain Road (NC 1242), 2,940 feet.

Peaks and Valleys

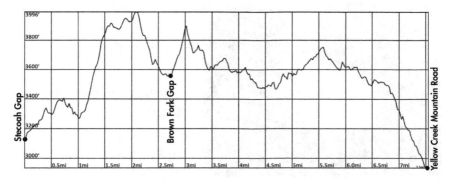

My Hiking Journal

MAY 2009: This is the second day of our three-day hiking trip.

On this sunny, breezy day, we meet many hikers. As we cross the road to go up the earthen path to begin our hike, we meet a backpacker with a black bowler hat. He tells us his trail name is "English Man."

"Where are you going?" Jim asks.

"Fontana Dam. I'm hiking the North Carolina section this year."

As we walk uphill, we listen to the breeze blowing through the trees and the birds calling to each other. When we get to the ridgeline, we rest and have lunch looking out over the mountains.

We meet a backpacker in her twenties with a rag doll hanging from her pack. When I ask about the rag doll, she tells us hikers gave her the trail name, "Dangling Legs," because the doll dangles off her pack.

Jim asks, "Where are you going?"

She smiles and answers, "Maine."

We hike up and down over the knobs as if we are rolling over waves in the sea.

Jim stops to takes pictures of the mushrooms and wildflowers hidden on the forest floor.

Purple fernleaf phacelia, May 2009

White-capped mushrooms, May 2009

We come upon two hikers resting in their hammocks on the side of the trail. The woman is writing in a journal. The man seems to be snacking.

Seeing their used bowls and stoves out, I ask, "Did you cook lunch?"

"Oh, yes," says the woman. "We fix our main meal at noon and then hike later in the day. We are going to the Fontana 'Hilton' Shelter tonight."

Before we know it, we are at Yellow Creek Gap, where we left the car. When we get back to the Hike Inn about four thirty, we shower and go to the Mexican restaurant in Robbinsville for dinner. Our host suggested this restaurant when we checked in yesterday.

On the way back, we stop by the store for some supplies and meet a thru-hiker from Florida. He tells us he is a jazz drummer and a roofer and that his trail name is "Drums."

Jim asks, "Where are you staying tonight?"

Drums replies, "At the Fontana 'Hilton.' I got off the trail so I could go to the store today. I'm going to the post office tomorrow in Fontana Dam to pick up my food drop. I was planning to hitch a ride to the shelter."

Some hikers pack dried food for meals and snacks in boxes, then ask friends or family members to ship the boxes to post offices along the A.T. Shipments are coordinated with the hikers' scheduled arrival times along the trail.

Jim asks, "Do you want a ride?"

"I would love a ride," Drums replies.

As we turn onto Fontana Dam Road, going toward the shelter, we see two older hikers who I think we passed earlier on the trail. I notice one is limping.

Jim stops the car and asks, "Would you like a ride?"

"Yes!" one of them replies.

After they get into the car, I ask, "Is your foot hurt?"

"Yes. I have blisters, and my feet are swollen. I could hardly get my boots on this morning. I may have to get off the trail."

We drop them at the sidewalk leading to the shelter, and we wish them well.

The Fontana "Hilton" Shelter was built in 1982 and is maintained by the TVA. It is a large shelter with two sleeping shelves on each side and an open breezeway in the middle. The shelter is in a picnic area overlooking Fontana Lake. You will find running water and flush toilets in a restroom building just off the sidewalk. There are showers at the Fontana Dam Visitors Center about a quarter of a mile down the road.

Carol's Reminders

- Be a Trail Angel.
- Take time to hear the stories of thru-hikers.

Nearest Towns

Fontana Dam is eleven miles from Yellow Creek Gap, the northern trailhead. Robbinsville is eight miles west of Stecoah Gap, the southern trailhead.

Directions to the Trailheads

SOUTHERN TRAILHEAD AT STECOAH GAP: GPS coordinates 35.35836, -83.71784. From the town of Fontana Dam, drive eleven miles on NC 28 South. Turn right on Sweetwater Road (NC 143) and drive two miles; parking is on left. The total trip is thirteen miles; allow fifteen minutes.

NORTHERN TRAILHEAD AT YELLOW CREEK GAP: GPS coordinates 35.41028, -83.76560. From Fontana Dam, drive eight miles on NC 28 South. Turn right on Tuskegee Road (NC 1242) and drive three miles to Yellow Creek Gap. There is a gravel parking lot on the left. The total trip is eleven miles; allow fifteen minutes.

If you plan to shuttle using two cars, leave one car at Yellow Creek Gap for the end of the hike. Drive the other car to Stecoah Gap for the beginning of the hike using the directions above.

ALTERNATIVE TRANSPORTATION: Arrange for a shuttle driver to meet you at Yellow Creek Gap, where you will leave your car for the end of the hike, and drive you to Stecoah Gap. See the list of shuttle-service providers in the **Hiker Essentials** sections for Wesser, Bryson City, Robbinsville, and Fontana Dam.

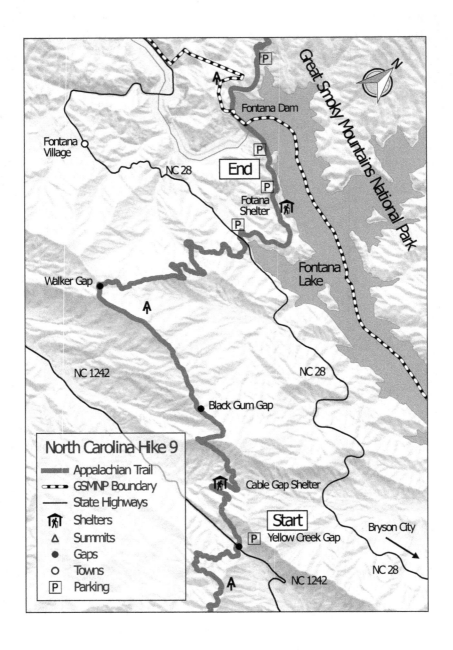

North Carolina Hike 9

Legend:
- Appalachian Trail
- GSMNP Boundary
- State Highways
- Shelters
- Summits
- Gaps
- Towns
- P Parking

Map labels:

Great Smoky Mountains National Park

P
Fontana Dam
Fontana Village
NC 28
P
End
P
Fotana Shelter
P
Walker Gap
Fontana Lake
NC 1242
NC 28
Black Gum Gap
Cable Gap Shelter
Start
P Yellow Creek Gap
Bryson City
NC 28
NC 1242

Yellow Creek Gap to Fontana Dam,
7.9 miles, Moderate

NC
HIKE
9

HIGHLIGHTS: Explore the hidden treasures you will find at the end of the hike, check out the Fontana "Hilton" Shelter, take in the views of Fontana Lake, and be sure to visit the Fontana Dam Visitors Center. Enjoy the natural beauty of the Nantahala National Forest, the creeks, ferns, and huge rock formations.

DISTANCE: 7.9 miles.   **HIKE TIME:** 5 to 6 hours.   **LEVEL OF EFFORT:** Moderate.

RECOMMENDED DIRECTION: South to north, from Yellow Creek Gap to Little Tennessee River at the southern boundary of the Great Smoky Mountains National Park.

DOWNHILL: 5.8 miles with an elevation loss of 3,010 feet. **UPHILL:** 2.1 miles with an elevation gain of 1,790 feet.

ALONG THE TRAIL: From Yellow Creek Gap, the earthen path rambles up and down through the diverse environs of the Yellow Creek Mountains. The trail descends into the moist creek valley, where you will find ferns, wildflowers, and marsh grasses, before crossing to the drier south-facing slope, where pink mountain laurels bloom. Finally, the trail descends down a steep, rocky ridge to Fontana Dam. Near the ridge tops, you will have views of Fontana Dam and the Smoky Mountains.

SHELTERS: There are two shelters, Cable Gap and Fontana Dam. The log-style Cable Gap Shelter was built in 1939 by the Civilian Conservation Corps and is less than a mile north of Yellow Creek Gap. A spring and privy are nearby. The Fontana Dam Shelter, known as the Fontana "Hilton," is just south of the trail and less than half a mile from the Fontana Dam Visitors Center. A restroom with running water and flush toilets is nearby, and showers are available in the visitors' center.

As the story goes, hikers gave the name Fontana "Hilton" to the shelter because of the unbelievable accommodations: four sleeping shelves; running water, flush toilets and showers nearby; and the magnificent view of Fontana Lake. You will not find another shelter like this anywhere along the 2,190 miles of the Appalachian Trail

Fontana "Hilton" Shelter on Fontana Lake, July 2010

Fontana Lake, May 2009

Fontana Dam Museum, May 2009

Follow the White Blazes

MILE 0.0: Yellow Creek Gap and NC 1242, 2,940 feet.

MILE 0.8: Cable Gap Shelter, water, privy.

MILE 2.2: Black Gum Gap, 3,420 feet.

MILE 3.6: Walker Gap and Yellow Creek Trail, 3,430 feet.

MILE 6.0: NC 28, 1,780 feet, Fontana Dam Marina.

MILE 7.1: Fontana Dam Shelter, water and flush toilets nearby.

MILE 7.5: Fontana Dam Visitors Center, 1,720 feet, water, showers, restrooms, gift shop, museum, tours of the dam. Fontana Dam was built in the 1940s by the Tennessee Valley Authority (TVA) because of the high demand for electricity during the war. It is the tallest dam east of the Rocky Mountains.

MILE 7.9: Southern boundary of the Great Smoky Mountains National Park, Little Tennessee River, Fontana Dam, 1,710 feet.

Peaks and Valleys

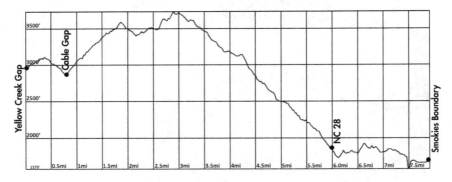

My Hiking Journal

MAY 2009: This is the first day of our three-day slackpacking trip. Jim and I drive up from Atlanta this morning. I worry it might storm like it did in Atlanta last night.

But It is a clear, sunny afternoon when we begin the hike about two o'clock.

We stop and inspect Cable Gap Shelter and look at the creative notes and pictures in the hiker register.

Hiker register entry at Cable Gap Shelter, May 2009

Spider web, May 2009

We take our time hiking up and down the slopes to see what we can see. Jim says, "This is an amazing spider web."

When we cross NC 28 and pass the Fontana Dam Marina, I say, "It should be all downhill from here."

As we go up a final hill before descending to the road again, Jim says, "I though you said it was all downhill. We should have just walked along the road to the Fontana Dam Visitors Center."

"Oh, well," I say, "The elevation profile does not show all the ups and downs."

As we near the visitors center about 7 o'clock, Jim says, "It is still open."

We catch up with the last docent tour and hear the story about the building of the dam and see pictures and diagrams depicting each stage of the construction. It is surprising that they could build this dam in just thirty-six months.

Tired, sweaty, and hungry, we jump into the car and drive two miles to Fontana Village Lodge, hoping the Montview Restaurant is still open. When we arrive at eight, Jim asks the desk clerk if the restaurant is still taking customers.

She replies, "If they are serving, they might seat you."

We hurry back to the dining room and learn that we're in luck. With a sigh of relief, we place our order with the hostess so we will get the order in before the kitchen closes. Jim goes to the bar and brings us glasses of pinot noir.

"What a fantastic way to end our hike," I say.

Carol's Reminders

- **Enjoy each hike one day at a time, stopping to savor the mystique of the A.T. Don't hurry.**
- **Enjoy the history of the small towns you are passing through.**

Nearest Town

The town of Fontana Dam is eleven miles north of Yellow Creek Gap, the southern trailhead and one mile from the southern boundary of the Great Smoky Mountains National Park, the northern trailhead.

Directions to the Trailheads

SOUTHERN TRAILHEAD AT YELLOW CREEK GAP: GPS Coordinates 35.41028, -83.76560. From the town of Fontana Dam, drive eight miles on NC 28 South. Turn right on Upper Tuskegee Road (NC 1242), drive three miles to

Yellow Creek Gap. There is a gravel parking lot on the left. The total trip is eleven miles; allow fifteen minutes.

NORTHERN TRAILHEAD AT THE SOUTHERN BOUNDARY OF THE GREAT SMOKY MOUNTAINS NATIONAL PARK: GPS coordinates 35.4604, -83.81104. From the town of Fontana Dam, drive one mile on NC 28 to Fontana Road (NC 1245). Turn left and drive for one mile, passing the Fontana Visitors Center on the left and crossing the dam. Turn right on the dirt road into trailhead parking.

If you plan to shuttle using two cars, leave a car at the Fontana Visitors Center or trailhead parking for the end of the hike. Drive the other car to Yellow Creek Gap. From the visitors' center, drive west on Fontana Road to NC 28. Turn left on NC 28 and drive south seven miles to Upper Tuskegee Road (NC 1242). Turn right and drive three miles to Yellow Creek Gap. There is a gravel parking lot on the south side of the gap.

ALTERNATIVE TRANSPORTATION: Ask a shuttle driver to meet you at the Fontana Visitors Center and drive you to Yellow Creek Gap. See the list of shuttle-service providers in the **Hiker Essentials** section for Wesser, Bryson City, Robbinsville and Fontana Dam.

Fine Wine and Accommodations
Fontana Dam and
Robbinsville

THE TOWN OF FONTANA DAM was incorporated in 2011, but the unincorporated village of Fontana Dam came into being in 1941 to house workers for the building of Fontana Dam. The dam was built to meet the new demands for electrical power that came with World War II.

The town is the home of the tallest dam east of the Rockies. It is also the site of Fontana Lake, the Little Tennessee River, and Fontana Village Resort. The town of Fontana Dam became an Appalachian Trail Community in 2015. The A.T. goes across the top of the dam.

ROBBINSVILLE is the sleepy county seat of remote Graham County in western North Carolina. The town has lodging, restaurants, grocery stores, shops, health-care facilities, the Junaluska Museum, and Lake Santeetlah. Stecoah Valley Cultural Arts Center is in nearby Stecoah Township. Robbinsville is eight miles west of Stecoah Gap.

Lodging and Restaurants within Five Miles of the Appalachian Trail

Lodging

THE CABIN IN THE WOODS: ½ $, hiker rate for mini cabin; $ with two-night minimum for 1BR/1.5BA cabin with Jacuzzi and for efficiency cabins; all cabins fully furnished with linens, toiletries, coffee and tea; hosts provide home-cooked breakfast for $6, dinner $8; laundry $3.50 per load; shuttle and slackpacking services; 301 Stecoah Heights Road, Robbinsville, about two miles from Stecoah Gap; 828-735-1930, www. thecabininthewoods.com.

APPALACHIAN INN B&B: $$ with full country breakfast; home-cooked lunch and dinner available for additional fee; charming mountain retreat with five luxury rooms, some with Jacuzzis; free Wi-Fi; non-smoking; 300 Knoll Top, Robbinsville, on the knoll overlooking Stecoah Gap and less than a mile from the A.T.; 828-735-1792 or 828-479-8450; www. appalachianinn.com.

CREEKSIDE PARADISE B&B: $ (hiker rate) with continental breakfast, lunch and dinner available for additional fee, three luxury rooms, Wi-Fi available, shuttle service, pet friendly, laundry and kitchen available for guest use, 259 Upper Cove Road, Robbinsville, two miles from Yellow Creek Gap, 828-346-1076, postandwilson@gmail.com

    A FRIEND WEIGHS IN: Fran says, "Jeff and Cynthia are wonderful hosts as well as great cooks. When we finished our hike from Clingmans Dome to Fontana Dam and spent the night at the B&B, they prepared a prime rib dinner with wine."

THE HIKE INN: $, hikers only, four old-style motel rooms with private baths, laundry, reservations required. Nancy, the owner, provides shuttle service, experience, enthusiasm, and encouragement to make your hike a success-ful one. She caters to thru-hikers and gives them rides to Robbinsville for dinner and to the post office in Fontana Dam. 3204 Fontana Road (NC 28), Fontana Dam, three to five miles from Stecoah Gap, Yellow Gap, and Fontana Dam, 828-479-3677, www.thehikeinn.com.

OUR EXPERIENCE: In May 2009, we stay at the Hike Inn when we slack-pack North Carolina Hikes 7, 8, and 9. The accommodations are basic but convenient. We enjoy talking with the owners, Nancy and Jeff, as they shuttle us. (Jeff died since we were there.)

They tell us about nearby restaurants, including the Mexican restau-rant in Robbinsville and Stecoah Diner, which is just down the road. They take all of their thru-hikers to the Mexican Restaurant.

On the first night, when we get back to the Hike Inn about nine thirty, Nancy says, "We've been worried about you and thought you might not have eaten. Everything around here closes early."

I reply, "We just barely made it to the restaurant at Fontana Village before it closed." It is good to be staying with people who care about us.

FONTANA VILLAGE RESORT: $$–$$$, family-focused resort with lodge rooms and cabins, two restaurants, bar, game room, swimming pools, ten-nis courts, marina, laundry facilities, sits in the Nantahala National Forest on the edge of the Great Smoky Mountains National Park and Fontana Lake, 300 Woods Road, Fontana Dam, 828-498-2211, www.fontanavillage.com.

Our experience in July 2010: After our three-day, thirty-three-mile, shelter-to-shelter A.T. backpacking trip in the Great Smoky Mountains National Park, we treat ourselves to the lodge's Sweetheart Room, which has a heart-shaped Jacuzzi. We relax in the Jacuzzi as we melt away the aches in our tired muscles. Then we reward ourselves with a gourmet dinner in the resort's Montview Restaurant. We have filet mignon with sides, champagne, wine, and a chocolate lava cake with vanilla-bean ice cream for dessert.

As we watch the sun set over the mountains, I say, "Today was a killer, going up and down those last thirteen miles. I'm glad we're finished with this part of the Smokies."

Selected Restaurants

STECOAH DINER: $, home-cooked Southern food, no beer or wine, 11 a.m. to 9 p.m. Mon through Sat, 1751 Highway 28, less than four miles east of Stecoah Gap, Robbinsville, 828-479-8430, www.facebook.com.

THE MONTVIEW RESTAURANT AT THE FONTANA VILLAGE RESORT: $$; American; 8 to 10:30 a. m., 11:30 a.m. to 2:30 p.m., and 5 p.m. to 9 p.m. daily; fine dining with a full bar, gourmet menu with local vegetables and meats, fresh baked goods and desserts; wonderful mountain views; 300 Woods Road, Fontana Dam; 828-498-2141; www.fontanavillage.com.

OUR EXPERIENCE IN MAY 2009: We have eaten here several times, but on this night we are running late for dinner because we stopped at the Fontana Dam Museum after hiking. We split an Asian-style tuna entree and a field-greens salad. We relax with glasses of pinot noir and enjoy our delicious meal. We top it off with dessert; I order crème brulee, and Jim orders ice cream with amaretto.

We talk about the Fontana Dam project and wonder how that kind of project could have been completed back in the forties. It was truly amazing.

THE WILDWOOD GRILL AT THE FONTANA VILLAGE RESORT: $, American, casual dining with beer and wine, 11 a.m. to 9 p.m. Wed through Sun seasonally, days and hours may change in summer. Dine outside and watch the sun set in the mountains. The resort sits in the Nantahala National Forest on the edge of the Great Smoky Mountains National Park and Fontana Lake. 300 Woods Road, Fontana Dam, 828-498-2211, www. fontanavillage.com.

OUR EXPERIENCE: In July 2010, we enjoy lunch on the deck under the clear blue sky. I order chicken salad, and Jim orders a chicken sandwich with fries and beer. The food is good and the atmosphere relaxing. The resort is crowded and the restaurant is humming.

Lodging and Restaurants in or West of Robbinsville

Lodging

PHILLIPS MOTEL: $ for rooms and efficiencies, $$ for cottages, family owned, microwaves, refrigerators, coffee makers. Hub's Restaurant will give guests a 10 percent discount. 291 Main Street, 828-479-3370, www.phillipsmotelonline.com.

SAN-RAN MOTEL: $, family owned, renovated rooms, microwaves, refrigerators, coffee makers; free Wi-Fi; swimming pool; 253 Rodney Orr Bypass (US 129), 828-429-3256, www.sanranmotel.com.

MICROTEL INN & SUITES BY WYNDHAM: $ with a continental breakfast, microwaves, internets, coffee & tea makers, pet friendly, 111 Rodney Orr Bypass (US 129), 888-293-6798, www.microtelinn.com.

Luxury Lodging Fifteen to Thirty Miles from the A.T. That You May Want to Enjoy after Your Hiking Trip

BLUE WATERS MOUNTAIN LODGE: $$ with breakfast, dinner for lodge guests with reservations, 292 Pine Ridge Road on pristine Lake Santeetlah, four miles north of Robbinsville , 828-475-8606, www.bluewatersmtnl.com.

SNOWBIRD MOUNTAIN LODGE: $$$, includes three gourmet meals, one of which is a packed lunch for your outdoor adventure. The main lodge has wood-paneled rooms with private baths and custom amenities. Wolfe Cottage and Chestnut Lodge have rooms with modern amenities, including hot tubs, decks, fireplaces, modern baths; tennis courts; 4633 Santeetlah Road, nine miles north of Robbinsville; 828- 479-3433; www.snowbirdlodge.com.

This secluded retreat, located on the mountaintop overlooking the mile-high Cherohala Skyway and Lake Santeetlah, is on the Register of Historic Places. The lodge was built in 1941with wood from local hardwood trees and stone from a nearby quarry. It was built by Arthur Wiley, who owned a travel agency in Chicago.

HISTORIC TAPOCO LODGE: $$-$$$, elegant rooms with Jacuzzi, beautiful views, cabins, family and pet friendly, restaurant on site, located on 120 acres in the Nantahala National Forest on the Cheoah River. The lodge was built in 1930 by the Aluminum Company of America for company functions and has been recently renovated as we go to press. Guests have many opportunities for hiking, biking, rafting, and fishing. 14981 Tapoco Road, fifteen miles north of Robbinsville, 828-498-2800, www.tapocolodge.com.

Selected Restaurants in Robbinsville

Graham County is dry and does not allow the sale of alcohol in restaurants or stores, except in restaurants and stores at selected resorts.

EL PACIFICO MEXICAN: ½ $, authentic Mexican dishes, 11 a.m. to 9 p.m. daily, 429 Rodney Orr Bypass, 828-479-8448.

OUR EXPERIENCE: In May 2009, after slackpacking this section of the A.T., we enjoy delicious chicken fajitas with fried ice cream for dessert.

FRIENDS WEIGH IN: Jeff and Nancy, owners of the Hike Inn, bring all of their thru-hikers here. Nancy says, "You will find good food served in healthy portions for hungry hikers at reasonable prices."

THE HUB OF WNC, LLC: $; American; 8 a.m. to 9 p.m. Sun through Thu; 8 a.m. to 9:30 p.m. Fri and Sat; fifties and sixties décor and music; happy, fun place to eat and shop for coffees and ice cream. Phillips Motel guests receive a 10 percent discount. 664 Rodney Orr Bypass, 828-479-0478.

LYNN'S PLACE: $, American, 11 a.m. to 9 p.m. Mon through Sat, 11 a.m. to 2:30 p.m. Sun, 237 East Main Street (across from the courthouse), 828-479-9777.

POP & NANA'S KITCHEN AND THE SCOOP: $, American home-cooked meals, 7 a.m. to 8 p.m. Mon through Thu, 7 a.m. to 9 p.m. Fri and Sat, 52 Rodney Orr Bypass, 828-479-8461.

SOUTHERN GALS COUNTRY COOKING: $, American, casual, 7 a.m. to 8:30 p.m. Mon through Sat, 400 Rodney Orr Bypass (Village Shopping Center), 828-479-9405.

TAPOCO RIVER GRILL IN THE HISTORIC TAPOCO LODGE: $–$$, American with full bar, casual, indoor and outdoor riverfront tables available on the banks of the Cheoah River, 11 a.m. to 9 p.m. Sun through Thu, 11 a.m. until closing Fri through Sun, 14981 Tapoco Road (fifteen miles north of Robbinsville), 828-498-2800, www.tapocolodge.com.

Hiker Essentials, Splurges, and Emergency Stops

Shuttle-Service Providers

The following lodging owners provide shuttle services to their guests as well as to other hikers. Lodging owners that provide shuttle services only for their guests are not listed here.

PHIL AND DONNA AT THE CABIN IN THE WOODS: 828-735-1930, www.thecabinin-thewoods.com.

JEFF AND CYNTHIA AT CREEKSIDE PARADISE B&B: 828-346-1076, postandwilson@gmail.com.

NANCY AT THE HIKE INN: 828-479-3677, hikeinn@graham.main.nc.us.

Outfitters

NANTAHALA OUTDOOR CENTER OUTFITTERS STORE: 8 a.m. to 8 p.m. daily, at the Nantahala River and US19/74 trailhead, 13077 West Highway 19, Wesser, 828-488-7230, A.T. Passport stamped here.

FONTANA VILLAGE GENERAL STORE: has a limited selection of hiking supplies. 9 a.m. to 7 p.m. Sun through Thu and 9 a.m. to 9 p.m. Fri and Sat seasonally, 300 Woods Road, Fontana Dam, 828-498-2148.

Groceries

FONTANA VILLAGE GENERAL STORE AND ICE CREAM SHOP: 9 a.m. to 7 p.m. Sun through Thu and 9 a.m. to 9 p.m. Fri and Sat seasonally, food, beer, hiking and camping supplies, unique gifts, 300 Woods Road, Fontana Dam, 828-498-2148.

INGLES MARKET: 7 a.m. to 10 p.m. daily, wide selection of groceries, deli, 2 Sweetwater Road, Robbinsville, 828-479-6748.

Wine and Beer Shops

None as the Graham County is dry.

ATMs

ATM: 457 Rodney Orr Bypass.

UNITED COMMUNITY BANK: 132 Rodney Orr Bypass.

Urgent Care and Emergency Services

TALLULAH HEALTH CENTER: primary-care services by appointment 7 a.m. to 6 p.m. Mon through Fri, walk-in clinic open noon to 4 p.m. Mon through Fri, 409 Tallulah Road, Robbinsville, 828-479-6434.

The nearest full service **Urgent Care Center and Emergency Services** are located in Bryson City.

SMOKY MOUNTAIN URGENT CARE AND FAMILY MEDICINE CENTER: 9 a.m. to 7 p.m. Mon through Fri, 9 a.m. to 5 p.m. Sat and Sun, 80 Veterans Boulevard, 828-538-4546.

SWAIN COUNTY HOSPITAL AND MEDICAL CENTER, EMERGENCY SERVICES: 24/7, 45 Plateau Street, 828-488-2155.

Fun Places to Visit

FONTANA DAM VISITORS CENTER AND OBSERVATORY: free, includes museum and self-guided tours of the power house, 9 a.m. to 6 or 7 p.m. daily Apr through Oct. The exhibit portrays the construction of the Fontana Dam on the Little Tennessee River in thirty-six months from 1942 to 1945 with workers toiling around the clock. The dam was built shortly after the bombing of Pearl Harbor to provide hydroelectric power to an aluminum plant in Alcoa, Tennessee, and to the atomic-bomb research facility in Oakridge, Tennessee. 71 Fontana Dam Road, Fontana Dam, 828-498-2234, A.T. Passport stamped here.

OUR EXPERIENCE, MAY 2009: Jim and I just happen to find this exhibit as we finish North Carolina Hike 9. It is incredible. It depicts the unbelievable accomplishments of the TVA in managing the thousands of people, equipment, supplies, housing, and food needed at this remote, sparsely populated western North Carolina site. Workers built the tallest dam east of the Rockies in thirty-six months. The volunteer docents are very knowledgeable and share stories with us.

JUNALUSKA MEMORIAL AND MUSEUM AND MEDICINE PLANT TRAIL: interpretive site along the Trail of Tears; memorial to Junaluska, the honored leader and distinguished Cherokee warrior; Cherokee museum; trail of medicinal plants used by the Cherokee; built at burial site of Cherokee warriors; 8 a.m. to 4:00 p.m. Mon through Sat; 1 Junaluska Memorial Drive, Robbinsville.

OUR EXPERIENCE: Jim and I find this museum when we are exploring Robbinsville after we complete this section of the A.T. The exhibits, with pictures of Cherokees from the 1800s, make me feel as if I can see the Cherokee people who lived in this valley and feel their sadness as they traveled the Trail of Tears to Oklahoma.

As a nurse, I find the Medicine Plant Trail to be an interesting way to learn about the plants used by the Cherokee to treat common illnesses. This trail is a path through a garden of medicinal plants with placards identifying the plants and describing what they were used for.

STECOAH VALLEY CULTURAL ARTS CENTER: 10 a.m. to 5 p.m. Mon through Sat; located in an old school built of native rock; includes the Stecoah Artisans Gallery and music on the Grand Olde Stage; hosts the Bluegrass Festival in May, the Harvest Festival in October, and An Appalachian Evening summer concert series each Saturday from the end of June until early September; 121 School House Road, Robbinsville; 828-479-3364, www.stecoahvalleycenter.com.

WORLD METHODIST MUSEUM AND SOUTHEAST JURISDICTION HERITAGE CENTER AND MUSEUM: free, largest collection of artifacts commemorating the earliest years of the Wesleyan movement in England and the United States. This building was a gift from the American Methodists to the World Council of Methodists. 9 a.m. 4 p.m. Tue through Sat, 575 North Lakeshore Drive, Junaluska, 828-456-7242.

YELLOW BRANCH POTTERY AND CHEESE: Yellow Branch Pottery is a working pottery studio with artisans producing functional stoneware such as tableware, ovenware, planters, lamps, sculpture, and ornaments. The Yellow Branch Farm produces Yellow Branch Farmstead cheeses from the milk of the farm's own herd in an herbicide-and-pesticide-free environment. The cheese has a mild flavor and goes well with many foods. Samplings are available. Cheese is sold in pottery containers. 11 a.m. to 5 p.m. Tue through Sat Apr through Nov, 1073 Old Yellow Branch Road, Robbinsville. Yellow Branch Pottery is down the hill from Yellow Branch Farm. 828-479-6710.

THE TAIL OF THE DRAGON AT DEALS GAP, THE CHEROHALA SKYWAY, AND MOONSHINER 28 in Graham County are three of the best motorcycle and sports car roads in America.

LAKE SANTEETLAH, CHEOAH RIVER, FONTANA LAKE, and area mountain streams are great places for boating, white water rafting, and fishing in pristine waters.

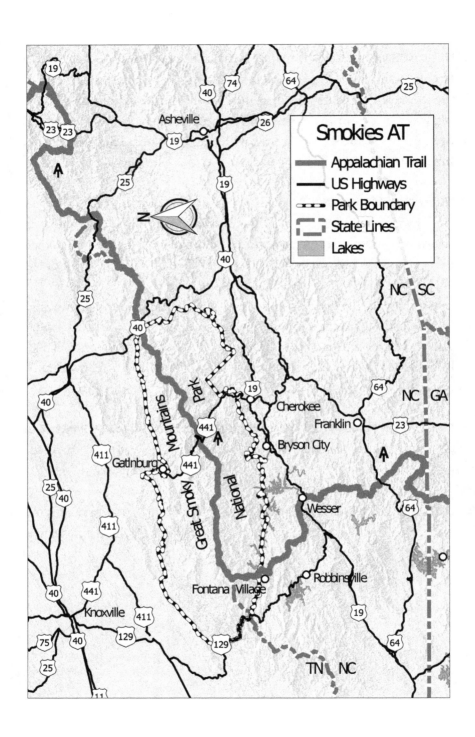

The Appalachian Trail through the Great Smoky Mountains National Park

The Appalachian Trail through the Great Smoky Mountains National Park (the Smokies) follows the ridgeline between North Carolina and Tennessee for seventy-two miles, from Fontana Dam to Davenport Gap. Only one road, US 441, crosses the A.T. This makes it challenging for slackpackers who want to day hike downhill to fine wine and accommodations each day. The one exception is an eight-mile section from Clingmans Dome to Newfound Gap. **Smokies Hike 1: Clingmans Dome to Newfound Gap** can be easily done as a day hike because Newfound Gap is on US 441 and there is an access road from US 441 to Clingmans Dome.

The other hikes in the Smokies described in this guidebook are three-to-four-day backpacking adventures. I have included them for those day hikers who want to complete the Appalachian Trail in the Smokies. Rather than day hiking, it is easier to do the southern section of the A.T., from Clingmans Dome to Fontana Dam, and the northern section, from Newfound Gap to Davenport Gap, as backpacking adventures, staying in shelters each night.

These sections could be completed with day hikes, but these day hikes would be long and challenging because you have to hike five miles or more on other trails to access or exit the A.T. Elizabeth Etnier, in her book ***Day Hiker's Guide To All The Trails In The Smoky Mountains,*** describes these day hikes on the A.T. There are three eighteen-to-twenty-mile day hikes for the thirty-three-mile section of the A.T. from Clingmans Dome to Fontana Dam. There are two sixteen-to-twenty-five-mile day hikes for the thirty-one-mile section of the A.T. from Newfound Gap to Davenport Gap.

The A.T. through the Smokies includes the highest point on the entire Appalachian Trail, Clingmans Dome at 6,643 feet, and the longest span of ridge trail above five thousand feet, the thirty-five- mile span from just north of Buckeye Gap to south of Camel Gap. You have

The Smokies, July 2010

spectacular views from the Clingmans Dome observation tower, the Mount Shuckstack Fire Lookout Tower, the Mount Cammerer Fire Lookout Tower, and rocky ridges along the trail. In the winter when the trees are bare, you can see from ridge top to ridge top.

You will see a vast array of plants and animals because the Smokies, with its copious rainfall, vast elevation changes, and old-growth forests, is one of the most biologically diverse habitats in North America. Here, you can find more than fifteen hundred species of flowering plants, more than a hundred species of native trees, over a hundred native shrub species, more than two hundred species of birds, more than sixty species of native fish, over sixty species of mammals, more than eighty types of reptiles and amphibians, and over two thousand different fungi.

You may see black bears, wild hogs, and elk. In 2001, elk were reintroduced to the park and are now thriving. All wild animals are dangerous. Do not approach them. Only look at them from afar. You should avoid them, and most of the time they will avoid you.

You should also be aware that, because of the copious rainfall and vast elevation changes, you will experience extreme temperature variations, brisk wind speeds, and more thunderstorm activity, especially at five thousand feet and above. If there is no rain or snow, the temperature will drop three to five degrees Fahrenheit for each thousand feet of elevation gain; for example, it may be fifty degrees at Fontana Dam and only twenty-five to thirty-five degrees at Clingmans Dome.

As this is the most visited national park, you can expect to meet fellow hikers along the way. The A.T. is marked with blazes that are easy to follow, and it is well maintained by the Smoky Mountains Hiking Club and the National Park Service. Overnight stays are limited to the shelters and designated campsites, where spots must be reserved in advance. No dogs except service dogs are permitted on the A.T. in the park. During the peak thru-hiking season (April–June), the National Park Service hires and trains "ridgerunners" to help hikers and protect the trail. These seasonal employees hike and camp along high-use sections of the A.T.

The Great Smoky Mountains National Park is a national treasure, made possible by the cooperative efforts of volunteers; private companies; and local, state, and federal governments.

President Calvin Coolidge authorized the creation of the Great Smoky Mountains National Park in 1926. His one stipulation was that park commissions in North Carolina and Tennessee purchase more than four hundred acres for the park from private citizens and private companies and then deed them to the federal government.

The Laura Spelman Rockefeller Memorial Fund, provided a $5 million dollar matching grant for land acquisition. Tennessee and North Carolina legislatures, private groups and individuals including school children donated the match for this grant. In 1940, President Franklin D. Roosevelt dedicated the park. He spoke from the Rockefeller Memorial at Newfound Gap. The United Nations Educational, Scientific, and Cultural Organization certified the Great Smoky Mountains National Park as a World Heritage Site in 1983.

Today we continue to enjoy the beauty of the Great Smoky Mountains National Park. More than eleven million people visited the park in 2016 and 2017. Take the opportunity to hike in this pristine, biologically diverse environment and meet those who work to protect and preserve it for future generations.

Smokies Hike 1, the only day hike in the Smokies in this guide, will give you a taste of the A.T. in the Smokies. If you want to be engulfed in this biologically diverse environment on the A.T. and if you are physically fit, take the backpacking, shelter-to-shelter adventures. The map on the adjoining page shows you all these hikes.

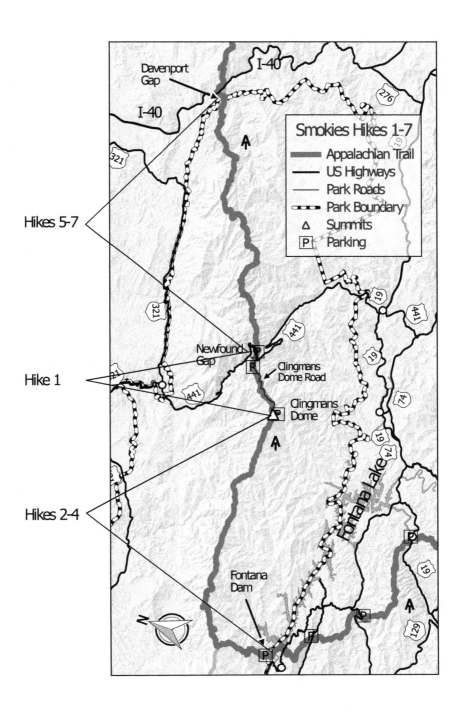

Davenport Gap

I-40

I-40

Hikes 5-7

Smokies Hikes 1-7
Appalachian Trail
US Highways
Park Roads
Park Boundary
△   Summits
P   Parking

Newfound Gap

Hike 1

Clingmans Dome Road

Clingmans Dome

Hikes 2-4

Fontana Lake

Fontana Dam

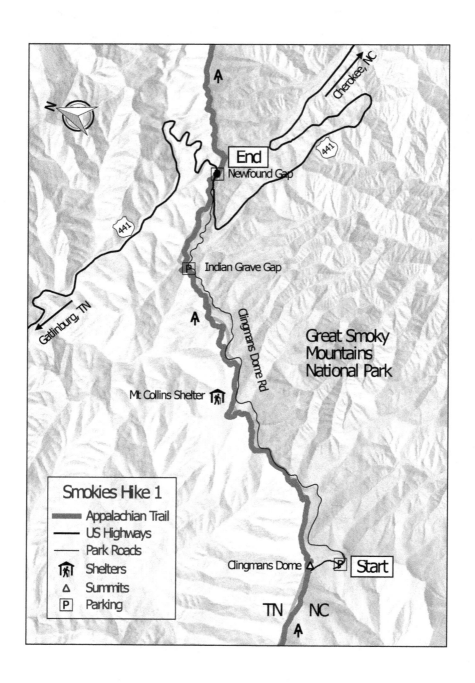

A Day Hike from Clingmans Dome to Newfound Gap,
7.5 miles, Moderate

SMOKIES
HIKE
1

HIGHLIGHTS: On the observation deck of Clingmans Dome, you have a 360-degree view of the Great Smoky Mountains National Park with signs and pictures to tell you what you are seeing.

Historic gaps are located along this portion of the A.T. At Indian Gap, you cross Road Prong Trail, a road once used by early settlers, traders, and the Confederate Army. This hike ends at Newfound Gap, near the middle of the Great Smoky Mountains National Park. Newfound Gap is where President Roosevelt dedicated the park in 1940 and is the site of the Rockefeller Memorial. The Rockefeller Memorial honors John D. Rockefeller's mother, Laura Spellman Rockefeller, for her donation of $5 million to complete the purchase of land for the park.

DISTANCE: 7.5 miles.　　　　**HIKE TIME:** 4 to 5 hours.

LEVEL OF EFFORT: Moderate, but when the weather turns cold and snowy, the trail can be challenging.

RECOMMENDED DIRECTION: South to north, from Clingmans Dome to Newfound Gap.

DOWNHILL: 5.8 miles with an elevation loss of 2,760 feet. **UPHILL:** 1.7 miles with an elevation gain of 1,185 feet.

ALONG THE TRAIL: At Clingmans Dome there is the observation tower, gift shop, and water. In the parking lot, there are modern waterless toilets.

From Clingmans Dome, the rocky Appalachian Trail descends through the spruce forest on log steps with switchbacks to Collins Gap, then climbs up Mount Collins. The trail then moves downward into Indian Gap before it ascends gradually to a ridge crest with views of Mount Le Conte. Finally, the trail goes down through the hardwood forest into Newfound Gap, where you can stop and look at the Rockefeller Memorial. Water and restrooms are located in the parking area at Newfound Gap.

SHELTER: Mount Collins Shelter was remodeled in 2009 with skylights and a covered porch. There is a privy and spring nearby.

Clingmans Dome observation deck, April 2011

Follow the White Blazes

MILE 0.0: Clingmans Dome, 6,643 feet, 360-degree views from the observation tower, the Great Smoky Mountains National Park Contact Center, waterless toilets.

MILE 0.6: Mount Love, 6,446 feet.

MILE 1.8: Collins Gap, 5,675 feet.

MILE 3.1: Sugarland Mountain Trail and a side trail, half a mile to Mount Collins Shelter with a privy and water nearby.

MILE 5.8: Indian Gap, 5,270 feet, Road Prong Trail. Clingmans Dome Road and parking are nearby.

MILE 7.5: Newfound Gap and US 441, 5,045 feet, water and restrooms. The North Carolina-Tennessee state line goes through Newfound Gap as do the Appalachian Trail and other trails.

Peaks and Valleys

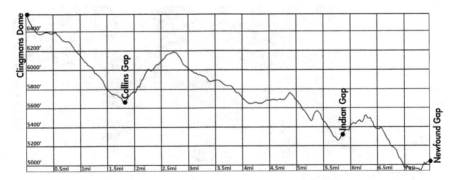

My Hiking Journal

APRIL 2011: We drive from Atlanta to the Smokies with friends Rana, Hadi, and Mo to complete two day hikes. These hikes will fill in gaps in our previous section hikes of the Appalachian Trail in North Carolina.

Today we will make a short eight-mile hike from Clingmans Dome to Newfound Gap. I estimate that it will take us about three hours.

It is a balmy day as we drive up through north Georgia and southwestern North Carolina. We expect a mild day in the Smokies too, but we have not checked the weather for Clingmans Dome, the highest point on the A.T.

We leave one car at Newfound Gap for the end of the hike before we drive toward Clingmans Dome where we will begin our hike. As we turn up Clingmans Dome Road, we see trees covered with snow and hear the wind howling through the branches. Before we get out of the car, we don our jackets, hats, and gloves. I wonder, *where did the warm weather go?*

As we enter the beautiful snow-covered spruce forest, we feel the bitter cold and notice that the forest floor is slick and icy. We proceed slowly and carefully, making sure we place our hiking poles firmly on the ground before we take our next steps. I watch as Rana's feet slide out from under her. Then all of a sudden, I am sitting on the forest floor.

Hadi, Rana, and me, April 2011

Luckily, neither one of us is hurt. We only have a few bumps and bruises. The guys are ahead of us and do not lose their footing.

When we come to a level resting spot, we stop to replenish our energy with snack bars and water. About two and a half hours later, we come to Indian Gap, where the sun is shining brightly and the snow has melted, but it is still cold.

We re-enter the forest for the last 1.7 miles downhill to Newfound Gap. Finally, we see car lights and know we are coming to Newfound Gap, where our hike will end.

What began at two o'clock as a "short" eight-mile hike ends at seven o'clock as a long and cold eight-mile trek along this section of the trail. We are happy to see our car, but we are very tired. Jim drives us back up Clingmans Dome Road to get the second car, and then we drive back to Cherokee slowly on the dark winding roads.

Our last challenge is to find a restaurant still open in Cherokee. We stop at the hotel to check in and ask the desk clerk for suggestions of what restaurants

Newfound Gap as the sun goes down, April 2011

might be open. She names a few restaurants that might be open and gives us a flyer for pizza delivery. We decide we want to try to find a restaurant.

As we drive through town, we notice that most restaurants have their lights turned off.

"Maybe that fried chicken place on the corner is still open," I say.

We park, and the guys go in to check it out. The server tells them that they have just closed. The clock shows 9:01. We know it is bad news when they come back to the car with their shoulders slumped and their mouths downturned.

"Let's try Wendy's," I say. As we approach the restaurant, I see that the sign says, "Open until 10 p.m." I sigh with relief.

When we get back to the hotel, we fall into bed.

I ask Jim, "Can you believe the challenges on the trail today?"

Carol's Reminders

- **Be aware of the significant changes in temperature and precipitation as the elevation climbs to five thousand feet and higher.** Be prepared with rain gear, warm jackets, gloves, and hats.
- **Plan to begin your hikes, even the short ones, by 10 or 11 a.m.** When the weather changes, even short hikes can become risky after the sun goes down.
- **Always take your maps, compass, flashlight, first aid kit, and safety equipment on every hike, even day hikes.** You never know when you will need them. It is better to be safe than sorry.
- **When planning a day hike, make a copy of this guide's list of nearby restaurants with their hours of operation. Bring it with you and leave it in the car.** You do not want to go to bed hungry. If possible, you want to end the day with fine dining or, at the very least, with fast food or pizza. Be prepared. Know your choices ahead of time.

Nearest Towns

Gatlinburg, Tennessee, is sixteen miles west of Newfound Gap, the northern trailhead and twenty-four miles from Clingmans Dome. Cherokee, North Carolina, is nineteen miles east of Newfound Gap and twenty-seven miles from Clingmans Dome.

Directions to the Trailheads

NORTHERN TRAILHEAD AT NEWFOUND GAP AND US 441: GPS coordinates 35.61108, -83.42484. From Cherokee, North Carolina, drive nineteen miles west on US 441 to Newfound Gap. From Gatlinburg, Tennessee, drive sixteen miles east on US 441 to Newfound Gap. The Rockefeller Memorial and parking area are on the north side of US 441.

SOUTHERN TRAILHEAD AT CLINGMANS DOME: GPS coordinates 35.55682, -8349612. From the parking area at Newfound Gap, turn left and go 0.2 miles to Clingmans Dome Road. Turn right and drive eight miles until the road dead-ends at the Clingmans Dome parking area. The Appalachian Trail is west of the paved path that leads to the Clingmans Dome observation tower.

If you plan to shuttle using two cars, leave one car at Newfound Gap, then drive the other car to Clingmans Dome, using the directions above.

ALTERNATIVE TRANSPORTATION: Hire a shuttle service to drive you from Newfound Gap, where you will leave your car, to Clingmans Dome, where you will begin your hike.

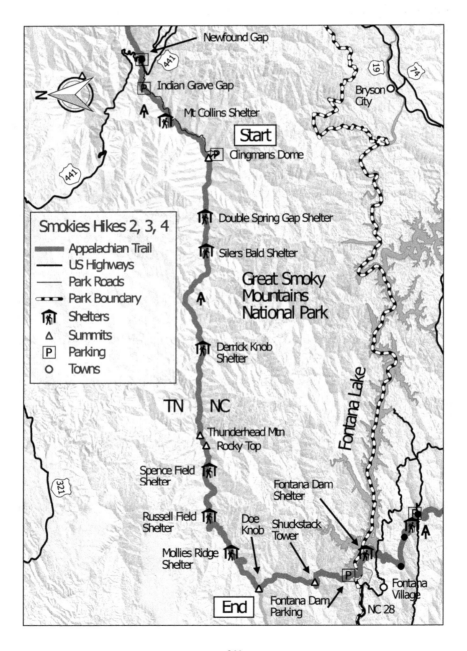

Newfound Gap

441

19

74

Indian Grave Gap

Bryson City

Mt Collins Shelter

Start

Clingmans Dome

Double Spring Gap Shelter

Silers Bald Shelter

Great Smoky Mountains National Park

Smokies Hikes 2, 3, 4

▬▬▬ Appalachian Trail
──── US Highways
──── Park Roads
●▬●▬● Park Boundary
🏠 Shelters
△ Summits
P Parking
○ Towns

Derrick Knob Shelter

TN   NC

Fontana Lake

Thunderhead Mtn

Rocky Top

Spence Field Shelter

321

Fontana Dam Shelter

Russell Field Shelter

Doe Knob

Shuckstack Tower

Mollies Ridge Shelter

Fontana Village

End

Fontana Dam Parking

NC 28

346

Overview of the Southern Smokies Three-Day Backpacking Adventure
from Clingmans Dome to Fontana Dam, 32.7 miles, Moderate

HIGHLIGHTS: This is a beautiful part of the Smokies and includes the crown jewel, Clingmans Dome, the highest point on the A.T. The forest changes from coniferous to hardwood, and the forest floor is full of plants. You can watch the haze and mist rising from the mountains and see why the area is known as "the Smokies." In the peak season, you will see many hikers.

The Smokies, July 2010

DISTANCE: 32.7 miles.   **HIKE TIME:** 3 or 4 days.

RECOMMENDED DIRECTION: North to south, from Clingmans Dome to Fontana Dam.

My Hiking Journal

JULY 2010: We ask our friends Rana and Mo and their ten-year-old son, Hadi, to join us on this adventure. As they are new to hiking and back-packing, I hold informal classes at their house on gear, food, physical preparation, safety, and first aid. We go on training hikes. I check out their packs. We exchange ideas on food to bring along.

After two months, we are ready. I make our reservations. A week before we leave, I check with the backcountry office to ask about

Fontana "Hilton" July 2010

water sources. The ranger tells me there is water available at all the shelters except Mollies Ridge. As this is one of the shelters that we have reserved, I ask about where there might be water nearby. The ranger assures me there is water near Russell Field Shelter before you get to Mollies Ridge Shelter.

We drive from Atlanta to Fontana Dam in two cars and leave one car in the long-term hiker parking area at the southern boundary of the Great Smoky Mountains National Park near Fontana Dam for the end of the hike. We check out Fontana Dam, the Fontana Dam Museum, and the Fontana "Hilton" Shelter.

I tell them that the Fontana "Hilton" is clean and new-looking with nearby running water, toilets, and showers, but that no other shelter on the Appalachian Trail has running water, flush toilets, and showers nearby. Many of the shelters in the Smokies were built in the thirties and forties with local stone and wood. Most have been refurbished with two sleeping shelves, fireplaces, and overhanging roofs with skylights. A few have not been refurbished and still have bear fences on them. There are no nearby bathroom facilities with running water; some do not even have privies.

Bear fences were originally put up to protect hikers from bears. But people would feed the bears through the fences, making the bears want to come to the shelters when there were signs of people. The Park Service has now taken down most of the fences and put up bear pulls for hikers to use to hang their packs, so that bears will not be attracted to the shelters.

After exploring the sites in the town of Fontana Dam, we drive to Gatlinburg. We check into our hotel and then wander through the shops in this tourist town and have dinner.

After dinner, Hadi wants to try out the swimming pool at the hotel. Jim and Mo join him. Rana and I fix our lunches for the next day. Jim and I will have peanut butter sandwiches, apple slices, and cookies. Rana, Mo, and Hadi will have hummus sandwiches and chips. We fill the water bladders, repack our packs, and check our lists for the three-day backpacking adventure.

The next morning, we rise early and drive to Clingmans Dome to begin our hike.

Carol's Reminders

- **Plan and prepare for the trip two to six months in advance**, especially if you are new to backpacking. For shelter reservations and backcountry permits, contact the Great Smoky Mountains National Park backcountry office at 865-436-1297 thirty days in advance of your trip. During the peak season, shelters fill up fast, and they save some slots for thru-hikers.
- **Check with the Great Smoky Mountains National Park** backcountry office a few days before you start your trek to see where water is available. In the summer, some springs and streams will be dry.
- **Arrive near the trailhead on the day before you begin your three-day backpacking, shelter-to-shelter adventure.** Arrive early so that you can relax, eat a good meal, and take in the sites, sounds, people, and history of the small communities near the A.T. At the end of the hike, you may be too tired to do so, or you may have to rush back home and not be able to take advantage of the local scenery.

Nearest Towns

Gatlinburg, Tennessee, is sixteen miles west of Newfound Gap, the northern trailhead. Cherokee, North Carolina, is nineteen miles east of Newfound Gap. Fontana Dam, North Carolina, is one mile from the southern boundary of the Great Smoky Mountains National Park, the southern trailhead.

Directions to the Trailheads

SOUTHERN TRAILHEAD, JUST NORTH OF FONTANA DAM, AT THE SOUTHERN BOUNDARY OF THE GREAT SMOKY MOUNTAINS NATIONAL PARK: GPS coordinates 35.46059, -83.81104. From the Fontana Dam Visitors Center, drive across the dam to the dirt road on the right. Turn right and drive to the parking area at the end of the road. The trailhead is at the north end of the parking area.

NORTHERN TRAILHEAD, CLINGMANS DOME: GPS coordinates 35.55682, -83,49612. From Cherokee, North Carolina, drive nineteen miles west on US 441 to Clingmans Dome Road. Turn left and drive eight miles until the road dead-ends into a large parking lot. The Clingmans Dome observation tower is half a mile west up a paved path. The A.T. is west of the paved path where you will see a small A.T. sign. For this hike, take the trail in the direction of Double Spring Gap Shelter. Do not take the trail in the direction of Mount Collins Shelter.

If you plan to shuttle using two cars, leave one car at the Fontana Dam hiker parking area at the southern trailhead and drive the second car to Clingmans Dome, the northern trailhead. From the southern trailhead drive west on Fontana Dam Road to NC 28, turn left and drive thirty-two miles southeast to US 19/74 near Bryson City. Turn left and drive eighteen miles to US 441/US 23. Turn left and drive nine miles to Cherokee. Continue on US 441 to Clingmans Dome Road. Turn left and drive eight miles on Clingmans Dome Road to the parking area at the end of the road. The total trip is sixty-seven miles; allow one and a half to two hours because of winding roads and possible tourist traffic.

As this is a long shuttle, you may wish to stay in Cherokee or Gatlinburg the night before the hike and drive to Clingmans Dome the next morning. From Cherokee, Clingmans Dome is twenty-seven miles. From Gatlinburg, it is twenty-four miles; with traffic, allow thirty to forty-five minutes.

ALTERNATIVE TRANSPORTATION: Leave one car at Fontana Dam hiker parking, and hire a shuttle driver to take you to Clingmans Dome to begin your hike. Find a list of shuttle drivers under **Hiker Essentials** for Cherokee, Gatlinburg, and Fontana Dam.

Day 1 of the Three-Day Backpacking Adventure,
Clingmans Dome to Derrick Knob Shelter, 10 miles, Moderate

SMOKIES HIKE

2

HIGHLIGHTS: Enjoy the panoramic views from Clingmans Dome and Mount Buckley. Delight in the variety of wildflowers, insects, and trees that you will see.

DISTANCE: 10.0 miles

HIKE TIME: 7 to 8 hours.

LEVEL OF EFFORT: Moderate.

DOWNHILL: 7.5 miles with an elevation loss of 3,435 feet.
UPHILL: 2.5 miles with an elevation gain of 1,705 feet.

ALONG THE TRAIL: At Clingmans Dome there is the observation tower, a gift shop, and water. In the parking area,

A monarch butterfly on a turk's cap lily, July 2010

there are modern waterless toilets. From Clingmans Dome, the narrow, rocky path descends southward through the trees. The background changes from fir and red spruce evergreen trees to beechnut, cherry, birch, and tulip poplar hardwood trees. Log steps have been built in some places to slow the erosion and to ease your hike.

SHELTERS: There are three shelters, spaced three to six miles apart: Double Spring Gap, Silers Bald, and Derrick Knob. Each has been renovated within the last few years and has an extended roof with a table and benches, skylights, two sleeping shelves, and a fireplace. Each shelter has a water source and bear pulls nearby. Double Spring Gap Shelter has a privy, but the other two shelters do not.

Derrick Knob Shelter, July 2010

Follow the White Blazes

MILE 0.0: Clingmans Dome, 6,643 feet, Great Smoky Mountains National Park Contact Center, waterless toilets.

MILE 0.5: Mount Buckley, 6,560 feet, views.

MILE 2.9: Double Spring Gap Shelter, water, privy.

MILE 4.2: Silers Bald, 5,590 feet.

MILE 4.5: Silers Bald Shelter, water.

MILE 7.1: Buckeye Gap, 4,800 feet, water nearby.

MILE 7.5: Cold Spring Knob, 5180 feet.

MILE 8.5: Hemlock Knob, 4,800 feet.

MILE 9.6: Sams Gap, 4,995 feet, water nearby.

MILE 10.0: Derrick Knob Shelter, 4,890 feet, water.

Peaks and Valleys

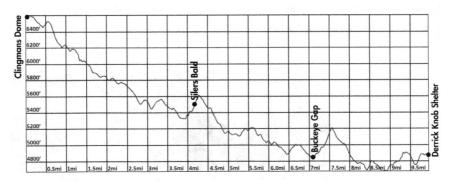

Alternate Shorter Hikes

SMOKIES HIKE 2.1:

Clingmans Dome to Silers Bald Shelter, 4.5 miles, Easy

DISTANCE: 4.5 miles.

HIKE TIME: 2 to 3 hours.

LEVEL OF EFFORT: Easy.

SMOKIES HIKE 2.2:
Silers Bald Shelter to Derrick Knob Shelter, 5.5 miles, Easy
DISTANCE: 5.5 Miles.
HIKE TIME: 3 hours.
LEVEL OF EFFORT: Easy.
DOWNHILL: 5.7 miles with an elevation loss of 600 feet.

My Hiking Journal

JULY 2010: We begin this trek on a clear but warm and humid day. We climb up the ramp to check out the Clingmans Dome observation tower and see Silers Bald, Thunderhead Mountain, and Shuckstack Mountain, all places that we will be hiking past in the next few days.

We walk down the trail and enter the forest of spruces and firs and pass lush grasses and wildflowers. We see red bee balm, yellow daisies, white fringed phacelia, turk's cap lilies, blackberries, and red, yellow, and purple mushrooms. We stop to take more pictures and eat blackberries.

Mo, Jim, Rana, Hadi, and me, July 2010

When we get to Double Springs Gap Shelter, we have lunch and check out the shelter. Jim shows Hadi the hikers register and reads a few entries.

After lunch we climb up and over sunny Silers Bald. We go down along the ridge into the hardwood forest and meet many hikers. Some are making loop hikes from the Clingmans Dome parking area to Silers Bald and back to Clingmans Dome. Others are backpackers.

About four thirty we come to Derricks Knob Shelter. Jim and Mo go down the slope to get water while Rana and I lay out the sleeping bags and start supper. Jim and I are having almond chicken and rice; Rana and family are having a vegan dish. Hadi picks up wood for the fire to roast marshmallows, just as every young boy loves to do. Rana has thoughtfully included marshmallows in the food she's brought along.

The shelter fills up with ten people. Three teenage boys, out for a few days in the woods, decide they will move on for the night. They don't tell us why, but the shelter may have been getting too crowded for them. They tell us they are going down the ridge trail to the road. When I look it up later, I find that Tremont Road is about six miles down the ridge trail and that there is a camping spot—but not a shelter—on the way.

As we are settling down for sleep, a group of guys arrive. One of them says, "We got a late start because we drove down from Michigan. I think we'll just sleep in our tents and not try to squeeze in with you." We hear them laughing and talking late into the night.

The next morning Rana says, "I hardly slept all night."

Carol's Reminders

- **Assign everyone tasks when you reach the shelter at night.** Even new hikers can feel good about doing their part. Assign some hikers to get water, some to lay out the sleeping bags, some to cook the meal, and some to check out the bear pulls to see how to hoist the packs.

- **Purify all water you take from springs and streams along the trail**. Water in the backcountry may be contaminated by microorganisms that can cause diarrhea or dysentery. Do not think that just because the water comes from a spring and is clear and pristine-looking that it does not contain invisible microorganisms that can cause disease. Boil the water or treat it using a filter, ultra violet light, or purifying tablets or solution.
- **Practice Leave No Trace.** Pack everything out you bring in, including plastic bags, wrappers, fruit peels, and used toilet paper. Do not try to burn plastics or aluminum foil in a fire ring. Do not throw banana and orange peels in the woods.
- **Resupply your bottles or water bladders each night.**
- **In bear-prone areas, hoist EVERYTHING high at night**. Any candy, food supplies, food scraps, or smelly articles like toothpaste and deodorant can attract bears and rodents.

Day 2 of the Three-Day Backpacking Adventure,
Derrick Knob Shelter to Russell Field Shelter, 9 miles, Moderate to Challenging

HIGHLIGHTS: Delight in the views all around you from Rocky Top, Brier Bald, and Little Bald, and watch the smoke rise from the mountains. Ramble through the grassy swag as you cross Spence Field. It is the largest grassy bald in the park.

DISTANCE: 9.0 miles.   **HIKE TIME:** 8 to 9 hours.

LEVEL OF EFFORT: Moderate to Challenging.

DOWNHILL: 5.7 miles with an elevation loss of 2,970 feet. **UPHILL:** 3.3 miles with an elevation gain of 2,435 feet.

ALONG THE TRAIL: From Derrick Knob the trail has many little ups and downs as it crosses several rocky balds and knobs that are thick with rhododendron bushes. Watch for the white blaze on the boulder that shows you the path across Spence Field.

SHELTERS: There are two shelters, Spence Field and Russell Field. Both have been renovated in the last few years. Workers have added extended roofs

Mo crossing Spence Field, July 2010

for picnic tables and benches and have also put in skylights. Neither shelter has a bear fence now. Each one has a water source and bear pulls nearby. Spence Field Shelter has a privy; Russell Field Shelter does not.

Follow the White Blazes

MILE 0.0: Derrick Knob Shelter, 4,880 feet, water.

MILE 0.3: Chestnut Bald, 4,950 feet.

MILE 1.0: Sugar Tree Gap, 4,435 feet.

MILE 1.7: Starky Gap, 4,550 feet.

MILE 2.3: Brier Knob, 5,070 feet.

MILE 3.2: Beechnut Gap, 4,830 feet, water nearby.

MILE 4.2: Thunderhead; 5,500 feet; the tallest peak in the southern end of the Smokies, where you have nice views. It is called Thunderhead because the rock formations here look like thunder clouds.

MILE 4.8: Rocky Top, 5,420 feet, views.

MILE 5.6: Jenkins Ridge Trail, 4,950 feet

MILE 6.3: 0.2 miles east to Spence Field Shelter on Eagle Creek Trail, Bote Mountain Trail to the west, 4,900 feet, views, water 0.2 west.

MILE 9.0: Russell Field Shelter, 4,350 feet. The shelter was named for Russell Gregory who built a cabin and grazed cattle here.

Peaks and Valleys

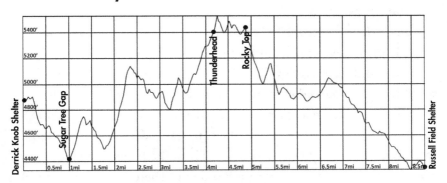

Alternate Shorter Hikes

SMOKIES HIKE 3.1:

Derrick Knob Shelter to Spence Field Shelter, 6.1 miles, Moderate

DISTANCE: 5.9 miles plus 0.2 miles from the trail to the shelter.

HIKE TIME: 4 hours.

LEVEL OF EFFORT: Moderate.

SMOKIES HIKE 3.2:

Spence Field Shelter to Mollies Ridge Shelter, 6.4 miles, Moderate

DISTANCE: 6.2 miles plus 0.2 miles from the shelter to the trail.

HIKE TIME: 3 hours.

LEVEL OF EFFORT: Moderate.

My Hiking Journal

JULY 2010: We have breakfast, stuff our packs, and set off on the trail about nine. It is another mild, sunny day, but we don't really feel the sun because we are under a canopy of hardwood trees.

Hadi points out many colored mushrooms and centipedes as we climb up over a little knob and then down into Starky Gap. We wait in the gap for Jim and Mo who lag behind.

When Jim comes up, he asks, "Did you see that snake on the steps?"

"No," I say. "Where?"

We turn and go back to see the snake, but it is no longer there.

"He must have crawled off into the grass," Jim says.

"How did we miss him?" I ask. "We were walking and talking and could have just walked over him. That's a little scary."

We huff and puff as we go up Thunderhead Mountain, climbing five hundred feet in less than a mile. The sun beams down on us. Streams of sweat pour down my face. Sweat seeps into the fringes of Hadi's curls. Mo covers his bald head with a bandana. There is no shade on this mountaintop, and there are no scenic views to look out upon, but it is covered with rhododendron plants that are taller than us.

Since we are hungry, we just sit down in the middle of the trail and have lunch. After lunch, we climb up Rocky Top, where there are views of the mountains and valleys all around us and beautiful white cumulus clouds overhead.

We walk down the trail under a canopy of hardwood trees, stopping to take pictures of fungi and artistic-looking configurations formed by the roots of fallen trees.

Jim stops to talk with a group of hikers. When he asks, "Where are you from?" one of them says, "I live in West Hartford, Connecticut."

As our son also lives there, Jim talks with her some more, and the rest of us go on.

When we come to a large rock outcropping, we look and look before we find the white A.T. blaze on a rock. (When there are no trees or posts,

Rattlesnake, July 2010

Me and Rana, July 2010

Mo and Hadi, Thunderhead Mountain, July 2010

Fungi, July 2010

blazes are often painted on rocks.) The blaze points the way across the grassy swag in the northern end of Spence Field. I'm a little hesitant to continue, because Jim hasn't caught up with us yet, but I decide to go on.

We cross the swag and stop at the next trail intersection to wait for Jim. It is two thirty already, and I have to decide how much farther I think we can hike today. We have six more miles to go, up and over another knob to Mollies Ridge Shelter, where we have reservations.

I decide we need to change our plans and stop at Russell Field Shelter, which is only three miles away. Since we do not have reservations there, I hope there will be room. Russell Field Shelter is an old shelter, so maybe there will not be too many people there.

After waiting twenty minutes or so, I say to our friends, "Go on to the shelter, and I'll come along when Jim catches up." I wait, watching the trail and checking my watch. I'm a little worried because I am afraid he may have missed the blaze directing him across the grassy swag.

After another twenty minutes, I smile when I see him coming.

When I ask him where he's been, he says, "I had trouble finding the blaze on the rocks."

"What did you learn from the hiker from Connecticut you were talking to?" I ask.

Jim replies, "She lived in the same condo complex as Harmon. She went to the University of Hartford and is a pianist." Harmon is our son. He went to the University of Hartford and is a cellist.

"What a small world," I say. "Who would have ever thought you would meet someone from West Hartford in the Smokies?"

When we get to the shelter about five thirty, our friends have arrived, but no one else is there. Rana is cooking their dinner. Hadi is collecting wood for a fire to roast marshmallows.

I start cooking our own dinner. The guys go down to the spring for water. After dinner, we hoist our packs on the bear pulls. We snuggle into our sleeping bags behind the bear fence.

Rain begins to fall. I don't remember rain being in the forecast, but in the Smokies, the weather pattern can change quickly. I'm glad we're under the shelter and not in a tent. I fall asleep listening to the rain fall softly on the tin roof.

The next morning, Jim and Rana talk about watching for bears all night and not sleeping well. I will admit that I only went around the corner of the shelter when I had to pee during the night. I did not want to take the chance of running into a bear.

When we talked with the ranger at the ***Oconaluftee Visitors Center*** before we started our hike, he warned us that bears were active around the shelters. He told us to be sure to hang our packs.

UPDATE: When we hiked this section, Russell Field Shelter still had one of the old bear fences over the front of the shelter, but the shelter has since been refurbished and the fence removed.

Carol's Reminders

- **Wait for all group members at major trail changes.** Ideally, all group members should remain within shouting distance of each other. If you have a large group, there should be a leader in the front and a sweeper in the back so that you can account for all members of the group at all times. In a small group, the leader should make sure he or she can always account for all members of the group.

- **Do not be afraid to change your hiking plans when the situation dictates**. For example, if the weather gets worse or if you end up hiking more slowly than expected, and darkness is approaching, select the closest shelter for the night; do not push on just because that is your plan. If possible, contact the backcountry office to see if there is room at the next shelter. The backcountry telephone number is the same one you use to make shelter reservations. Keep this number and the park emergency number with you when you are hiking. Unfortunately, you may not have cell-phone service in the backcountry.

Day 3 of the Three-Day Backpacking Adventure,
Russell Field Shelter to Fontana Dam and Little Tennessee River, 13.7 miles, Moderate to Challenging

HIGHLIGHTS: There are magnificent panoramic views from Shuckstack Mountain.

DISTANCE: 13.7 miles.   **HIKE TIME:** 8 to 9 hours.

LEVEL OF EFFORT: Jim rates this as challenging because of the length of the hike and the many little ups and downs. I rate it as moderate because of the overall downhill direction of the hike and the fact that we made the hike in only eight hours.

DOWNHILL: 10.7 miles with an elevation loss of 4,805 feet. **UPHILL:** 3.0 miles with an elevation gain of 2,145 feet.

ALONG THE TRAIL: From Russell Field Shelter the path is narrow, earthen, and rocky. It goes up and down over several knobs. Several trails cross the A.T. in this section; follow the white blazes.

Views of the Great Smoky Mountains, July 2010

Mo and Hadi taking pictures, July 2010

SHELTERS: Russell Field Shelter and Mollies Ridge Shelter have been renovated in the last few years and have skylights and extended roofs for picnic tables and benches. Neither shelter has a privy. There are water sources near the shelters and near Ekaneetlee Gap and Birch Spring Gap. But during the dry season, these may be unreliable.

Follow the White Blazes

MILE 0.0: Russell Field Shelter, 4,350 feet, water.

MILE 1.4: Little Abrams Gap, 4,100 feet.

MILE 2.6: Devils Tater Patch, 4,750 feet. This is a ragged ridge. No one knows the origin of the name.

MILE 3.1: Mollies Ridge Shelter, 4,580 feet, water.

MILE 4.8: Ekaneetlee Gap, 3,850 feet, water nearby. An old Indian and buffalo trail crosses the A.T. here.

MILE 6.1: Doe Knob, 4,520 feet, Gregory Bald Trail crosses the A.T. here.

MILE 8.4: Birch Spring Gap, 3,760 feet.

MILE 9.3: Sassafras Gap, 3,680 feet. Twenty-Mile Trail goes to the west, and Lost Cove Trail goes to the east.

MILE 9.7: Shuckstack Mountain, 3,840 feet. You can take a steep side trail 0.1 miles up to see views from the fire lookout tower. From afar, the mountain peak looks like a bundle of corn stalks, thus the name Shuckstack.

MILE 13.7: Southern boundary of the Great Smoky Mountains National Park, 1,700 feet, Fontana Dam, Fontana Lake, Little Tennessee River.

Peaks and Valleys

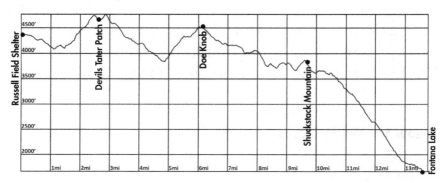

Alternate Shorter Hikes

SMOKIES HIKE 4.1:
Russell Field Shelter to Mollies Ridge Shelter, 3.1 miles, Moderate
DISTANCE: 3.1 miles.
HIKE TIME: 2 hours.
LEVEL OF EFFORT: Moderate.

SMOKIES HIKE 4.2:
Mollies Ridge Shelter to Fontana Dam, 10.6 miles, Moderate
DISTANCE: 10.6 miles.
HIKE TIME: 6 hours.
LEVEL OF EFFORT: Moderate.

My Hiking Journal

JULY 2010: Today is the last day of our three-day backpacking adventure. Our friends need to get back home tonight, so we pick up our pace. Everyone seems ready to get back to civilization.

We have breakfast, stuff our packs, and set off on the trail about eight. Fortunately, it is an overcast day. Under the canopy of hardwood trees, it is not hot, but the trail starts off uphill.

Ten-year-old Hadi says, "I cannot make it up this hill."

Jim issues him a challenge: "Let's see if you can keep up with me."

Hadi hurries up the trail. He and Jim talk about computers and electronic games, and the miles fly by.

We stop for an early lunch at Mollies Ridge Shelter, and I say, "I am really glad we did not try to make it here last night over that last knob."

As we come to the top of Doe Knob, we see beautiful wildflowers waving in the sunlight. We admire an orange turk's cap lily, a blue-purplish spiderwort, and little white flowers that look like paper umbrellas. After a short break, the guys take off at a fast clip down the rocky trail. The last seven miles are downhill under the trees.

Hadi finds a black centipede and some grey earthworms. Then in the middle of the trail, we come to a rattlesnake with its head cut off. We all stop to examine it.

Jim, Mo, and Hadi go ahead. Rana and I walk along, talking.

All of a sudden we hear, "Stay back!"

"I think that's Jim," I say.

We wait for Jim to come back and tell us what's happening.

Soon he comes back and explains with excitement in his voice. "I round the bend in the trail and see what I think is a wild hog. I yell, and it stands up and goes down the mountain. It's a bear."

Black centipede July 2010   *Rattlesnake,*

371

We all talk at once about the bear. Hadi is quiet, but his eyes are big as saucers. We eat a few snacks to try to calm our nerves.

We stay together as we continue down the trail, not wanting to be separated if the bear comes close. We look across the valley through the trees and see the bear about six hundred feet away, walking down the mountain parallel to our path. When the trail turns at Shuckstack Mountain, we can't see him anymore.

Today the trail has been filled with surprises.

About five o'clock, we make it to the trailhead. We pose for pictures, smiling broadly.

We pile into the car and ask our friends to drop us at the Fontana Village Resort. They have to be back in Atlanta tonight, and we don't want them spending time taking us to get our car at Clingmans Dome. We call the Hike Inn shuttle service and arrange for a driver to take us there tomorrow.

Rana, Hadi, and Mo, July 2010

Luckily, the resort has a room available. We treat ourselves to a room with a heart-shaped hot tub. We go by the bar and get some wine and then relax in the hot tub before dinner. This has been a long hike, and we are ready for the comforts of the resort.

Carol's Reminders

- **Good friends, conversation, and beautiful views make challenging hikes easier.**
- **Be cautious when you come upon wild animals.** Stop, make noise, and warn your fellow hikers. Do NOT approach a wild animal.
- **Be prepared with phone numbers for the backcountry office and shuttle drivers** in case your plans change. But be aware that you may only have cell phone reception on mountaintops or when you get back to town.
- **Treat yourselves at the end of your adventure.**

Fine Wine and Accommodations
Cherokee, North Carolina

CHEROKEE is the eastern gateway to the Great Smoky Mountains National Park and the headquarters of the Eastern Band of the Cherokee Indians. Located on the Qualla Boundary land trust in western North Carolina, it is steeped in Cherokee history and tourism. With the opening of Harrah's Cherokee Casino in 1995, the economy improved dramatically. More than three million people visit the casino yearly.

Lodging within Twenty Miles of Newfound Gap

Local Hotels and Motels

CHEROKEE LODGE MOTEL: $–$$, king and queen rooms with refrigerators and microwaves, pool, 1593 Acquoni Road, 828-449-8915, www.cherokee-lodgenc.com.

PINK MOTEL: $, senior and military discounts, located on the river, coffee makers and microwaves in rooms, pool, 1306 Tsali Boulevard (US 441), 828-497-3530, www.facebook/pinkmotel/.

RIVER'S EDGE MOTEL: $–$$, AAA and AARP discounts, king and double rooms with refrigerators and coffee makers, free Wi-Fi, 1026 Tsali Boulevard (US 441), 828-497-7995, www.riversedgecherokee.com.

ROLLING HILLS LODGE: $–$$; hiker, AARP, and AAA discounts; mountain views; queen and king rooms with refrigerators; free Wi-Fi; convenient to attractions; 739 Tsali Boulevard (US 441 North); 1-800-255-5371; www.rollinghillslodge.com.

National Chain Hotels

BAYMONT INN AND SUITES: $-$$ with complimentary continental breakfast; king and queen rooms; suites with sleeper sofas; microwaves, refrigerators, and coffee makers in rooms; free Wi-Fi; outdoor pool; 1455 Acquoni Road, 828-497-2101, www.baymontcherokee.com.

OUR EXPERIENCE, APRIL 11: We stay here while we are making two day hikes. When we come back late the first night, the staff members are helpful. They tell us which restaurants might be open and give us a brochure for pizza-delivery service.

JULY 2011: We stay here just before we begin our three-day backpacking adventure in the northern part of the Smokies. We get up early to try their free breakfast. It is delicious with boiled eggs, toast, bagels, and fresh bananas. We walk from the hotel to the bus stop where the Cherokee Transit will take us to Newfound Gap. Unfortunately, the Cherokee Transit no longer runs between Cherokee and Gatlinburg.

Baymont Inn has nice, clean, up-to-date rooms, and is priced reasonably.

FRIENDS WEIGH IN: In 2016, Fran and Deborah stay here. Fran says the hotel is very nice and quiet. Plus, there are two good restaurants located up the street, The Little Princess and Sassy Sunflowers Café.

COMFORT SUITES: $–$$ with complimentary breakfast; mini refrigerators, microwaves, and coffee makers in rooms; pool and laundry facilities; 1223 Tsali Boulevard (US 441); (828) 497-3500; www.choicehotels.com/north-carolina/cherokee/comfort-suites-hotels/NC042.

MICROTEL INN & SUITES BY WYNDHAM: $–$$ with continental breakfast; queen rooms with flat screen TVs and refrigerators; suites come with flat screen TVs, refrigerators, microwaves and coffee makers; some suites have Jacuzzis; business center; Wi-Fi; pet friendly; outdoor saltwater pool; shuttle service to casino for guests for a fee; 674 Casino Trail; 828-497-7800; www.microtelinn.com.

There are more than thirty other national and local hotels in Cherokee.

Selected Restaurants

The Cherokee Reservation is dry and does not serve alcoholic beverages in any restaurants except for those at the casino.

Restaurants at Harrah's Cherokee Casino, 777 Casino Trail

BRIO TUSCAN GRILLE: $$, Italian, full bar, brunch on Sat and Sun, 11:30 a.m. to 10 p.m. Sun through Thu, 11 a.m. to 11 p.m. Fri and Sat, 828-497-8233.

RUTH'S CHRIS STEAK HOUSE: $$–$$$ American, full bar, casual-elegant, New Orleans-inspired appetizers, steaks, seafood, homemade desserts, 5 to 10 p.m. Mon through Thu, 5 to 11 p.m. Fri and Sat, 4 to 9 p.m. Sun, 828-497-8577, reservations suggested.

CHEFS STAGE BUFFET: $–$$, international, full bar, gluten-free and vegan options, 4:30 to 10 p.m. Mon and Thu, 4:30 to 11 p.m. Fri, 11 a.m. to 11 p.m. Sat.

Restaurants in or near Cherokee

WISE GUYZ GRILLE: ½ $, American, hamburgers, sandwiches, wings, pizza, 11 a.m. to 8 p.m. Mon through Sat, 11 a.m. to 4:30 p.m. Sun, 68 Big Cove, 828-497-2838.

GRANNY'S KITCHEN: $–$$, Southern buffet, vegetarian friendly, 7 a.m. to 8 p.m. Tue through Sat, 7 a.m. to 3 p.m. Sun, middle of Mar through middle of Dec, 1098 Paint Town Road (US 19), 828-497-5010.

THE LITTLE PRINCESS: $–$$, American, country-style diner with buffet, 8 a.m. to 6 p.m. daily, 1681 Acquoni Road, 828-497-9000.
  FRIENDS WEIGH IN: Fran and Deborah say food is very good.

NEWFOUND LODGE RESTAURANT: $, American, 7 a.m. to 8:30 p.m. daily, 1303 Tsali Boulevard (US 441), 828-497-4590.
  OUR EXPERIENCE, JULY 2010: We check out this restaurant for lunch. It is clean, and many local cars are there, which we take as a good sign. The menu has the basic lunch choices: a salad bar, soup, and sandwiches. I order a BLT with a trip to the salad bar. Both are good. Jim and I split a piece of apple pie with ice cream. It is homemade and delicious.

PAUL'S FAMILY RESTAURANT: $, cash only, American, buffalo burgers, Indian tacos, trout, 11 a.m. to 8:30 p.m. daily, 1111 Tsali Boulevard, 828-497-9012.

RANCHO VIEJO: $, Mexican, 11 a.m. to 9 p.m. daily, 16 Cherokee Crossing, Suite 5, Whittier (off US 441, south of US 19), 828-497-0343.

There are over thirty other restaurants, including fast-food establishments, in or near Cherokee.

Hiker Essentials, Splurges, and Emergency Stops

Shuttle-Service Providers

BILL JOHNSON, APPALACHIAN SERVICES: 828-741-9658, AppalachianServices@ msn.com or www.appalachianservices.biz.

CHEROKEE CAB: 24/7, 828-269-8621, cherokeecabs@gmail.

Car Rental Agency

ENTERPRISE RENT-A-CAR: 8 a.m. to 5:30 p.m. Mon through Fri, 9 a.m. to noon Sat, 1188 West Main Street, Sylva (16 miles southeast of Cherokee), 828-631-0142.

Outfitters

RIVER'S EDGE OUTFITTERS: 8 a.m. to 5 p.m. Mon through Fri, 61 Big Cove Road, 828-497-9300.

Groceries

FOOD LION: 7 a.m. to 11 p.m. daily, no beer or wine, 16 Cherokee Crossing Road, Suite 1 (US 441 & Business US 441), Whittier, 828-497-4743.

CATAMOUNT TRAVEL CENTER: sells snacks and a limited supply of groceries as well as beer and wine, banking services, 6 a.m. to midnight Mon through Fri, 7 a.m. to midnight Sat and Sun, 3385 US 441, Whittier (not on the Cherokee Reservation), 828-497-0800.

Wine and Beer Shops

None as the Cherokee Nation is dry.

ATMs

CHEROKEE FIRE GRILL AND WISE GUYZ PIZZA: 68 Big Cove Road.

CHEROKEE LODGE MOTEL: 1593 Acquoni Road.

FIRST CITIZENS BANK: 701 Tsali Boulevard (US 441 N), 828-497-2041.

HARDEE'S: 1607 Acquoni Road.

HARRAH'S CHEROKEE CASINO & HOTEL: 777 Casino Trail.

MOUNTAIN CREDIT UNION: 3533 US 441 North, Whittier.

SHELL SERVICE STATION: 510 Paint Town Road.

Urgent Care and Emergency Services

FAMILY CARE CENTER: 8 a.m. to 4:30 p.m. Mon through Fri, 77 Paint Town Rd. (US 19), 828-554-5565.

HARRIS URGENT CARE IN SYLVA: 8 a.m. to 6:30 p.m. daily; only closed Christmas Day, Thanksgiving Day, and New Year's Day; 176 Walmart Plaza (in Walmart) on Asheville Highway; Sylva (16 miles southeast of Cherokee); 828-631-9462.

CHEROKEE INDIAN HOSPITAL: Emergency services, 24/7, 188 Hospital Road, 828-497-9163.

GREAT SMOKY MOUNTAINS NATIONAL PARK: emergency number, 865-436-9171.

Fun Places to Visit in and near Cherokee

CHEROKEE VISITORS CENTER: 8 a.m. to 5 p.m. daily, tourist brochures, coffee, 498 Tsali Boulevard (US 441 N), 1-800-438-1601.

MOUNTAINSIDE THEATRE, "UNTO THESE HILLS" OUTDOOR HISTORICAL DRAMA: $23.75 for adults, $13.75 for children 6–12, free for children 5 and under; box office 9 a.m. to 10:30 p.m. Mon through Sat, performances 8 p.m. Mon through Sat, June–August; 564 Tsali Boulevard, 828-497-2111 or 1-866-554-4557.

MUSEUM OF THE CHEROKEE INDIANS: Cherokee art, history, and culture, educational offerings, handicapped accessible, no pets, 9 a.m. to 5 p.m. daily, 589 Tsali Boulevard (US 441 North), 828-497-3481.

OUR EXPERIENCE: We stop to learn more about the Cherokees. The displays tell the story of the Trail of Tears and those who escaped and hid in these mountains.

OCONALUFTEE INDIAN VILLAGE: $20 for adults, $12 for children 6–12, free for children 5 and under. Tour an authentic 1760s working village with dwellings, artisans, and handmade crafts. Tours are led by Cherokee High School student guides whose interpretation of Cherokee culture is based on tradition and research. 11 a.m. to 5:30 p.m. Mon through Sat, May through Oct, 218 Drama Road, 828-497-2111.

QUALLA ARTS AND CRAFTS MUTUAL: quality handmade Cherokee arts and crafts; 8 a.m. to 7 p.m. Mon through Sat and 9 a.m. to 5 p.m. Sun, Jun through Aug; 8 a.m. to 5 p.m. Mon through Sat and 9 a.m. to 4:30 p.m. Sun, Sep through Dec and Mar through May; closed Jan and Feb; 645 Tsali Boulevard (US 441 North); 828-497-3103; www.quallaartsandcrafts.com.

OUR EXPERIENCE: This shop has beautiful handcrafted items. I buy one of their baskets.

HARRAH'S CHEROKEE CASINO: 24/7, 777 Casino Trail, 828-497-7777.

FLY-FISHING IN CHEROKEE TROUT STREAMS: You must register and buy a permit. 828-554-6110.

SEQUOYAH NATIONAL GOLF COURSE: Robert Trent Jones II design championship golf course,18 holes, par 72, $45 in winter, $64 to $85 in spring and summer, $60 to $65 for seniors, 79 Cahons Road, Whittier, 828-497-3000, www.sequoyahnational.com.

SMOKY MOUNTAIN CLUB GOLF COURSE: 18 holes, par 71 golf course, designed by Thomas Walker, $49 for non-residents, book online; pro shop, Permission Grill; 1300 Conleys Creek Road, Whittier; 828-497-7622; www.caro-linamountaingolf.com .

MINGO FALLS: the most stunning cascading waterfall in the region, five miles north of Cherokee on Big Cove Road.

Visitor Centers and Historic Grist Mills within the Great Smoky Mountains National Park

OCONALUFTEE VISITOR CENTER: ranger-led programs, exhibits, bookshop, back-country permit station; 8 a.m. to closing daily, closing time varies from 4:30 to 6 p.m. depending on the season, closed on Christmas Day; two miles north of Cherokee on US 441, 828-497-1904.

OUR EXPERIENCE, JULY 2010: We stop here with friends to get an update on water sources and to fill out our backcountry permits. The rangers are very helpful and give us the latest information, warning us that the water source near Mollies Ridge Shelter is dry and that we will need to stop at Russell Field Shelter for water. They also tell us that bears are active and to hang our bags on the bear pulls at night.

We check out the exhibits. There is a great exhibit about the mountains and all the trails. We see the A.T. in all its three-dimensional glory as it winds through the mountains.

The bookshop has a wonderful collection of books and music with a Smokies theme. We find the Appalachian Trail map produced by the Great Smoky Mountains Association. It has a nice trail profile, details about the trail as it passes through the Smokies, and pictures of all the shelters. I buy several inexpensive pamphlets with colorful pictures of wildflowers and trees. I like to know the names of the plants and trees that I am seeing along the trail.

SUGARLANDS VISITOR CENTER: ranger-led programs, twenty-minute film about the Smokies, natural history exhibits, museum, hiker information, backcountry permit station; 8 a.m. until closing daily, closing time varies from 4:30 to 7:30 p.m. depending on the season, closed on Christmas Day; two miles south of Gatlinburg and thirty-three miles north of Cherokee on US 441; 865-436-7318, park recording at 865-436-1200.

OUR EXPERIENCE: We stop and check out the exhibits as well as the movie, which tells about how the Great Smoky Mountains National Park came to be. The exhibits highlight plants and animals in the park.

CLINGMANS DOME VISITOR CONTACT STATION: bookstore and shop; 10 a.m. to 6 p.m. daily, Apr through Oct (closing at 6:30 p.m. in July), 9:30 a.m. to 5 p.m. daily, Nov; Clingmans Dome observation tower with 360-degree views, located on top of Clingmans Dome at 6,643 feet, the highest peak in the Smokies; 24/7 Apr through Nov; eight miles south of US 441 on Clingmans Dome Road; 865-436-7318, ext. 326.

OUR EXPERIENCE, APRIL 2016: On a visit to the Clingmans Dome observation tower, we stop to check out this visitor contact station. It has a good collection of books and refreshments. We need cool drinks. I find some storybooks for my young neighbors.

CADES COVE VISITOR CENTER: 9 a.m. to closing daily, closing time varies from 4:30 to 7:30 p.m. depending on the season, closed Christmas Day; located near the midpoint of the eleven-mile one-way Cades Cove Loop Road; 865-436-7318, ext. 320.

CABLE MILL IN CADES COVE: water-powered gristmill, built in the 1870s; 10 a.m. to 6 p.m. daily, Apr through Oct, 9:30 a.m. to 5 p.m. Fri through Sun, Nov.

MINGUS MILL NEAR OCONALUFTEE VISITORS CENTER ON US 441: turbine-powered gristmill, built in the 1880s; 9 a.m. to 5 p.m. daily, middle of Apr through Oct, 9 a.m. to 5 p.m. Fri through Sun, Nov.

Fine Wine and Accommodations
Gatlinburg, Tennessee

GATLINBURG is the western gateway to the Great Smoky Mountains National Park. With the creation of the national park in 1934, the small logging town of Gatlinburg was transformed into a major tourist destination. To accommodate more than eleven million visitors yearly, Gatlinburg has many hotels, restaurants, and attractions, including an aquarium and the only ski resort in Tennessee. It also has a trolley service. The town, along with its estimated four thousand residents, welcomes visitors and is making a recovery after the devastating fires of 2016.

Lodging near the Western Gateway to the Smokies

Selected Hotels, Lodges, and Inns

BEARSKIN LODGE: $–$$$, prices vary seasonally, free continental breakfast, king and queen rooms, fireplaces in some rooms, whirlpool tubs, free Wi-Fi, outdoor heated pool, on river, 840 River Road, 877-795-7546, www.TheBearskinLodge.com.

GATLINBURG INN: $$, complimentary hot breakfast, historic building dating back to 1937, double and king rooms and suites, free Wi-Fi, outdoor pool, child friendly, 755 Parkway, 865-436-5133, www.gatlinburginn.com.

FRIENDS WEIGH IN: Linda says, "I have stayed here and it is great. Convenient walking distance to many places."

RIVERHOUSE AT THE PARK: $–$$ with complimentary in-room homemade breakfast, whirlpool tubs, refrigerators, microwaves, Wi-Fi, outside pool, within walking distance to downtown, 205 Ski Mountain Road, 865-436-2070, www.riverhousemotels.com/riverhouse_at_the_park.php

National Hotel Chains

HAMPTON INN OF GATLINBURG: $–$$$ with complimentary breakfast, free Wi-Fi, outdoor pool, fitness center, 967 Parkway, 865-436-4878, www.hamptoninn.hilton.com/gatlinburg.

HILTON GARDEN INN: $$–$$$; rates vary seasonally; made-to-order breakfast; refrigerators, microwaves, and coffee makers in rooms; free Wi-Fi; restaurant and lounge on site; indoor saltwater pool; laundry; within walking distance of many attractions; 635 River Road; 865-436-0048; www.gardeninn.hilton.com/en/hotels/tennessee/hilton-garden-inn-gatlinburg-GATGIGI/index.html.

COURTYARD BY MARRIOTT GATLINBURG: $$–$$$, rates vary seasonally, breakfast for fee, king and queen rooms and suites, refrigerators, high-speed internet, heated pool, hot tub, fitness center, business center, bar and lounge, 315 Historic Nature Trail, 865-436-4008, www.marriott.com.

THE PARK VISTA DOUBLETREE BY HILTON HOTEL: $–$$, rates vary seasonally, queen and king rooms with private balconies to enjoy the sunrise or sunset, bar and lounge next to a fireplace to enjoy drinks and warm cookies, restaurant, laundry, pool, 705 Cherokee Orchard Rd., 865-436-9211, www.parkvista.com.

OUR EXPERIENCE, APRIL 2016: While attending the Wildflower Pilgrimage, we stay at this unusual-looking round hotel up on a hill. Rooms have been recently updated, and there are beautiful views of the mountains. We enjoy having a restaurant and bar on site. For breakfast, there are many choices on the buffet with a chef to cook your eggs in any style. I have a delicious omelet with spinach and mushrooms.

HOLIDAY INN CLUB VACATIONS, SMOKY MOUNTAIN RESORT: $$–$$$; villas with 1 or 2 BR, 1BA, full kitchen, DR/LR area, private balconies; free internet; self-service laundry; spa tub; heated pool; fitness center; 404 Historic Nature Trail; 865-908-1700, www.ihg.com/holidayinnclubvactions/hotels/us/en/gatlinburg/glbcv/hoteldetail

There are more than seventy-five national and independent hotels and resorts in Gatlinburg and the surrounding area.

B&Bs, Lodges, and Inns

These are a little farther away from the Appalachian Trail than the hotels listed above. You might enjoy staying at one of these after your hiking trip.

BUCKHORN INN BED AND BREAKFAST: $$–$$$; free breakfast; friendly, romantic atmosphere in the forest with mountain views; free Wi-Fi; kitchen in rooms; fitness center; hot tub; restaurant on site with fine dining; 2140 Tudor Mountain Road; 865-436-4668, www.buckhorninn.com.

THE LODGE AT BUCKBERRY CREEK: $$–$$$, rustic charm, luxurious suites with fireplaces and mountain views, on-site restaurant, 961 Campbell Lead Road, 865-430-8030, www.buckberrylodge.com.

LAUREL SPRINGS LODGE B&B: $$, award-winning bed and breakfast with a history dating back to the 1930s, free breakfast entrée that changes daily with fresh fruits and breads, hot tub, free Wi-Fi, easy walk to town, near a trolley stop, 204 Hill Street, 888-430-9211, www.laurelspringslodge.com.

FOXTROT BED & BREAKFAST: $$–$$$, gourmet breakfast, located on a mountaintop three miles from downtown, luxurious rooms with balconies, 1520 Garrett Lane, 865-436-3033, www.thefoxtrot.com.

HIPPENSTEAL'S MOUNTAIN VIEW INN: $$, free delectable breakfasts, special desserts in the evening, quiet and relaxing rooms with great mountain views, free Wi-Fi, beautiful porch. Vern Hippensteal's watercolors are featured throughout the inn. 4201 Tatern Marr Way, Sevierville, 865-436-5761, www.hippensteal.com.

Selected Restaurants

BENNETT'S PIT BBQ: $–$$, American, full bar, 8 a.m. until closing Sun through Thu, closing time varies from 8-10 p.m.; 8 a.m. until closing Fri and Sat, closing time varies from 9 to 11 p.m.; closing time varies by season; 714 River Road, 865-436-2400, www.bennetts-bbq.com.

CALHOUN'S GATLINBURG: $, American, full bar, craft beers, specializes in ribs, 11 a.m. to 10 p.m. daily, 1004 Parkway, Suite 101, 865-436-4100, www.calhouns.com.

CHEROKEE GRILL: $–$$, American, full bar, steak, chicken, seafood, homemade bread baked daily, casual dress, 4 to 9:30 p.m. Mon through Fri, 11 a.m. to 11 p.m. Sat and Sun, 1002 Parkway, 865-436-4287.
    OUR EXPERIENCE, APRIL 2015: In town for the Wildflower Pilgrimage, I find this wonderful restaurant, which offers fine dining in a quiet atmosphere.

I enjoy a glass of pinot noir and then my dinner of grilled trout and garden vegetables. It is delicious.

The Wildflower Pilgrimage brings serious botanists together each year to witness spring bursting forth in the Smokies.

THE PEDDLER STEAKHOUSE: $$–$$$, American, full bar, steak, chicken, seafood, 5 to 9 p.m. Sun through Fri, 4:30 to 10 p.m. Sat and Sun, 820 River Road, 865-436-5794, www.peddlergatlinburg.com.

SMOKY MOUNTAIN TROUT HOUSE: $–$$; American; family-style restaurant known for their trout but also serving chicken, ham, and steak; beer and wine; 5 to 9 p.m. daily; 410 Parkway; 865-436-5416; www.gatlinburgtrouthouse.com.

BUCKHORN INN RESTAURANT: $$–$$$, American, fine dining, full bar, four-course dinners, 7 p.m. seating daily, 2140 Tudor Mountain Road, 865-436-4668, www.buckhorninn.com.

THE RESTAURANT AT BUCKBERRY CREEK: $$$, American, fine dining, chef changes menu daily, full bar, spectacular views in a rustic setting, days and hours vary seasonally, 961 Campbell Lead Rd., 865-430-8030, www.buckberrylodge.com.

OUR EXPERIENCE, APRIL 2016: When my friend Ginny and I are here for the Wildflower Pilgrimage, we decide to check this restaurant out. With the GPS, we make it up the mountain to this hidden gem. The building looks old, but it was built to look like a rustic New England lodge with fireplaces and outside seating. Unfortunately, we did not know there was outside seating when we made our reservations. There are wonderful views of the forest and of Gatlinburg.

We are pleasantly surprised with the meal and the surroundings. Ginny has a martini, and I order wine. We decide to share several appetizers and a salad. Then we treat ourselves to a delectable dessert. I think, "This is what fine dining is all about."

Hiker Essentials, Splurges, and Emergency Stops

Shuttle-Service Providers

A WALK IN THE WOODS: 9 a.m. to 5 p.m., 865-436-8283, Vesna@awalkinthe-woods.com or www.awalkinthewoods.com.

ALL PARK TAXI: 865-436-5893, allparktaxi@aol.com.

A2Z TAXI: 865-323-9708.

DRIVERZ TAXI SERVICE: 865-809-9186.

Car Rental

The nearest locations are in Sevierville, fifteen miles west of Gatlinburg.

ENTERPRISE RENT-A-CAR: 7:30 a.m. to 6 p.m. Mon through Fri, 8 a.m. to 4 p.m. Sat, 736 West Main Street, Sevierville, 865-908-3102.

HERTZ RENT-A-CAR: 7:30 a.m. to 6 p.m. Mon through Fri, 708 Winfield Dunn Parkway, Sevierville, 865-774-0919.

Outfitters

THE DAY HIKER: one-stop shop for affordable outdoor and hiking products, 10 a.m. to 9 or 10 p.m. daily May through Oct, 10 a.m. to 6 p.m. Nov through April, 634 Parkway #1, 865-430-0970.

NANTAHALA OUTDOOR CENTER (NOC) GATLINBURG: 18,000-square-foot store with gifts, gear, and guidance for people planning hiking, biking, and water excursions; 10 a.m. to 9 p.m. daily; 1138 Parkway; 865-277-8209.

Groceries

FOOD CITY: 6 a.m. to midnight, daily, groceries, beer and wine, 1219 East Parkway, 865-430-3116.

OLD DAD'S GENERAL STORE: groceries, beer and wine, 7 a.m. to midnight daily; short order grill selling picnic-style lunches, sandwiches, hamburgers, biscuits and gravy, 7 a.m. to 5 p.m. daily; 1127 Parkway, 865-430-1644.

OUR EXPERIENCE: For lunch my friend Ginny and I share a sandwich piled high with turkey, lettuce, and tomatoes. It is delicious. We treat ourselves to homemade oatmeal cookies for dessert.

I tell Ginny, "If I were day hiking on the A.T., this would be a good place to pick up supplies and lunch for the trail. It is open early and near by."

WHOLE EARTH GROCERY: organic groceries and natural medicines, café with vegan and vegetarian selections, no beer or wine, 10 a.m. to 6 p.m. Mon through Fri, 10 a.m. to 5 p.m. Sat, 446 East Parkway, 865-436-6967.

Wine or Beer Shops

SMOKY MOUNTAIN BREWERY: homemade beer, fresh-squeezed citrus and berry drinks, full bar, pizza, burgers, sandwiches, High-Definition TVs, band on weekends, 11:30 to 1 a.m. daily, 1004 Parkway #501, 865-436-4200.

OUR EXPERIENCE: My friend Ginny and I check out the Smoky Mountain Brewery for lunch and have delicious flatbreads with cheese and vegetables. We also try one of their brews. We peek in at their beer tanks; everything is quiet and clean.

SMOKY MOUNTAIN WINERY: East Tennessee's oldest producer of premium wines, free tastings of more than twenty award-winning wines, unique shop,

10 a.m. to 8 p.m. daily in summer, days and hours vary seasonally, 450 Cherry St., 865-436-7551.

SUGARLAND CELLARS: handcrafted wines and fine gifts, free wine tasting, tours, 10 a.m. to 8 p.m. daily, 1133 Parkway, 865-325-1110.

ATMs

ATM: 542 Parkway.

ATM (BBT): 625 and 815 Parkway.

BBT: 1001 Parkway.

CARDTRONICS ATM: Downtown Market, 762 Parkway.

MONEYTREE ATM: 919 Parkway.

Other ATMs located at more than twelve banks in Gatlinburg.

Urgent Care and Emergency Services in Gatlinburg or Nearby

FIRST MED FAMILY PRACTICE: 8 a.m. to 5 p.m. Mon through Fri, 9 a.m. to 1 p.m. Sat and Sun, 1015 East Parkway, 865-436-7267.

PIGEON FORGE MEDICAL CLINIC: 8:30 a.m. to 5 p.m. Mon through Fri, 9 a.m. to 1 p.m. Sat, 190 Community Center Drive, #102, Pigeon Forge (six miles west of Gatlinburg), 865-453-1924.

LE CONTE MEDICAL CENTER (FT. SANDERS-SEVIER MEDICAL CENTER), EMERGENCY SERVICES: 24/7, 742 Middle Creek Rd., Sevierville (eleven miles west of Gatlinburg), 865-446-7000.

WELL-KEY URGENT CARE (SMOKY MOUNTAIN URGENT CARE): 8 a.m. to 8 p.m. daily, walk-ins welcome, 1787 Veterans Boulevard, Sevierville, 865-428-2773.

URGENT FAMILY CARE: 8 a.m. to 8 p.m. Mon through Sat, 8 a.m. to 6 p.m. Sun, 707 Dolly Parton Parkway, Sevierville, 865-428-2014.

GREAT SMOKY MOUNTAINS NATIONAL PARK: emergency number, 865-436-9171.

Fun Places to Visit

ARROWMONT SCHOOL OF ARTS AND CRAFTS GALLERIES: national arts and crafts educational center, workshops available weekdays and weekends, 8:30 a.m. to 5 p.m. Mon through Fri, call for weekend hours, 556 Parkway, 865-436-5860. Two buildings were destroyed by fire in 2016.

OUR EXPERIENCE: My friend Ginny and I check out the exhibit spaces while we are here for a reception for the Wildflower Pilgrimage. The exhibit includes a small but interesting display of modern work by artists from the Arrowmont School. The artists have made use of eclectic materials such as cloth, stones, marbles, paper, and metal to create their works.

PAUL MURRAY ART GALLERY: 10:30 a.m. to 6 p.m. Mon through Sat, noon to 3 p.m. Sun, 1103 Glades Road, 865-436-8445.

GREAT SMOKY ARTS & CRAFTS COMMUNITY: This is the largest group of independent artisans in North America. The eight-mile trail of shops starts on Glades Road at East Parkway. Shops are open year round. Art forms include whittling, painting, sewing, casting, weaving, and carving.

GREAT SMOKY MOUNTAINS HERITAGE CENTER: $7 for adults, $5 for seniors, $5 for children 6–17, free for children under 6; dedicated to the cultural heritage of Eastern Tennessee and the Great Smoky Mountains, check website for special events; 10 a.m. to 5 p.m. Mon through Sat, noon to 5 p.m. Sun; 123 Cromwell Drive, Townsend, Tennessee; www.gsmheritagecenter.org.

FORBIDDEN CAVERNS: tours, 10 a.m. to 5 p.m. Mon through Sat, Apr through Nov, 455 Blowing Cave Road, Sevierville.

TENNESSEE MUSEUM OF AVIATION: $12.75 for adults, $9.75 for seniors, $6.75 for children six to twelve, free for children under six, 10 a.m. to 6 p.m. Mon through Sat, 1 to 6 p.m. Sun, historic aircraft collection, live demonstrations, tours available, gift shop, 135 Air Museum Way, Sevierville, 865-908-0171 and 866-286-8738.

OUR EXPERIENCE, MAY 2013: Jim and I stop to see the museum on our way home from day hikes in southwest Virginia. The museum tells the story of aviation in southeastern Tennessee with exhibits of antique aircraft and pictures. It is interesting to see the story of women who flew in the early days and how the airport in Sevierville came to be.

A WALK IN THE WOODS: guided nature walks by Vesna and Erik Plakanis, experts on the ecology of the Great Smoky Mountains National Park. You will see waterfalls, majestic forests, mountain streams, old home sites, and graveyards. 865-436-8283.

BENT CREEK GOLF COURSE: 18 holes, par 72, tee times 8 a.m. to 8 p.m. daily, call to reserve tee times and ask about fees, 3919 East Parkway, 865-436-3947 and 1-800-767-3574.

RAFTING IN THE SMOKIES: Pigeon River rafting, ziplining and family adventures, certified and trained rafting guides; see prices on website; 813 East Parkway 1-800-776-7238, https://raftinginthesmokies.com.

ROARING FORK MOTOR NATURE TRAIL IN GREAT SMOKY MOUNTAINS NATIONAL PARK: most popular driving tour in the Smokies, log cabins, near waterfall; turn off the parkway in Gatlinburg at traffic light #8 onto Historic Nature Trail Road to the Cherokee Orchard entrance to the national park, follow the one-way Roaring Fork Motor Nature Trail; closed in winter; 865-436-1200.

SMOKY MOUNTAIN OUTDOORS: white water rafting on the Pigeon River, breathtaking scenery with rafting thrills for the whole family, 453 Brookside Village Way, 1-800-771-7238.

SMOKY MOUNTAIN ANGLER: guided fishing trips, oldest fly-fishing store in Sevier County, open year round, 466 Brookside Village Way, Suite 8, Gatlinburg, 865-436-8746. Call 865-332-6270 to book a trip.

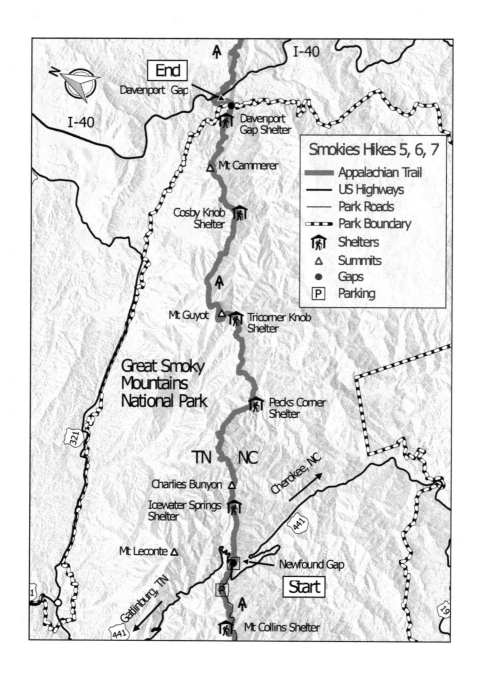

Overview of the Northern Smokies Three-Day Backpacking Adventure

from Newfound Gap at US 441 to Davenport Gap, 30.8 miles, Challenging

HIGHLIGHTS: This is a beautiful but challenging section of the Appalachian Trail. It begins at Newfound Gap and runs up and down along the ridgeline above five thousand feet before it descends into Davenport Gap. You are rewarded by spectacular views from rocky crags such as Charlies Bunion and from the Mount Cammerer fire lookout tower. In the peak season of April through June, you will pass many hikers.

DISTANCE: 30.8 miles on the A.T.
HIKE TIME: 3 to 4 days.

RECOMMENDED DIRECTION: South to north, from Newfound Gap to Davenport Gap.

Jim makes funny faces as we wait for the bus to Newfound Gap, July 2011

My Hiking Journal

We drive up from Atlanta for our second three-day backpacking adventure in the Smokies. Jim didn't want to make this trip without our friends Mo, Rana, and Hadi, who came with us last year on our backpacking adventure in the southern part of the Smokies. They couldn't join us this year. I am a little uncertain about how this adventure will go.

We arrive the day before the hike so we can leave our car at Davenport Gap for the end of the trek and be ready to start our hike the next day at Newfound Gap. We stay overnight in Cherokee and take the Cherokee Transit to Newfound Gap on the morning of the hike. The Cherokee Transit no longer runs from Cherokee to Gatlinburg with a stop at Newfound Gap.

Carol's Reminders

- **Plan and Prepare for the trip two to six months in advance.**
- **Contact the Great Smoky Mountains National Park Backcountry Office thirty days** before your hike to secure your shelter reservations and obtain your backcountry permit. During the peak season, shelters fill up fast, and officials save some slots for thru-hikers.
- **Check with the National Park Service before you start your trek** to see which water sources are reliable. In the summer, some will be dry.
- **Arrive near the trailhead the night before** you begin your three-day backpacking adventure. Get an early start to the trailhead on the first day.

Nearest Towns

Gatlinburg, Tennessee, is sixteen miles west and Cherokee, North Carolina, is nineteen miles east of Newfound Gap, the southern trailhead.

Hartford, Cosby, and Newport, Tennessee, are six, fifteen, and twenty miles respectively to the west and Waterville and Maggie Valley, North Carolina, are two and thirty-five miles respectively to the east of Davenport Gap, the northern trailhead.

Directions to the Trailheads

SOUTHERN TRAILHEAD AT NEWFOUND GAP: GPS coordinates 35.61108, -83.42484. The A.T. crosses US 441 at Newfound Gap. From Cherokee drive west nineteen miles on US 441 and from Gatlinburg drive east sixteen miles on US 441 to Newfound Gap. The Rockefeller Memorial and parking area are on the north side of US 441 at Newfound Gap.

NORTHERN TRAILHEAD AT DAVENPORT GAP: GPS coordinates 36.7674, -83.1334. Take I-40, exit 451 (Waterville, North Carolina). Drive through Waterville on NC 1332 and then west on NC 1397 to Davenport Gap. Because of reported instances of vandalism, do not leave your car at the Gap. Park at the Big Creek Ranger Station or nearby at Standing Bear Farm Hostel.

If you plan to shuttle using two cars, leave one car at the Big Creek Ranger Station or Standing Bear Farm Hostel. Drive the second car to Newfound Gap. Retracing your route from the gap to I-40, drive east on I-40 to Exit 20. Turn right on US 276. At Dellwood, turn right on US 19/US 276 and drive twenty-four miles to Cherokee. Turn right on US 441 and drive nineteen miles to Newfound Gap. Parking is on the north side of the road where the A.T. crosses US 441.

ALTERNATIVE TRANSPORTATION: Hire a shuttle driver to pick you up at either the Big Creek Ranger Station or Standing Bear Farm Hostel where you can leave a car near Davenport Gap. Have the driver take you to Newfound Gap to start your hike.

Day 1 of the Three-Day Backpacking Adventure, Newfound Gap to Pecks Corner Shelter,
10.6 miles, Challenging

HIGHLIGHTS: The views of the valleys, gorges, and mountain ranges are splendid from the ridgelines. You can watch the blue smoke rise from the Smoky Mountains.

DISTANCE: 10.2 miles plus 0.4 miles to the shelter on Hughes Ridge Trail.

HIKE TIME: 8 to 10 hours.

LEVEL OF EFFORT: Challenging because of the 900-foot climb in less than three miles from Newfound Gap to the Boulevard Trail.

DOWNHILL: 5.3 miles with an elevation loss of 2,410 feet. **UPHILL:** 5.3 miles with an elevation gain of 2,610 feet.

ALONG THE TRAIL: From Newfound Gap, the earthen trail ascends through a canopy of spruce and fir trees to the ridgeline then becomes narrow and rocky. When the trail splits into the Boulevard Trail to left and the Appalachian Trail to the right, take the less traveled A.T. to the right.

SHELTERS: There are two shelters: Icewater Spring Shelter and Pecks Corner Shelter. Both shelters have been renovated and have extended roofs with tables and benches, skylights, and two sleeping shelves. There are privies, springs, and bear pulls nearby.

Follow the White Blazes

MILE 0.0: Newfound Gap, 5,045 feet, water and restrooms.

MILE 1.7: Sweat Heifer Trail to the right. Years ago, cattle sweated as they were driven up this trail in the summers to pastures on the balds.

MILE 2.4: Mount Ambler, 6,100 feet.

MILE 2.7: Boulevard Trail to Mount Le Conte splits off to the left. Another side trail goes left to Mount Kephart, and the A.T. splits to the right. 6,030 feet.

MILE 3.0: Icewater Spring Shelter with water and a privy, 5,900 feet.

MILE 3.9: Charlies Bunion, 5,500 feet. Take the loop trail to the left for a profile view of Charlies Bunion. This rock sticks out from the ridgeline like a bunion might stick out from your foot. The famed naturalist Horace Kephart named it for his hiking partner Charlie Conner. Conner, as you might guess, had a bunion on his foot.

MILE 4.2: Dry Sluice Gap, 5,380 feet. In this gap, the stream flows underground most of the year, and the gap is dry. In heavy rains, the gap handles the overflow.

MILE 4.3: Dry Sluice Gap Trail to right.

MILE 5.2: Porters Gap, 5,370 feet.

MILE 7.7: Laurel Top, 5760 feet.

MILE 8.3: Bradley's View, 5,200 feet.

MILE 10.2: Hughes Ridge Trail to Pecks Corner Shelter , 0.4 miles east, 5,280 feet. Trail named for the Hughes family who lived here in the 1800s.
MILE 10.6: Pecks Corner Shelter with water and privy nearby.

Peaks and Valleys

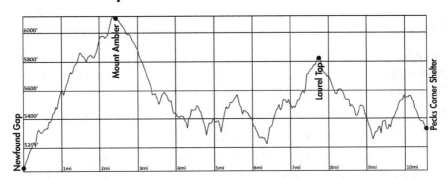

Alternate Shorter Hikes

SMOKIES HIKE 5.1:
Newfound Gap to Icewater Spring Shelter, 3 miles, Challenging
DISTANCE: 3 miles.
HIKE TIME: 2 to 2.5 hours.
LEVEL OF EFFORT: Challenging.

SMOKIES HIKE 5.2:
Icewater Spring Shelter to Pecks Corner Shelter, 7.6 miles, Moderate
DISTANCE: 7.2 miles on the A.T. plus 0.4 miles to the shelter.
HIKE TIME: 4 hours.
LEVEL OF EFFORT: Moderate.

My Hiking Journal

JULY 2011: The sky is overcast when we head up the trail from Newfound Gap through a tunnel of spruce and fir trees. The trail is wet from the rain that has fallen the last few days.

We have maps, but there are many trails that intersect the A.T. in the Smokies. I wonder, "Will we make the correct turns?" In less than three miles, we come to a fork. One wide trail continues to the left. A smaller side trail goes left as well, and another small trail goes to the right. We select the wide trail to the left because it looks like the one that gets the most use.

After a mile or so, we meet another hiker and stop to talk with him.

"Where are you going?" Jim asks.

"Oh, back to the car. I have been to Mount Le Conte," he says.

It is then that we realize that we went the wrong way at the fork. We took the Boulevard Trail, which goes to Mount Le Conte, and not the Appalachian Trail. We look at the map and retrace our steps.

Soon after we rejoin the A.T., we reach the Icewater Spring Shelter and stop for lunch. When we leave the shelter, we look for the white A.T. blazes so that we know we are still on the trail.

As we are going down the rocky trail with Icewater Spring Creek flowing down through it, we come upon an older, overweight hiker sitting in the middle of the trail with his backpack off.

I ask, "Are you all right?"

"No," he said. "I have twisted my knee! I have sent some of the boys from my scout troop for the other leaders. I'm just going to wait right here until they come back and help me to the car."

Soon we come to Charlies Bunion, a rock outcropping named for Charlie Conner, a local mountaineer. We walk carefully out onto the black slate ledge to see the spectacular views of gorges and mountaintops. Suddenly, there is a big clap of thunder. We hurry off the ledge and back to the trail.

As we enter the forest, it begins to rain lightly. We decide it is too warm for our rain jackets and put up our umbrellas.

A hiker passes us and we ask where he's headed. He tells us he's going to Pecks Corner Shelter.

Jim says, "We are too."

He says, "I'll save you two spots at the shelter."

"Please make it on the lower sleeping shelf," I say.

We go up and down and up and down before we reach the side trail to Pecks Corner Shelter. It is starting to get dark, so we stop and put on our headlights.

Jim on Charlies Bunion, July 2011

We finally get to the shelter about seven thirty. Our muscles are tired and aching.

Barry, the hiker we met earlier, is already there. "I used my rain gear to save you two spots on the lower sleeping shelf," he says.

"Thanks," I say.

Every spot on both sleeping shelves has a sleeping bag on it except for our spots. Boy, am I glad Barry saved us these two places.

A junco on Charlies Bunion, July 2011

Jim goes down the hill for water, and I lay out our pads and sleeping bags and start supper. We are having rice with salmon and vegetables tonight.

Jim comes back from the spring with mud on his pants.

"What happened?" I ask.

"I slipped on the rocks," he says.

"Are your hurt?" I ask.

"No," he replies.

I tell him, "Supper's ready."

We eat and toast our hike with a little wine. I brought one small plastic bottle of wine so we could celebrate each day.

We clean up quickly and crawl into our sleeping bags.

Carol's Reminders

- **Start early on your first day of a multiple-day hike.**
- **If possible, make the first day a short day**. Even with training, your body will need to adjust to the backpack and to the miles of ups and downs on the trail.
- **Watch the white A.T. blazes closely.** If you have hiked for fifteen minutes or longer without seeing a blaze, retrace your steps until you see one. You may have missed a turn.
- **Have your pack well organized.** For easy access, have your rain jacket and umbrella near the top. Color-code the small bags in your pack with different colors for food, water, and cooking equipment so that you can find them quickly once you reach the shelter.
- **Pack lightly.** For a short backpacking trip, keep the weight at thirty pounds or less.
- **Test your recipes for your evening meals, and keep them simple.** I use minute rice and add chicken or salmon and dry vegetables or soup for seasoning. It is easy to cook and tasty.

Day 2 of the Three-Day Backpacking Adventure, Pecks Corner Shelter to Tri-Corner Knob Shelter,
5.5 miles, Moderate

HIGHLIGHTS: If it is not foggy, the views from Eagle Rocks and Mount Sequoyah will be great.

DISTANCE: 5.1 miles on the A.T. plus 0.4 miles from the shelter to the A. T.

HIKE TIME: 4 hours.

The Smokies, July 2011

LEVEL OF EFFORT: Moderate. You will hike a short distance but have a long uphill climb.

DOWNHILL: 2.3 miles with an elevation loss of 1,160 feet. **UPHILL:** 3.2 miles with an elevation gain of 1,745 feet.

ALONG THE TRAIL: From Pecks Corner Shelter on the Hughes Ridge Trail, the A.T. goes up and down over rocks to the viewing spot known as Eagle Rocks. These craggy, weathered, round rocks look like an eagle on a perch. On this section of the trail the rocks have turned from slate to sandstone over millions of years.

Over the next four miles, the trail goes down to Copper Gap, up six hundred feet to Mount Sequoyah, down to Chapman Gap, up 400 feet on a rocky steep path to Mount Chapman, and then down a rocky path to Tri-corner Knob Shelter.

SHELTERS: Pecks Corner Shelter is at the beginning of this hike, and Tri-corner Knob Shelter is at the end. Each has been refurbished with an overhanging roof, two sleeping shelves, and benches. A privy, water source, and bear pulls are near each shelter. Tri-corner Knob Shelter, in the coldest section of the park, is one of the least visited shelters.

Follow the White Blazes

MILE 0.0: Pecks Corner Shelter with water and privy nearby.

MILE 0.4: A.T. and Hughes Ridge Trail

MILE 1.4: Eagle Rocks, 5,800 feet, views. These rocks look like an eagle on a perch.

MILE 2.1: Copper Gap, 5,500 feet.

MILE 2.8: Mount Sequoyah, 5,960 feet. Sequoyah was the leader who developed the Cherokee written language.

MILE 3.8: Chapman Gap, 5,800 feet.

MILE 4.5: Mount Chapman, 6,240 feet. Colonel David Chapman was an early promoter of the park in the 1920s and is considered by some to be the "Father of the Park."

MILE 5.5: Tri-Corner Knob Shelter, 5,920 feet. Three counties and three ridge crests converge here.

Peaks and Valleys

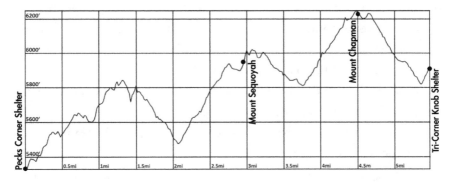

My Hiking Journal

When we get up and move around this morning, we both feel tired and dragged out.

"I guess my body is just getting adjusted to hiking again," I say.

This is the first challenging hiking trip we have made in the last three months. We hiked up and down Stone Mountain and the trail that goes around the Westminster campus several times with our packs, but have done nothing as strenuous as this hike. We are asking our muscles to do more than they normally do every day. This puts stress on our bodies.

We finally start down the trail about ten. As we walk down the trail through the fog, I have an eerie feeling. It is like we are floating through the fog. If Jim walks more than twenty feet ahead, he looks like a blur.

We hike slowly up and down Mount Sequoyah and Mount Chapman. It begins to rain lightly, and the fog finally lifts. We stop to take pictures.

When we reach Tri-corner Knob Shelter in midafternoon, we decide to stay. It is two o'clock, and it has taken us four hours to hike these last five miles. If we were to hike the next 7.7 miles as planned, we would be walking over a rocky path along a six-thousand-foot ridgeline, and it would take us another five or six hours. This could be unsafe as the light wanes.

I am too tired to go any further, and I know Jim is too.

Since I have time, I wash up and rest. Jim relaxes and gathers wood for a fire. Trey, a ridgerunner, arrives at the shelter.

Jim says to him, "We would like to stay here tonight instead of Cosby Knob Shelter where we have reservations."

Trey replies, "It's good that you stopped here because we have a bear problem at Cosby Knob Shelter."

Jim tells Trey that we need to let Curtis, our shuttle driver, know we will be arriving late tomorrow and to change our hotel reservations in Cherokee.

I say to Jim, "We are really lucky to have stopped here and that Trey is here and can help us."

While on the radio with the backcountry office, Trey checks the weather and says, "Tomorrow is projected to be clear and no rain."

We relax and cook supper. Other hikers join us, including Ed, a writer; his eight-year-old son, Ethan; and Tom, a teacher from Ohio who hikes in the Smokies frequently and is experimenting with lightweight equipment. Ethan reads us a scary story as we snuggle in our sleeping bags.

Just as we are about to fall asleep, a group of three hikers comes into the shelter. They seem new to backpacking and are sharing information with each other about the food and supplies they have found for this trip. I enjoy listening to them. But we are so tired that we drift off to sleep, even though they are still cooking, talking, and settling down for the night.

Carol's Reminders

- **Listen to your body.** When you are tired, change your plans and adjust the next day's schedule so it is less strenuous.
- **Take extra food and supplies for emergencies.** We take an extra day of food just in case we stay out longer than expected.
- **When you make your shelter reservations, ask about the availability of ridgerunners on the trail.** Ridgerunners are seasonal employees hired to help hikers, handle problems, and protect the trail. They tell hikers about the principles of Leave No Trace, and they pick up trash.

Day 3 of the Three-Day Backpacking Adventure, Tri-Corner Knob Shelter to Davenport Gap,
15.5 miles, Moderate

HIGHLIGHTS: In June and July, there are beautiful rhododendrons and wildflowers in bloom. Along the six-thousand-foot ridge crest and from Mount Cammerer, there are grand panoramic views. You can see Mount Guyot and the Mount Sterling Fire Lookout Tower to the southwest, Snowbird Mountains to the east, and the town of Cosby to the west.

Beautiful rhododendrons, July 2011

The Mount Cammerer historic stone fire lookout tower is .6 miles north of the A.T. on a side trail. This fire lookout tower was built over a period of time between 1937 and 1939 by the Civilian Conservation Corps and refurbished in 1995 by the Friends of the Smokies. It is an amazing structure.

Mount Cammerer Fire Lookout Tower, Wikipedia 2016

DISTANCE: 15.5 miles.   **HIKE TIME:** 8 to 9 hours.

LEVEL OF EFFORT: Moderate. This is a downhill but lengthy hike.

DOWNHILL: 11.4 miles with an elevation loss of 5,060 feet. **UPHILL:** 4.1 miles with an elevation gain of 1,960 feet.

ALONG THE TRAIL: From Tri-Corner Shelter, the path along the ridge crest is rocky, but the trail becomes earthen as it winds downhill through rhododendron tunnels. The trail passes through sandstone outcroppings and large sandstone slabs. After Cosby Knob, the forest changes from evergreen to hardwood trees. At Sunup Knob, there are grey rocks speckled with dark chips called greywacke along with black and grey slate rocks. These rocks are common in the Smokies.

SHELTERS: Cosby Knob Shelter has been refurbished with an extended roof, skylights, two sleeping shelves, benches, and a table. A privy, spring, and bear pulls are nearby. Davenport Gap Shelter has been refurbished with two sleeping shelves and skylights, but it still has a bear fence.

Follow the White Blazes

MILE 0.0: Tri-Corner Knob Shelter with water and privy, 5,900 feet.

MILE 1.2: Mount Guyot Spur, 6,330 feet.

MILE 1.9: Guyot Spring, 6,230 feet.

MILE 2.1: Mount Guyot side trail, 6,395 feet.

MILE 2.8: Deer Creek Gap, 6,050 feet, views of Mount Sterling, Mount Guyot, and Big Creek Basin.

MILE 3.3: Metal remnants of a 1984 Air Force jet crash.

MILE 3.9: Inadu Knob, 5,800 feet, Snake Den Ridge Trail leads five miles to Cosby Campground. Inadu is the Cherokee word for snake. There are copperhead and rattlesnake dens in the area.

MILE 5.3: Camel Hump Knob, 5,050 feet.

MILE 6.2: Camel Gap and Camel Gap Trail, 4,600 feet, views of the Big Creek watershed.

MILE 7.4: Cosby Knob, 5,000 feet.

MILE 7.6: Cosby Knob Shelter with a spring and privy, 4,700 feet.

MILE 8.4: Low Gap, 4,270 feet. Low Gap Trail leads two and a half miles north to Cosby Campground and hiker parking.

MILE 9.7: Sunup Knob, 4,850 feet.

MILE 10.6: Mount Cammerer side trail, 5,000 feet. This trail will take you 0.6 miles west to a restored fire lookout tower with views. Mount Cammerer was named for Arno B. Cammerer, the third director of the National Park Service and a friend of John D. Rockefeller.

MILE 11.1: Spring, 4,300 feet.

MILE 12.5: Spring east of A.T., 3,700 feet.

MILE 13.6: Chestnut Branch Trail.

MILE 14.8: Davenport Gap Shelter, 2,600 feet, water.

MILE 15.5: Davenport Gap, 1,975 feet, park boundary, TN 32 to the west and NC 1397 to the east.

Peaks and Valleys

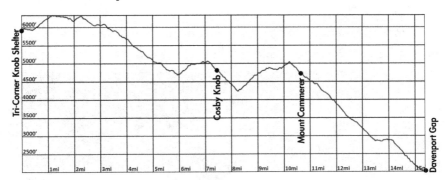

Alternate Hikes

SMOKIES HIKE 7.1:
Tri-Corner Knob Shelter to Cosby Knob Shelter,
7.6 miles, Moderate

DISTANCE: 7.6 miles. **TIME:** 4 hours. **LEVEL OF EFFORT:** Moderate.

SMOKIES HIKE 7.2:

Cosby Knob Shelter to Davenport Gap, 7.9 miles, Moderate to Easy

DISTANCE: 7.9 miles.   **HIKE TIME:** 4 hours.

LEVEL OF EFFORT: Moderate to Easy with a long downhill trek.

My Hiking Journal

I wake up early this morning feeling refreshed. Jim gets up and begins to pack. When I go to heat the water for tea, I realize the gas canister is out.

I ask, "How can this be?"

Tom, the teacher staying at the shelter, says, "Use my stove and pot after I finish."

I put out our cereal and then heat our water. By eight thirty, we are ready to leave.

Jim says, "I am ready for a steak and champagne tonight."

Jim leads the way and walks at a fast clip. We have almost sixteen miles to go to Davenport Gap. I follow along at a slower pace. My left

Jim's body language says that we need to stop at Cosby Knob Shelter for a break, July 2011

knee has started to hurt. I catch up with Jim when he stops for snacks and to talk with other hikers.

We stop and have lunch at Cosby Knob Shelter and check the structure out. It is an old, worn-looking shelter with one sleeping shelf, an outdoor picnic table, and a fire ring. I'm really glad we did not stay here last night as we had planned.

Jim remembers that the ridgerunner told us yesterday that a bear was active around this shelter. Jim bangs his poles to ward off the bear. We don't see a bear.

When we come to the Mount Cammerer side trail, I say, "I am going to pass this up. My knee is hurting."

Jim runs up the side trail. "I'm going to check this fire lookout tower out and get a few pictures," he says.

We begin our final, five-mile downhill stretch. We pass many hikers coming up the trail for the weekend. Jim stops to talk, but I hike on, moving slowly down the trail. I finally stop, wait for him, and rest my knee. In a little while, down he comes, but with only one hiking pole.

"Where is your other pole?" I ask, but to my surprise, there is no answer. Later on I ask him again, but there is still no answer. I guess he doesn't want to talk about whatever happened.

Jim calls Curtis, the shuttle driver, and says, "We'll be there by seven."

When we get to Davenport Gap, we only have to wait a few minutes before Curtis rolls up. We both smile broadly and jump in the car. He takes us to our car at Standing Bear Farm Hostel.

We change clothes behind our car and hit the road.

"I hope we find fine dining in Maggie Valley," I say.

Maggie Valley is thirty-five miles away and it is almost eight o'clock. Fortunately, we find a restaurant called J. Arthur's and celebrate completing the A.T. in the Smokies with champagne and a delicious dinner.

Carol's Reminders

- **Plan a wonderful meal, hotel stay, or sightseeing trip at the end of your hiking adventure.** With this plan in mind, you may find that your hiking partner is willing to tackle greater mileage in order to finish the hike on the expected day and not have to stay in a shelter another night.
- **Have phone numbers for nearby emergency services, hotels, restaurants, and shuttle services.** We are glad we had these numbers with us so we could ask the ridgerunner to change our reservations when we decided to change our plans while hiking on the trail.
- **For a three-day backpacking adventure, be safe and take extra supplies and food.**

Fine Wine and Accommodations
Hartford, Cosby, and Newport, Tennessee

HARTFORD is a small community at the Tennessee–North Carolina border along I-40 in the narrow Pigeon River Valley of rural Cocke County. It has a hostel, cabins for rent, groceries, refueling stations, restaurants, and rafting companies.

COSBY is an unincorporated community of around 5,000 people in Cocke County at the northwestern border of the Great Smoky Mountains National Park. It has restaurants, small motels, B&Bs, and cabin rentals.

NEWPORT is the county seat of Cocke County, with a population of about seven thousand. It has many hotels and restaurants.

Lodging and Restaurants, Hartford

Lodging

STANDING BEAR FARM HOSTEL: ½ $, rustic bunkroom, cabins, campground available, hot showers, privy, no flush toilets, laundry, microwave, grill, small resupply store, free Wi-Fi, parking, shuttle service, 4255 Green Corner Road (just west of where the A.T. crosses Green Corner Road), 423-487-0014. All business must be done by phone and not online. Reservations are required for shuttles.

FOXFIRE RIVERSIDE CAMPGROUND: operates mid March to mid Nov; ½ $ for tent sites with shower house and restrooms; $$ for cabins with sleeping loft and 1BA or cottage with 2BR,1BA; furnished kitchens, TVs, DVD players, and linens; picnic area; gas grill; concession stand on site; fishing; rafting; kayaking. On Pigeon River at 3541 Hartford Road at I-40, Exit 447, 502-641-5369, www.foxfireriversidecamp.com.

PIGEON RIVER CAMPGROUND: ½ $ for tent site, $ for RV site, $–$$ for camping cabins with bunk beds, AC/Heat, no linens, picnic tables, pool, bathhouse, laundry room, 3375 Hartford Rd. at I-40, Exit 447, 844-766-2267, 1-888-827-3404, www.campinginthesmokymountains.com.

Restaurants

PIGEON RIVER SMOKEHOUSE: $, American, 7 a.m. to 7 p.m., barbeque and Krispy Krunchy chicken, catfish, boxed dinners, lunches to go, sodas, beer, located inside a BP convenience store, 3105 Big Creek Rd. at I-40, exit 447, 423-487-0061, www.pigeonriversmokehouse.com.

OUR EXPERIENCE: In April 2011, we pick up our car at Standing Bear Farm Hostel about six thirty after a long day of hiking with our friends, Rana, Mo, and Hadi. We ask Maria, the hostel owner, if there is a restaurant nearby.

She says, "The only place open is the barbeque restaurant at the next exit." The next exit is about five miles away.

We jump in the car and drive to the next exit and look for the restaurant. We discover that it's in a BP convenience store. We rush in and see a food counter and tables in the back, but there is no one working behind the counter there.

Jim asks the cashier, "Is the restaurant open?"

He replies, "We close at seven, but I'll send someone back to fix something for you."

We look at the menu board: fried chicken, fried fish, barbeque, vegetables, and sandwiches.

Since our friends are vegan, I ask them, "Can you find something you can eat?"

Rana replies, "I think so."

Jim and I have a beer while we are waiting. I order fried fish, Jim orders fried chicken, and our friends order vegan sandwiches and chips. Jim and I top our meals off with ice cream. The food is okay. But since we are hungry, it is good.

Lodging and Restaurants in Cosby

Selected Lodging

CREEKWALK INN AT WHISPERWOOD FARM B&B: $$ with full breakfast; cozy, rustic rooms and cabin with whirlpools, hot tubs, and fireplaces; free Wi-Fi; children welcome; indoor pool; business center; conference rooms; on-site chapel; library; piano; laundry room; 166 Middle Creek Road; 1-800-962-2246; 865-696-4000, www.whisperwoodretreat.com.

COSBY CREEK CABIN RENTALS: $$, 1BR to 4BR with 1 BA, full kitchens, linens, TVs, Wi-Fi, located on Cosby Creek at 4376 Cosby Highway, 423-487-3333, 1-800-508-8844, www.cosbycreekcabins.com. Cosby Creek is stocked with trout.

GARDEN OF EDEN CABINS: $ with three-night minimum; rustic 1 or 2BR, 1 BA cabins; full kitchens; linens; TVs; outside fire pits and grills; pet friendly; no Wi-Fi. Situated on a creek at 467 Laurel Spring Road, 423-487-2617, www.gardenofedencabins.com.

HUMMING BEAR CABINS: $ with two-night minimum, 3 BR, 2BA, some with kitchenettes, some with fully furnished kitchens, linens, whirlpool tubs, fireplaces or outside fire pits, VCR and DVD players, panoramic views, snowmobile trail, no pets, on top of the mountain at 283 Costner Road, 423-794-7206, www.hummingbearcabins.com.

SERENITY FALLS CABIN RENTALS: $$ with two-night minimum, rustic 1 or 2BR with 1BA, kitchens, linens, pet friendly, located on falls and a creek at 4555 Redwood Road, 423-487-2990, www.serenityfallscabinrentals.com.

WILDWOOD MOUNTAIN ACRES LOG CABIN RENTALS: $–$$, 1BR to 4 BR with 1BA to 3BA, kitchens, hot tubs, linens, views of Smokies, discounts for guests at Rafting on Smokies, no pets, sits on thirty acres at 4410 Wildwood Drive, 1-800-423-2030, www.wildwoodmountain.com.

Selected Restaurants

CARVER'S ORCHARD, APPLEHOUSE RESTAURANT AND COUNTRY STORE: $, American, Southern comfort classics, home cooking, apple-based desserts, no wine or beer, 8 a.m. to 8 p.m. daily, 3460 Cosby Hwy, 423-487-2710.

MAGNOLIA TREE AND COUNTRY STORE: $, American, no beer or wine, 11 a.m. to 7:30 p.m. Sun through Tue and Thu through Sat, 4925 Hooper Highway, 423-487-2519.

SUBSTATION ITALIAN RESTAURANT & SANDWICH SHOP: $–$$, Italian, pizza, sandwiches, BBQ sandwiches, meals, ice cream, desserts, 11 a.m. to 8 p.m.

Mon through Sat, 11 a.m. to 7 p.m. Sun, 4410 Hooper Highway, 423-465-7142.

Lodging and Restaurants in Newport

Selected Lodging

CHRISTOPHER PLACE RESORT B&B: $$–$$$ with gourmet breakfast, free Wi-Fi, beautiful guest rooms designed for comfort and relaxation with whirlpools and sitting areas, garden or mountain views, restaurant on site, tennis court, hiking trail, on 200 acres at 1500 Pinnacles Way, 423-623-6555, 1-800-595-9441, www.christopherplace.com.

COMFORT INN: $–$$, seasonal rates, free hot breakfast, outdoor pool, fitness center, pet friendly, 1149 Smoky Mountain Lane at I-40, Exit 432A, 423-623-5355, www.choicehotels.com/tennessee/newport.

BEST WESTERN NEWPORT INN: $$, seasonal rates, free full breakfast, hot tub, outside pool, free high-speed internet, pet friendly, 1015 Cosby Highway at I-40, Exit 435, 423-623-8713.

HOLIDAY INN EXPRESS: $$, seasonal rates, ask about hiker discount, free breakfast, microwaves, refrigerators, indoor saltwater pool, fitness center, 1022 Cosby Hwy at I-40, Exit 435, 423-623-2121, www.hiexpress.com/newport.

Selected Restaurants

SAGEBRUSH STEAKHOUSE: $, American, Black Angus steak and burgers, ribs, BBQ, seafood, chicken, sandwiches, soups, salads, full bar, cowboy vibe,

11 a.m. to 10 p.m. Sun through Thu, 11 a.m. to 11 p.m. Fri and Sat, 201 Heritage Boulevard, 423-613-4900, www.sagebrushsteakhouse.com.

MILANOS PIZZA & ITALIAN: $, American and Italian, no beer or wine, 10:30 a.m. to 8:30 p.m. Mon through Thu, 10 a.m. to 9:30 p.m. Fri and Sat, 11 a.m. to 8 p.m. Sun, 465 West Broadway, 423-625-3472.

MONTERREY MEXICAN RESTAURANT: $, Mexican, full bar, 11 a.m. to 10 p.m. daily, 130 Newport Towne Center, 423-623-0104.

RUBY TUESDAY: $, American, full bar, 11 a.m. to 10 p.m. Mon through Thu, 11 a.m. to 11 p.m. Fri and Sat, 11 a.m. to 9 p.m. Sun, 1005 Cosby Highway, 423-613-0769, www.rubytuesday.com.

Hiker Essentials, Splurges, and Emergency Stops in Southeastern Tennessee near Davenport Gap

Shuttle-Service Providers

AAA HIKER SERVICE: Joshua Newman and Seth Rodgers: More than twenty-eight years driving in and around the Smoky Mountains, Cosby, 423-487-3112 or 865-322-0691 (cell), email shuttle@AAAHIKERSERVICE.com.

HIGHLANDS SHUTTLE SERVICE, RON MCGAHA: Very experienced in local area, Newport, 423-625-739 or 865- 322-2752 (cell), email mdron@bellsouth.net, www.highlandsshuttleservice.com.

STANDING BEAR FARM HOSTEL: Hartford, 423-487-0014.
OUR EXPERIENCE, JULY 2011: We use them when we do our three-day backpacking adventure from Newfound Gap to Davenport Gap. We leave

our car at the hostel the day before we plan to begin our hike. They take us back to Cherokee, where we stay overnight.

Near the end of our hike, we call them as we are approaching Davenport Gap. Curtis, one of the owners, picks us up minutes after we arrive at the gap.

They are friendly, accommodating to hikers' needs, and timely. Plus, they have reasonable rates.

Car Rental Agencies

ENTERPRISE RENT-A-CAR: 8 a.m. to 6 p.m. Mon through Fri, 864 West Highway 25/70, Newport, 423-613-5647.

Outfitters

THE DAY HIKER: one-stop shop for affordable outdoor and hiking products, 10 a.m. to 9 or 10 p.m. daily May through Oct, 10 a.m. to 6 p.m. Nov through April, 634 Parkway #1, Gatlinburg, 865-430-0970.

NANTAHALA OUTDOOR CENTER (NOC): Gatlinburg, 18,000- square-foot store carrying everything for people planning hiking, biking, and water excursions, including gifts, gear, and guidance; 10 a.m. to 9 p.m. daily; 1138 Parkway, Gatlinburg, 865-277-8209.

Groceries in Hartford

DOWNTOWN HARTFORD CITGO STATION: convenience store, snacks, souvenirs, no beer or wine, 6:30 a.m. to 11 p.m. daily, 3155 Big Creek Rd. (north of I-40, Ext. 447), 423-487-0192.

PIGEON RIVER SMOKEHOUSE AND CONVENIENCE STORE, BP STATION: groceries, fast food, beer, camping supplies, 7 a.m. to midnight daily, 3601 Hartford Road (south of I-40, Exit. 447), 423-487-0061.

Groceries in Cosby

A&M FAMILY GROCERY AND EXXON STATION: groceries, snacks, beer, 5:30 a.m. to 10 p.m. daily, 3066 Cosby Highway #B, 423-487-3158.

Groceries in Newport

BROCK'S OPEN AIR MARKET: organic and farm-fresh fruits and vegetables, home-made vegetable soup, subs, biscuits and gravy, beer, 24/7, 601 East Broadway, 423-623-2870.

FOOD CITY: groceries, beer and wine, 6 a.m. to midnight daily, 181 Western Plaza Drive, 423-623-4705 and 423-623-3356, 416 Eastern Plaza Way.

SAVE-A-LOT: discount grocery, no beer or wine, 8 a.m. to 9 p.m. daily, 1043 Cosby Highway (south of exit 435), 423-625-2060.

WALMART SUPERCENTER: groceries, camping supplies, beer, wine, 24/7, 1075 Cosby Hwy (south of exit 435), 423-623-0429.

Wine or Beer Shops in Newport

NEWPORT PACKAGE STORE: wine, beer, and spirits; 9 a.m. to 10 p.m. Mon through Sat; 203 Cosby Highway; 423-625-1532.

WEST END PACKAGE STORE: 8 a.m. to 9 p.m. Mon through Thu, 8 a.m. to 10 p.m. Fri and Sat, 335 West Broadway Street, 423-623-0449.

ATMs

Hartford

DOWNTOWN HARTFORD CITGO STATION: 6:30 a.m. to 11 p.m. daily, 3155 Big Creek Rd. (north of I-40, Ext 447).

PIGEON RIVER SMOKEHOUSE, BP STATION: 7 a.m. to midnight daily, 3601 Hartford Road (south of I-40, Exit 447).

Cosby

ATM: 3066 Cosby Highway.

Newport

US BANK: 301 East Main Street.

ATM EXPRESS: 243 East Main Street.

ATM: 366 West Broadway Street.

ATM: 447 West Broadway Street.

ATM NETWORK, INC.: 424 Heritage Boulevard.

PIT STOP MOBIL MART: 405 and 774 Cosby Highway

KENJO MARKET ATM: 1004 Cosby Highway

ATM, EXXON: 905 Cosby Highway.

Urgent Care and Emergency Services in Newport

FAST PACE URGENT CARE CLINIC: walk-ins welcome, urgent or primary health care, 8 a.m. to 8 p.m. Mon through Fri, 8 a.m. to 6 p.m. Sat, 1 to 5 p.m. Sun, 756 Cosby Highway, 423-237-6546.

NEWPORT MEDICAL CENTER, EMERGENCY DEPARTMENT: 24/7, 435 Second Street, 423-625-2200.

Fun Places to Visit in Southeastern Tennessee, West of Davenport Gap

BIG BEAR RAFTING: 10 a.m. to 7 p.m. Tue, Wed, Thu, and Sat; 3165 Big Creek Road; Hartford; 844-799-7238.

BIG CREEK EXPEDITIONS: white water adventures, scenic floats, no previous experience needed, 3541 Hartford Road, Hartford, 423-487-0178.

NANTAHALA OUTDOOR CENTER PIGEON RIVER OUTPOST: rafting, must weigh more than seventy pounds and be over eight years old, 3485 Hartford Road, Hartford, 1-800-232-7238.

RAFTING IN SMOKIES OUTPOST: 3595 Hartford Road, Hartford, 1-800-776-7238.

WILDWATER PIGEON RIVER: rafting and zip lining; 9 a.m. to 6:30 p.m. Tue, Wed, Thu, and Sat; 3555 Hartford Road, Hartford; 1-800-451-0072.

FORBIDDEN CAVERNS: tours, 10 a.m. to 5 p.m. Mon through Sat, Apr through Nov, 455 Blowing Cave Road, Sevierville.

TENNESSEE MUSEUM OF AVIATION: $12.75 for adults, $9.75 for seniors, $6.75 for children six to twelve, free for children under six, 10 a.m. to 6 p.m. Mon through Sat, 1 to 6 p.m. Sun, historic aircraft collection, live demonstrations, tours available, gift shop, 135 Air Museum Way, Sevierville, 865-908-0171 and 866-286-8738.

OUR EXPERIENCE, MAY 2013: Jim and I stop to see this museum on our way home from our day hikes in southwest Virginia. The museum tells the story of aviation in southeastern Tennessee with antique aircraft exhibits and pictures. It is interesting to see the story of women who flew in the early days and how the airport in Sevierville came to be.

Fine Wine and Accommodations
Waterville and Maggie Valley, North Carolina

WATERVILLE is a small village on the North Carolina-Tennessee border, I-40, Exit 451. It is the home of Walters Dam and Hydroelectric Plant. The Great Smoky Mountains National Park Big Creek Ranger Station, Big Creek Campground, and Big Creek Country Store are nearby.

MAGGIE VALLEY is a small friendly town in the Smoky Mountains. It is the home of the Cataloochee Ski Resort and the Ghost Town in the Sky amusement park. It has many lodging and restaurant choices.

Lodging

Lodging near Waterville

BIG CREEK CAMPGROUND: Great Smoky Mountains National Park, first-come-first-served policy, tent pads, fire rings, grills, picnic tables with nearby flush toilets, water, cold-water sinks, emergency phone, two miles northeast of Davenport Gap, I-40, Exit 451. Enjoy the gentle waters of Big Creek running alongside the campground. Activities include hiking, fly-fishing, and horseback riding.

Lodging in or near Maggie Valley

MISTY MOUNTAIN RANCH B&B: $–$$ with full mountain breakfast, menu changes daily, suites and 2 BR cabins have refrigerators, microwaves, coffee makers, whirlpools, fireplaces, and decks overlooking a waterfall. 561 Caldwell Drive, 828-926-2710, 1-855-516-1093, www.mistymtnranch.com.

TIMBERWOLF CREEK BED & BREAKFAST: $$–$$$ with creative, delicious breakfasts; luxury rooms with queen or king beds, whirlpool tubs, refrigerators, private decks, free Wi-Fi and internet. Fall asleep to the sound of a nearby stream. Hosts greet you with smiles and humor. 391 Johnson Branch, 828-926-2608, 1-888-525-4218, www.timberwolfcreek.com.

BEST WESTERN MOUNTAINBROOK INN: $ with complimentary continental breakfast; rooms with sofa beds, microwaves, refrigerators, balconies with rocking chairs and breathtaking views, and satellite TVs with HBO; Wi-Fi; high- speed internet; outdoor heated pool and hot tub; picnic area with grills; 3811 Soco Road (US 19), 828-926-3962, www.bestwestern.com.

FIVE STAR INN: $–$$; rooms with refrigerators, microwaves, and coffee makers; public Wi-Fi; rocking chairs on porch; creek-side swings, hammocks, and fire pit; 2474 Soco Road (US 19); 828-926-3816, www.fivestarinnnc.com.

FOUR SEASONS INN: $–$$ with complimentary breakfast; rooms with refrigerators, microwaves, and coffee makers; some have whirlpool tubs; heated outdoor pool; 4040 Soco Road (US 19); 828-926-8505, www.fourseasonsinn.com.

JONATHAN CREEK INN AND VILLAS: $–$$; rooms with flat- screen TVs, refrigerators, microwaves, and coffee makers; rocking chairs on porch; indoor pool; outdoor hot tub; 4324 Soco Road (US 19), 1-800-577-7812, www.jonathancreekinn.com.

MAGGIE VALLEY CREEKSIDE LODGE: $; rooms with microwaves, refrigerators, and coffee makers; some rooms have whirlpool tubs; indoor and outdoor pools; 2716 Soco Road (US 19); 828-926-1301; www.creeksidelodge.com.

MAGGIE VALLEY INN & CONFERENCE CENTER: $–$$ with complimentary breakfast, outdoor pool, on-site restaurant, bar, lounge, covered parking, 70 Soco Road (US 19), 866-926-0201, www.maggievalleyhotel.com.

CABINS: numerous individual cabins are available for rent. Check www.airbnb.com, www.vibo.com, or www.tripadvisor.com.

Selected Restaurants in Maggie Valley

J. ARTHUR'S RESTAURANT: $–$$, American, family-operated, steak, seafood, pasta, salad entrées, known for their gorgonzola cheese salad and prime rib, full bar, 4 to 9 p.m. daily during season, 4:30 to 8 p.m. Thu through Sat and noon to 7 p.m. Sun in the winter, 2843 Soco Road (US 19), 828-926-1817, www.jarthurs.com.

OUR EXPERIENCE, JULY 2011: When we finish our three-day backpacking adventure at Davenport Gap, we are ready for fine dining, but it is late. We don't know what we will find on our way back to Cherokee where we are staying for the night. We hope to find something in Maggie Valley.

We see J Arthur's with a big sign saying, "Prime Rib Special." At 8:30 p.m., the lights are still on and there are cars in the parking lot.

We go in and Jim asks, "Are you still open?"

"Sure," Martha, our waitress, says and shows us to a table. We only see people at two other tables.

I say, *"We are really lucky."*

We relax and order drinks. Jim has a glass of champagne, and I have a glass of pinot noir. My wine has a smooth, fruity taste. Jim orders prime rib, and I order filet mignon. Martha brings us our salads and we begin talking with her.

When she finds out we have been hiking the A.T., Martha says, "A friend and I maintain that section of the A.T. from Davenport Gap to Green Corner Road."

"That's interesting. How did you start doing that?" I ask.

"I hiked the Georgia and North Carolina part of the A.T. about ten years ago. When I moved back to Maggie Valley, I wanted to get involved with the trail. I joined the Carolina Mountain Club and started doing trail maintenance."

She tells us they work on the two-and-a-half-mile stretch of the trail about once a month.

The entrées arrive and we eat every morsel. What a wonderful end to a long day of hiking "Downhill to Fine Wine and Accommodations."

CARVER'S MAGGIE VALLEY RESTAURANT AND RV PARK: \$–\$\$, American, specializing in favorite Southern dishes, daily specials, family-operated, no beer or wine; 7 a.m. to 9 p.m. daily, 2804 Soco Road (US 19), 828-926-0425, wwww.maggievalleyrestaurant.net.

RENDEZVOUS RESTAURANT: \$, American, fish, grilled favorites, chicken, pasta, large variety of appetizers, full bar, 11:30 a.m. to 9 p.m. Sun through Thu, 11:30 a.m. to 11 p.m. Fri and Sat, located inside the Maggie Valley Hotel & Conference Center at 70 Soco Road (US 19), 828-926-0201, www.maggievalleyhotelrendezvousrestaurant.com.

SNAPPY'S ITALIAN RESTAURANT & PIZZERIA: $; Italian and American; pizza, traditional Italian entrées, and steaks; served in an informal setting; 4 to 9 p.m. Mon through Thu; 4 to 10 p.m. Fri and Sat; 2769 Soco Road, 828-926-6126, www.snappysitalian.net.

Hiker Essentials, Splurges, and Emergency Stops in Southwestern North Carolina near Davenport Gap

Car Rental Agency

ENTERPRISE RENT-A-CAR: 8 a.m. to 6 p.m. Mon through Fri, 9 a.m. to noon Sat, 491 Russ Ave, Waynesville, 828-452-0004.

Outfitters

BLACKROCK OUTDOOR COMPANY: everything you need for hiking, fishing, and camping; 9 a.m. to 6 p.m. Mon through Sat; noon to 5 p.m. Sun; 570 West Main Street, Sylva; 828-631-4453.

OUR EXPERIENCE: When the Appalachian Trail Conservancy Biennial Conference is at nearby Western Carolina University, we walk through Sylva and browse in this store. They have a wide variety of quality hiking apparel and gear. They are having a sale, and we buy a hiking shirt and pants.

Groceries near Waterville

BIG CREEK COUNTRY STORE: deli sandwiches, cooked and freeze-dried food, camping gear, fuel, propane tanks, 10 a.m. to 5 p.m. Thu through Sat, noon to 5 p.m. Sun, 67 Mount Sterling Road (one mile northeast of Davenport Gap), 828-476-4492.

Groceries in Maggie Valley

SOCO GROCERIES & MEAT MARKET: groceries, beer and wine, 6 a.m. to 9 p.m. Sun through Thu, 6 a.m. to 11 p.m. Fri and Sat, 4593 Soco Road (US 19) in the Shell station, 828-926-9485.

TEAGUES GROCERY & CAFÉ: groceries, gas, fresh meat, café, no beer or wine, 7 a.m. to 10 p.m. Sun through Fri, 7 a.m. to 10:30 p.m. Sat, 130 Soco Road (US 19) in the Shell station, 828-926-1147.

Wine or Beer Shop

ABC STORE: 9 a.m. to 9 p.m. Mon through Sat, 3931 Soco Road (US 19), 828-926-3481.

ATMs in Maggie Valley

BBT BANK & ATM: 2451 Soco Road.

ATM AT MAGGIE VALLEY TOWN HALL: 3987 Soco Road.

ATM AT SOCO GROCERIES & MEAT MARKET: 6 a.m. to 9 p.m. Sun through Thu, 6 a.m. to 11 p.m. Fri and Sat, 4593 Soco Road (US 19) in the Shell station.

ATM AT TEAGUES GROCERY & CAFÉ: 7 a.m. to 10 p.m. Sun through Fri, 7 a.m. to 10:30 p.m. Sat, 130 Soco Road (US 19) in the Shell station.

ATM IN SHELL RAPID LUBE: 2650 Soco Road.

Urgent Care and Emergency Services

URGENT CARE: 8 a.m. to 6:30 p.m. daily, 556 Hazelwood Avenue, Waynesville, 828-452-8890.

HAYWOOD MEDICAL CENTER EMERGENCY DEPARTMENT: 24/7, 262 Leroy George Drive, Clyde, 828-456-731.

Fun Places to Visit East of Davenport Gap in Western North Carolina

WHEELS THROUGH TIME MUSEUM: premier collection of more than 350 rare and historic American vintage motorcycles, $15 for adults, $12 for seniors, $6 for children, 9 a.m. to 5 p.m. Thu through Mon, April through Oct, 62 Vintage Lane, Maggie Valley, five miles off the Blue Ridge Parkway, 828-926-6266.

CATALOOCHEE SKI AREA: open daily during season, skiing, tubing, snowboarding, 1080 Ski Lodge Road, 828-926-0285.

TROUT FISHING IN DESIGNATED MOUNTAIN HERITAGE STREAMS: Purchase a three-day $5 fishing license at the **Maggie Valley Visitors Center**. 9 a.m. to 4:30 p.m. daily, 2551 Soco Road, Maggie Valley, 828-926-1207.

References

Adkin, Leonard M. 1997. *The Appalachian Trail: A Visitor's Companion.* Birmingham: Menasha Press.

Adkin, Leonard M. 1999. *Wildflowers of the Appalachian Trail.* Birmingham: Menasha Press.

The Appalachian Trail. 2015. New York: Rizolli International Publications, Inc.

Bowman, Amanda. 2011. "Origin of the Trail into the Hearts of America." *A.T. Journeys* 7(1): 18-23.

Chazin, Daniel D, ed. 2016. *Appalachian Trail Data Book 2017.* Harpers Ferry, WV: Appalachian Trail Conservancy.

Chew, V. Collins 1993. *Underfoot: A Geologic Guide to the Appalachian Trail.* Harpers Ferry, WV: Appalachian Trail Conservancy.

Chew, V. Collins, ed. 2013. *Appalachian Trail Guide to Tennessee-North Carolina*. Harpers Ferry, WV: Appalachian Trail Conservancy.

Hart, Allen de. 2005. *North Carolina Hiking Trails*. Boston: Appalachian Mountain Club.

Etnier, Elizabeth L. 2015. *Day Hiker's Guide To All The Trails In The Smoky Mountains*. Knoxville: Elizabeth Etnier.

Fisher, Ronald M. 1972. *The Appalachian Trail*. Washington, DC: National Geographic Society.

"Does Elevation Affect Temperature?" Joel Gratz, August 18, 2016, Mountain News Corporation, ONTHESNOW, www.onthesnow. com/news/a/15157/does-elevation-affect-temperature-

Gove, Doris. 2012. *Exploring the Appalachian Trail, Hikes in the Southern Appalachians, Georgia, North Carolina, Tennessee*. Mechanicsburg, PA: Stackpole Books.

Hutson, Robert W., William F. Hutson, and Aaron J. Sharp. 2013, *Great Smoky Mountains Wildflowers*. Northbrook, IL: Windy Pines Publishing, LLC.

Ketelle, Richard H., Don O'Neal, and Lisa Williams, eds. 2011. *Appalachian Trail Guide to North Carolina-Georgia*. Harpers Ferry, WV: Appalachian Trail Conservancy.

"Leave No Trace Principles," American Hiking Society, americanhikingsociety.org/resources/leave-no-trace, accessed June 1, 2017.

MacKaye, Benton. 1921. "An Appalachian Trail: A Project in Regional Planning." *Journal of American Institute of Architects* 9:325-330.

Miller, David. 2017. *The A.T. Guide, 2017 Northbound.* Titusville, FL: Jerelyn Press.

Parham, Jim. 2012. *Day Hiking the North Georgia Mountains.* Almond, NC: Milestone Press.

Schoning, Polly. 2010. *The Appalachian Trail by Day Hikes—Tips for the Timid.* Manhattan, KS: AG Press Inc.

Smith, Dave. 2003. *Don't Get Eaten—The Dangers of Animals that Charge or Attack.* Seattle: The Mountaineers Books.

Sylvester, Robert, ed. 2016. *Appalachian Trail Thru-Hikers' Companion 2017.* Harpers Ferry, WV: Appalachian Trail Conservancy.

Tilton, Buck. 2007. *Backcountry First Aid.* Guildford, CT: Falcon Guides.

Resources

National Hiking Organizations

AMERICAN HIKING SOCIETY: Silver Spring, MD, 301-565-6704, www.americanhiking.org.

APPALACHIAN TRAIL CONSERVANCY: Harpers Ferry, WV, 304-535-6331, www.appalachiantrail.org.

Hiking Clubs in Georgia, North Carolina, and Tennessee that maintain the trail from Springer Mountain, Georgia, to Davenport Gap, Tennessee

GEORGIA APPALACHIAN TRAIL CLUB: www.georgia-atclub.org.

NANTAHALA HIKING CLUB: www.nantahalahikingclub.org.

SMOKY MOUNTAINS HIKING CLUB: 423-558-1341, www.smhclub.org.

Maps of the Appalachian Trail

APPALACHIAN TRAIL CONSERVANCY: 304-535-6331, www.appalachiantrail.org.
NATIONAL GEOGRAPHIC MAPS: 1-800-962-1643, maps@ngs.org.

National Park Service

GREAT SMOKY MOUNTAINS NATIONAL PARK: Gatlinburg, TN, weather forecasts and other information: 865-436-1200, backcountry office: 865-436-1297, emergency number: 865-436-9171, www.nps.gov/grsm.

United States Forest Service

CHATTAHOOCHEE-OCONEE NATIONAL FOREST, FOREST SUPERVISOR'S OFFICE: Gainesville, GA, 9 a.m. to noon, 1 to 4 p.m. Mon through Fri, 770-297-3000, www.fs.usda.gov/conf.
BLUE RIDGE RANGER DISTRICT: Blairsville, GA, 8 to 11:30 a.m., 12:30 to 4:30 p.m. Mon through Fri, 706-745-6928.
CHATTOOGA RIVER DISTRICT: Lakemont, GA, 8 a.m. to noon, 1 to 4:30 p.m. Mon through Fri, 706-754-6221.

Nantahala National Forest

CHEOAH RANGER DISTRICT: Robbinsville, NC, 8 a.m. to 4:30 p.m. Mon through Fri, 828-479-6431.
NANTAHALA RANGER DISTRICT: Franklin, NC, 8 a.m. to 4:30 p.m. Mon through Fri, 828-524-6441.
NATIONAL FORESTS IN NORTH CAROLINA: Asheville, 8 a.m. to 4:30 p.m. Mon through Fri, 828-257-4201, www.fs.usda.gov/nfsnc.

Weather Services

NATIONAL WEATHER SERVICE: www.weather.gov.
THE WEATHER UNDERGROUND: www.wunderground.com.

Acknowledgements

We want to thank Anna Huthmaker, founder of Trail Dames, for writing the inspiring Foreword; Chris Bogan, our graphic artist and nephew, for creating our amazing book cover and social media pieces; Stewart Holt, our map guru, for creating the detailed maps and trail profiles; Kimberly Martin, our self-publishing coach and owner of Jera Publishing, for guiding us through the publishing process; the Roswell Authors Group for encouraging us; Mary Beth Bishop, our editor, for critically examining our drafts during the conceptual editing phase and making valuable suggestions, and for conducting the crucial line and proof editing; Stephanie Anderson, Jera's design guru for creating an outstanding interior layout; Michael Blyler, our friend, for providing technical support; Linda Harp, our gregarious friend, for making the endless phone calls to check the facts about each business listed in the Fine Wine and Accommodations sections; Frances Laprade, Deborah Morgan, Lee Graham, and Betty Brewer-Calvert, our hiking and photographer friends for sharing their photographs; Roxanne Parrott, our communications expert and outdoor lover, for reviewing our drafts; Harmon Steiner, our thru-hiker son, for being our hiking coach and for thoughtfully examining our drafts and recommending changes;

Peg McKenna, Lee Graham, Catherine Bergman, and Lisa Robinson, our beta readers, for reviewing the initial draft and providing invaluable feedback; Ginny Parks and Vicky Childs, my walking partners, for being my impartial listening ears; John and Janice Wilsky, Rana Bayakly, Mohamed and Hadi Qayad, Vicky and John Childs, our hiking partners, for hiking parts of the Appalachian Trail in Georgia, North Carolina and Tennessee with us; members of the Georgia Appalachian Trail Club, the Nantahala Hiking Club, and the Smoky Mountains Hiking Club for maintaining the Appalachian Trail so caringly and sharing with us their knowledge about the Appalachian Trail; staff of the Chattahoochee National Forest, the Nantahala National Forest, and the Great Smoky Mountains National Park for being caretakers of the forests and parks and advocates for hikers. Publishing a day hikers' guide takes a village of friends and family who are willing and ready to share their expertise, joy, and laughter.

We dedicate our guide to those who aspire to day hike the Appalachian Trail, to Benton MacKaye and his vision for creating the Appalachian Trail, to Myron Avery and the trail clubs who blazed the Trail, and to the thousands of volunteers who have maintained the Trail over the last eighty years and who will continue to be stewards of the Trail for future generations.

About the Authors, Carol and Jim Steiner

Carol is the writer, hiker, trip planner, and speaker. Jim is the electronic geek, photographer, treasure hunter, and hiker. In photos, he captures the beauty and details along the trail for Carol to bring to life on paper. Together they crafted *The Appalachian Trail Day Hikers' Guide: Downhill to Fine Wine and Accommodations, Georgia, North Carolina, and Tennessee.*

Carol and Jim have hiked more than eight hundred miles of the Appalachian Trail. Their slackpacking adventure began in 2007. They hike several sections of the trail yearly so they can savor the mystique of the A.T., research segments for their next book, and explore the hidden treasures of Appalachian communities.

When asked, "How long do you think it will take you to finish the Appalachian Trail?" Jim laughs and says, "Our son hiked the trail in a hundred and twelve days. Carol thinks we can hike it in a hundred and twelve years." Their goal is to enjoy each hike, one day at a time, and to explore the small towns along the way, but not necessarily to complete the entire Appalachian Trail from end to end.

Carol is a retired state public health section director, former college professor, and public health nurse. She has authored more than a dozen articles for scientific and professional journals. In 1991, she received the Dorothy Barfield Award for scholastic achievement in the promotion of public health in Georgia.

Jim is a computer consultant, developing computer systems, programs, and training materials, and conducting computer classes. He is the co-author of *The CDP Review Manual, Second Edition,* published by *Van Nostrand Reinhold Company.*

Carol and Jim love exploring the outdoors and traveling to new places. They grew up hiking in the piney woods of Northwest Florida, boating and skin diving in the Gulf and inland water ways. When they married and moved to Cape Canaveral, they explored the Atlantic for sunken Spanish galleons and hidden treasures. Carol became a private pilot and explored the airways from California to New York in the Power Puff Derby, the Bahamas on vacations, and small Georgia towns as a public health nurse educator. They love the challenge of exploring new places and finding natural wonders in nature and discovering the art, music, and culture of small towns in the Appalachian Mountains. Every day hiking trip along the Appalachian Trail is an adventure to be shared with their readers.

Index

CPSIA information can be obtained
at www.ICGtesting.com
Printed in the USA
JSHW012056280323
39617JS00001B/3